AF323717

# MULTIMODAL INTERFACE FOR HUMAN–MACHINE COMMUNICATION

# SERIES IN MACHINE PERCEPTION AND ARTIFICIAL INTELLIGENCE*

*Editors:* **H. Bunke** (Univ. Bern, Switzerland)
**P. S. P. Wang** (Northeastern Univ., USA)



*For the complete list of titles in this series, please write to the Publisher.

Series in Machine Perception and Artificial Intelligence – Vol. 48

# MULTIMODAL INTERFACE FOR HUMAN–MACHINE COMMUNICATION

Editors

## P. C. Yuen

## Y. Y. Tang

*Hong Kong Baptist University*

## P. S. P. Wang

*Northeastern University, USA*

*Published by*

World Scientific Publishing Co. Pte. Ltd.

P O Box 128, Farrer Road, Singapore 912805

*USA office:* Suite 1B, 1060 Main Street, River Edge, NJ 07661

*UK office:* 57 Shelton Street, Covent Garden, London WC2H 9HE


**British Library Cataloguing-in-Publication Data**
A catalogue record for this book is available from the British Library.



ISBN 981-02-4594-7


Printed in Singapore.

# List of Contributors

**A Armstrong**
*School of Computing*
*University of Glamorgan*
*UK*

**Jeffrey T Cohn**
*Robotics Institute, Carnegie Mellon*
*University and*
*Department of Psychology, University*
*of Pittsburgh*
*USA*

**Trevor Darell**
*Artificial Intelligence Laboratory*
*Massachusetts Institute of Technology*
*USA*

**John W Fisher III**
*Artificial Intelligence Laboratory*
*Massachusetts Institute of Technology*
*USA*

**G C Feng**
*School of Computing*
*University of Glamorgan*
*UK*

**Wen Gao**
*University of Science and Technology*
*China*

**Jianmin Jiang**
*School of Computing*
*University of Glamorgan*
*UK*

**Insu Kang**
*Department of Computer Science and*
*Engineering*
*Pohang University of Science and*
*Technology*
*Korea*

**Oh-woog Kwon**
*Department of Computer Science and*
*Engineering*
*Pohang University of Science and*
*Technology*
*Korea*

**Takeo Kanade**
*Robotics Institute*
*Carnegie Mellon University*
*USA*

James A Landay
*Department of Electrical Engineering
and Computer Science
University of California, Berkeley
USA*

J H Lai
*Department of Mathematics
Zhongshan University
China*

Geunbae Lee
*Department of Computer Science and
Engineering
Pohang University of Science and
Technology
Korea*

Jong-Hyeok Lee
*Department of Computer Science and
Engineering
Pohang University of Science and
Technology
Korea*

A Chris Long
*Human Computer Interaction Institute
Carnegie Mellon University
USA*

Robert Mariani
*Kent Ridge Digital Laboratory
Singapore*

Sharon Oviatt
*Center for Human-Computer
Communication
Oregon Graduate Institute of Science
and Technology
USA*

Lawrence A Rowe
*Department of Electrical Engineering
and Computer Science
University of California, Berkeley
USA*

Yuan Y Tang
*Department of Computer Science
Hong Kong Baptist University
Hong Kong*

Daniel Thalmann
*Computer Graphics Laboratory
EPFL
Switzerland*

Yian-ti Tian
*Robotics Institute*
*Carnegie Mellon University*
*USA*

Chunli Wang
*University of Science and Technology*
*China*

**Pong C Yuen**
*Department of Computer Science*
*Hong Kong Baptist University*
*Hong Kong*

P S P Wang
*College of Computer Science*
*Northeastern University*
*USA*

# Introduction to Multimodal Interface for Human–Machine Communication

Pong C Yuen[+], Yuan Y Tang[+] and P S P Wang[*]

[+] Department of Computer Science
Hong Kong Baptist University, Hong Kong

[*]College of Computer Science
Northeastern University
USA

Multi-modal interface for human machine communication is an interdisciplinary research area. Basically, it consists of two parts, namely, multimodal input and multimedia output. In that sense, research on multimodal input involves image and video analysis (vision), speech analysis (voice), pen-based analysis (handwritten analysis) and other sensor-based input analysis. The multimedia output consists of speech synthesis, image-based synthesis, computer graphics and animation.

As you may see, in order to build a practical multimodality system for human machine communication, we need to build up fundamental algorithms in each of the above mentioned areas, in which many researchers have been working on for years. The second problem that we need to solve is how to integrate the output in each modal to draw a final conclusion.

## Motivations

It has been foreseen that many potential new applications will be developed based on the structure of mutlimodal input and multimedia output, and the concept of synthesis by analysis. One of the applications is the multimodal input interface for human communications with machine. It can be further categorized into four areas namely, education, entertainment, business and public services. In education sector, web-based or on-line learning is the direction in future education. By integrating the multimodal interface (MI) into the system, the new learning system is able to understand the student's feeling such as being interested, bored or puzzled, when the student is studying each section or answering each question. Knowing these, the rest of the course can be tailor made for the student. In the entertainment sector, the MI can be used in the game/toys industry and provide a more natural communication between players and machine. On the business side, MI can be added into the unmanned multimedia sale kiosk. In public services, MI can be used as monitoring systems in public areas.

## Overview of the Book

This book consists of four parts, namely, algorithm, single modality systems, information retrieval and multimodality systems.

There are three contributed articles in the algorithm part for multimodal interface. Mariani reports a face detection and recognition system based on Tangent Distance. Tian et al.'s article focuses on the facial expression recognition and their algorithm in recognizing action units is reported. The last article in this part is related to face synthesis. Feng et al. report a view synthesis based on a single image.

Part II consists of two single modality systems. Gao and Wang report a vision-based Chinese sign language recognition system. Long et al. designed and developed a pen-based user interface.

Two articles on information retrieval are reported in Part III. Kang et al. developed a cross-language text retrieval by query translation using term re-weighting. Feng et al. developed a feature extract technique in DCT domain. This algorithm is further applied in online web image retrieval.

The last section reports three mutlimodality systems. Oviatt reports the Quickset system, which makes use of the speech and pen as multimodal input. Fisher et al. discuss the information-theoretic fusion for multimodal interfaces. The last article is related to virtual and augment reality. Thalmann makes use of virtual humans for multimodal communication in virtual reality and augment reality.

Hope you enjoy reading the book.

# Contents

# Part IV  Multimodality Systems                              201

# Part I  Algorithms

# A Face Location and Recognition System Based on Tangent Distance

Robert Mariani

*Kent Ridge Digital Labs, 21 Heng Mui Keng Terrace, 119613 Singapore.*
*Real World Computing Partnership, Multimodal Function Lab, Japan*

## Introduction

The difficulties of automatic face recognition lie in the variability of the face characteristics (age, gender, and race), geometry (distance, viewpoint), image quality (resolution, illumination, signal-to-noise ratio), and image content (background, occlusion, disguise) [Takacs and Wechsler]. Because of such complexity, most face recognition systems assume a well controlled environment and recognize only near frontal faces. Reliable means of automatic identification of people in dynamic environments are becoming more and more vital to face the challenges that lie ahead in security and access control systems. Significant efforts have been made over the years to recognize faces automatically under restricted environments. A bottleneck in building a robust face recognition system is to find an algorithm that can reliably compensate for environmental changes, facial expressions and feature localization errors as a whole.

In this paper, we describe a complete face location and face recognition system, robust to the lighting conditions, the changes of expressions and the changes of poses. This system is integrated into the mobile robot JIJO-II [Asoh] developped by the Electrotechnical Laboratory, evolving in an uncontrolled indoor environment. Here, the lighting conditions and the time that separates the registration of the person from the recognition (days, months ...) are of critical importance.

The system relies on a precise face location and uses an intensive face registration technique. The face recognition is achieved by combining a template-matching with a feature-matching techniques.

In the first section, we describe the face location system. In the second section, we present the registration algorithm, and in the third section we detail the face recognition algorithm. In the fourth section, we establish the performances of the system on the ORL  and on the MV2TS databases, and on a database of 1500 images representing 40 persons under 16 lighting conditions. The performances achieved show that our system is robust to the changes of facial expressions, the little changes of poses and, most importantly, to the changes of lighting conditions. In the fifth section, we conclude with the improvements and the future challenges to solve.

## Face Location in a Cluttered Background

Two categories of algorithms are used to detect a face in a cluttered background, namely the feature-based and template-based algorithms. Prior image filtering using skin color [Sun] and/or motion [Jordao] can be used to accelerate the detection process.

The feature-based algorithms consider a face as a set of facial features such as the eyes, the nose and the mouth, spatially organized according to anthropometric rules [Huang and Mariani] or within an ellipsis [Sirohey]. Eventually, multiresolution schemes have been proposed to detect face-like structures in the image, and to validate with a subpixellic eye detector [Huang and Mariani]. Other techniques are based on image feature extraction, like Gabor wavelets [Manjunath], and on the use of specific similarity measures between feature vectors, like the Mahalanobis distance [Brunelli], the elatisc graph matching [Elagin], the decision trees [Huang]...

In the template matching techniques, the face is examined as a whole, usually using model-based vision techniques. A probabilistic or statistic model can be used to analyze the pixels intensity of each subwindow of the image. This model can be built with different methods: neural networks [Feraud][Rowley][Sung], principal component analysis [Moghaddam], support vector machines [Osuna], linear discriminant analysis [Mariani][Hotta].

We have developped a feature-based system that locates accurately the eyes positions. The accurate localization of the eyes is crucial for a recognition algorithm, and, to be more specific, the error of the system in locating the eyes (in pixels), is directly used as *a priori* knowledge during the face registration. The faces are detected in 640x480 pixels grey level images, as color-based techniques are not suitable for the kind of lighting conditions we address (cf. Figure 1). We have constrained the face location system such that it extracts faces of a given size, typically situated between 0.8m to 1.5m from the camera. For these sizes of faces, the recognition scores are reliable. For such faces, the interocular distance varies between 60 to 160 pixels, and the maximum face tilt allowed is 20 degrees. For a greater interocular distance, the face usually exceeds the frame. For a lower distance, accuracy in eyes detection is not guaranteed. For both cases, the face recognition becomes unreliable. Given these constraints, the geometrical constraints are integrated in an early stage in the system and the thresholds have been tuned optimally, providing a fast and reliable face locator.

**Figure 1: Various Lighting Conditions**

We proceed in three steps: 1) we build a set of possible eyes $E = \{(x_1,y_1),...(x_n,y_n)\}$ using a point extraction algorithm, that combines image characteristics and eye model; 2) we generate a set of face hypothesis $F = \{f_1,..f_k\}$, subset of ExE, using image similarity, geometrical constraints, and template matching; 3) we select the best face hypothesis $f_i \in F$ according to a cost function. These three steps are described in the following subsection.

## *Eye Hypothesis Extraction*

As the eyes are represented by small areas, with relatively high variance, we first segment the original image, to discard the large areas of the image that are homogeneous, as well as the areas of low variance. The result is a binary mask, where all the pixels set to 1 represent the possible eyes' center positions. Each hypothesis of eye center is then validated or rejected using an eye model, where we combine robust contour correlation and eye template matching. Finally, a clustering algorithm is applied to reduce the number of hypothesis, when these hypothesis are very close to each other.

Segmentation by Connected Component Analysis.

The eyes are represented by small connected components, darker than the surrounding skin. By resampling the grey levels between [0,16], where each grey level $i$ represents the grey levels [16*i, 16*(i+1)[, and by selecting the small connected components of the image, we achieve the first step of the eye extraction. Large areas of the cluttered background, the face skin and the hair (if the face is large enough) will be discarded by this operation. The remaining components are small and their pixels have roughly the same intensity.

Given a connected component R, having a grey level 1, 1 $\in$ [0,16], obtained by 8-connected raster scan, R is accepted if the five following constraints are respected:

$$n < 400; \, w < 35; \, h < 35; \, w > 0.5h; \, n > 0.5(w*h) \quad (1)$$

where $n$ is the number of pixel of the component $R$, and $w$ and $h$ are respectively the width and the height of the bounding box of $R$. The constant values of the thresholds have been fixed experimentally, according to the size of the faces we are looking for.

We start with a mask M initialized to 0 everywhere. Then, we set to 1 all the pixels that are present within a disc of ray 12 pixels, centered at the centroid of the component. At the end, we obtain a binary mask, where all the pixels set to 1, are potential centers of eyes.

  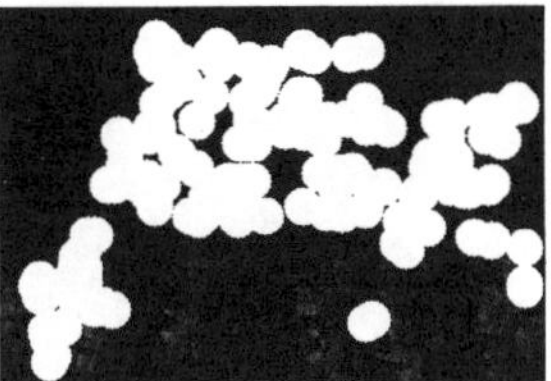

**Figure 2: Connected Component Analysis**

## Segmentation by Image Derivative Analysis

After smoothing the input image and computing the vertical derivative, the eye areas are represented by regions having a high standard deviation. Using derivative images with zero mean and unit standard deviation, a simple binarization provides additionnal ways to filter the eyes' position.

Because the convolution operator * commutates with the derivative operators, ie $\delta_y(g*f) = \delta_y g * f = g * \delta_y f$, where $\delta_y$ denotes the vertical derivative operator, and because the gaussian operator is separable, an efficient computation is obtained by convolving the input image, horizontally with the one-dimensional gaussian filter G, then vertically with the one-dimensional derivative of G. Satisfactory results were obtained with gaussian filters with a standard deviation of 4. This filter transforms the eyes in a dark line-like structure, presenting strong standard deviation.

We start from the mask $M$ obtained at the previous step. Let $(\mu,\sigma)$ the mean and standard deviation of the image $\delta_y I(x,y)$. For each pixel $(x,y)$ of the mask, a test is realized to decide whether or not the pixel $(x,y)$ is a potential eye center:

$$M'(x,y) = \begin{cases} M(x,y) \ \text{if} \ \dfrac{\partial_y I(x,y) - \mu}{\sigma} \leq -0.68 \\ 0 \ \textit{otherwise} \end{cases} \qquad (2)$$

This test verifies if the previously selected pixels $(M(x,y)=1)$ belong to a darker area (below the average $\mu$) with a high standard deviation. At the end, we obtain the mask $M$, where the pixels set to 1, are potential eye center.

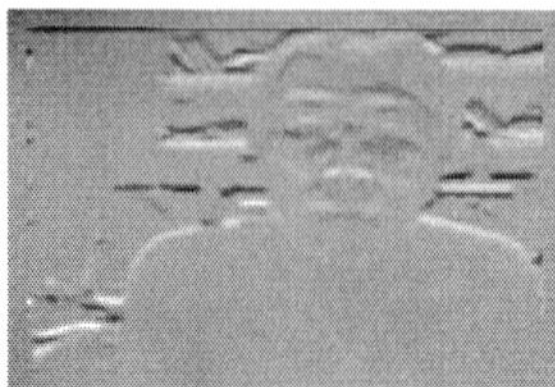

**Figure 3: Image Derivative Analysis**

## Validation by Eye Template Matching

Given an hypothetical eye center $(x,y)$, for which $M(x,y)=1$, we measure the correlation between an image region centered at $(x,y)$, and an eye template, using the coefficient of correlation, invariant to the linear shifts of grey levels existing between the template and the image region. The coefficient of correlation between two random variables $X$ and $Y$ is defined by

$$\rho(X,Y) = \frac{E(XY) - E(X)E(Y)}{\Gamma(X)\Gamma(Y)} \quad (3)$$

where $E(.)$ is the expectation and $\Gamma(.)$ the standard deviation. $\rho$ varies within [-1,1], where 1 is the perfect match. This coefficient is estimated at 3 different scales, 16x16 pixels, 20x20 pixels and 24x24 pixels, using three different templates. The score associated to $(x,y)$ is defined as the maximum of the three correlation scores. When this score is below a threshold, the eye position $(x,y)$ is rejected, and the mask $M$ is updated: $M(x,y)=0$.

## Validation by Contour Correlation Technique

Given an hypothetical eye center $(x,y)$, for which $M(x,y)=1$, we verify if $(x,y)$ is the center of a circle in the edge map obtained using the Canny-Deriche edge detector [Deriche]. For each circle $C(x,y,r)$, where $r$ is the ray, we estimate an angular correlation score, that counts the number of pixels $(x',y')$ of the edge map, that have a likely gradient direction, compared to the theoretical gradient at that point. For a point $(x',y')$ of the circle centered in $(x,y)$, the theoretical gradient is

$$\theta_{th}(x',y') = \tan^{-1}\left(\frac{y'-y}{x'-x}\right) \quad (4)$$

This value varies within $[-\pi,\pi]$. When we apply the edge detector, we obtain two information: the edge magnitude and the edge direction maps. We define for a point $(x_i,y_i)$ of the circle $C(x,y,r)$, an angular correlation score, combining the edge magnitude and edge direction values:

$$\alpha_i(xi,yi) = \begin{cases} \pi & if \quad Edge(xi,yi) = 0 \\ \left\| \theta(xi,yi) \right| - \left| \theta_{th}(xi,yi) \right\| & otherwise \end{cases} \quad (5)$$

This values varies within $[0, \pi]$, $\pi$ corresponding to the worst match. Then, given a digital circle $C(x,y,r) = \{(x_1,y_1),...(x_{nr},y_{nr})\}$, containing $nr$ points, we obtain $nr$ angular correlations $\{\alpha_1(x_1,y_1),...,\alpha_n(x_n,y_n)\}$. The angular correlation score $\alpha(x,y,r)$ associated to the circle $C(x,y,r)$, is defined as the $i^{th}$ lowest angular score. The final score associated to $(x,y)$ is defined as the lowest angular score over the considered rays, here from 3 to 10 pixels:

$$\alpha(x, y) = \min_{r=3}^{r=10} \alpha(x, y, r) \quad (6)$$

In practice for each circle $C(x,y,r)$ we select the angular score corresponding to 35% of the points of the circle. In this way, we can deal with interrupted or partial contours. Finally, if the score is too high, then the eye hypothesis $(x,y)$ is rejected and $M$ is updated: $M(x,y)=0$.

Local Maxima Filtering

A final step consists in reducing the number of hypothesis, using a local maxima algorithm. Let $G=(X,U)$, the graph where the each node $(x,y) \in X$ is an eye hypothesis $(x,y)$ $(ie\ M(x,y)=1)$, and each edge $(p,q) \in U$ links two points $p$ and $q$ of $X$, such that their euclidean distance $d(p,q)$ is below a threshold D. Let $\{C_1,C_2,...,C_n\}$ the $n$ connected components of $G$. By definition, each connected component $C_i$ containing $ki$ points is defined as:

$$C_i = \{\{p_{i1},p_{i2},...,p_{ik}\}/\forall p_{in} \in C_i, \exists p_{im} \in C_i, 0 < d(p_{in},p_{im}) < D\} \quad (7)$$

Each component $C_i$ is replaced by one point $e_i$, for which the angular correlation score is minimum (cf. Eq (6)):

$$e_i = \arg\min_{j=1..ki} \alpha(p_{ij} = (x_j,y_j)) \quad (8)$$

At the end, we obtain a set of n points $H=\{e_1=(x_1,y_1),...,e_n=(x_n,y_n)\}$, each point being one representative of each connected component $\{C_1,C_2,...,C_n\}$.

**Figure 4 : Eyes Hypothesis Extraction**

## *Face Hypothesis Extraction*

The next step of the face location, is to consider all the couples of eyes hypothesis, and to verify if they are within a face or not. Formally, given the set of eye hypothesis $H=\{(x_1,y_1),...,(x_n,y_n)\}$, we construct the set of potential faces $F=HxH$, where 'x' denotes the cartesian product, and we filter it, by applying geometrical constraints, intra-image constraints, and model-based constraints. The resulting set $F' \subset F$, contains all the faces that verify these constraints. Then, using a quality measure, we select the best face among all the faces of F'.

Filtering Using Geometrical Constraints.

Let $f_{ij} = ((x_i,y_i),(x_j,y_j))$, a face hypothesis described by the two potential eyes $(x_i,y_i)$ and $(x_j,y_j)$, $d$, the euclidean distance between $(x_i,y_i)$ and $(x_j,y_j)$, and $\theta$, the angle between the line $((x_i,y_i),(x_j,y_j))$ and the horizontal. $f_{ij}$ is accepted if the following conditions are verified:

$$\begin{cases} d_{min} \leq d \leq d_{max} \\ |\theta| \leq \theta_{max} \\ Polygon(x_1,y_1,x_2,y_2,x_3,y_3,x_4,y_4) \subset Window(0,0,640,480) \end{cases} \quad (9)$$

The first rule defines the interval of interocular distance $[d_{min},d_{max}]$ that we allow. The second rule specifies the maximum authorized horizontal tilt of the face $[-\theta,\theta]$, and the third rules verifies if the important part of the face is completely within the image frame. The polygon $(x_1,y_1,x_2,y_2,x_3,y_3,x_4,y_4)$ is constructed using the eyes position $(x_i,y_i)$ and $(x_j,y_j)$ in the following way. Let *(mx,my)* the middle of the segment $[(x_i,y_i),(x_j,y_j)]$. Referring to an horizontal segment of length $d$, where the middle is given by *(mx,my)*, we obtain the rectangle $[(x_{left},y_{high}), (x_{right},y_{low})]$ where:

$$\begin{cases} x_{left} = mx - \lambda_x * d \quad y_{high} = my - \lambda_{y1} * d \\ x_{right} = mx + \lambda_x * d \quad y_{low} = my + \lambda_{y2} * d \end{cases} \quad (10)$$

Rotating this rectangle about *(mx,my)* by the angle $\theta$, provides the polygon $(x_1,y_1,x_2,y_2,x_3,y_3,x_4,y_4)$ enclosing the face. Here, $\lambda_x{=}0.6$, $\lambda_{y1}{=}0.5$ and $\lambda_{y2}{=}1$.

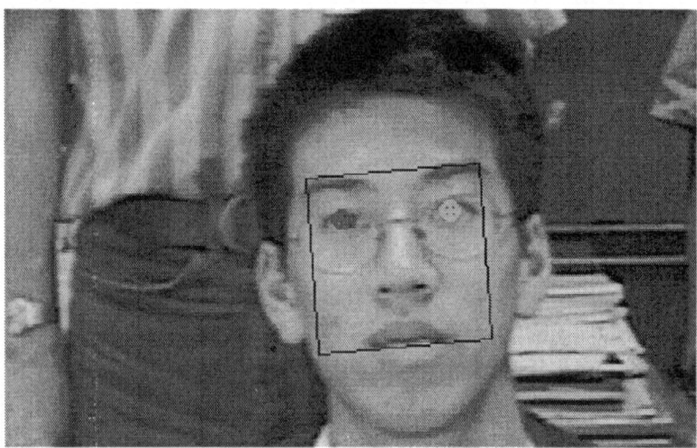

**Figure 5: Eyes Detection and Bounding Box**

Filtering Using Image Measures

Given a face hypothesis $f_{ij} = ((x_i,y_i),(x_j,y_j))$, described by the two potential eyes $(x_i,y_i)$ *and* $(x_j,y_j)$, $f_{ij}$ is accepted if the three image properties are verified: 1) the two eyeballs surrounding $(x_i,y_i)$ and $(x_j,y_j)$ are similar; 2) the two eye regions surrounding $(x_i,y_i)$ and $(x_j,y_j)$ are similar; 3) the face region is vertically symmetric. The measures 1) and 2) are based on the same technique, but applied on two different size of subimages; the measure 3) is based on the correlation between the left and the right parts of the face.

*Eyeball and Eye Region Similarity*

To determine whether two regions of the same image $I$ are similar, we count the number of times two corresponding pixels have similar grey levels. We obtain a score between 0 and 1, where 1 is a perfect match. We have:

$$S((x_i,y_i),(x_j,y_j)) = \frac{1}{N}\sum_{v=-m}^{v=m}\sum_{w=-n}^{w=n}\partial(I(x_i+v,y_i+w),I(x_j+v,y_j+w))$$

$$where\quad \partial(u,v) = \begin{cases} 1 & if\,|u-v| < Th \\ 0 & otherwise \end{cases} \qquad (11)$$

The number of couple of pixels explored is $N=(2*m+1)*(2*n+1)$, where $m$ and $n$ are defined according to the distance between the two eyes. In our case, we use $m=n$. For the eyeball similarity, $m$ varies between 3 to 6 pixels, and for the eye region similarity, $m$ varies between 15 to 20 pixels. Finally, a face hypothesis is rejected if the eyeball or eye region similarity is too low.

*Face Symmetry*

The face symmetry, valid for frontal faces and near frontal faces, is an important criteria, to select faces that are appropriate for a reliable face recognition. However, due to the variability of the lighting conditions that affect this estimation, we mainly use it to reject trivial cases, rather than detecting good cases. This computation is based on the statistical correlation (cf Eq (3)) between the left part and the right parts of the face, defined within the rectangle obtained using Eq.10.

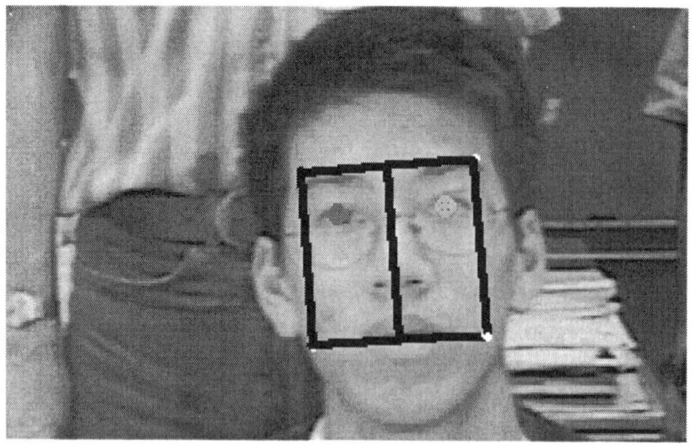

**Figure 6: Face Symmetry**

Given a polygon $(p_1,p_2,p_3,p_4) = ((x_1,y_1),(x_2,y_2),(x_3,y_3),(x_4,y_4))$, and the middle vertical segment defined by $[m_1,m_2]$ where $m_1 = (m_{x1},m_{y1}) = ((x_1+x_2)/2,(y_1+y_2)/2)$ and $m_2 = (m_{x2},m_{y2}) = ((x_3+x_4)/2,(y_3+y_4)/2)$, the left region $X$ is defined by the polygon $X=(p_1,m_1,m_2,p_4)$. The symmetric region $Y$ of $X$ about $[m_1,m_2]$ is defined by the polygon $Y=(m_1,p_2,p_3,m_2)$. We define the symmetric correlation between $X$ and $Y$ as

$$\rho_{sym} = \frac{E_{sym}(XY) - E(X)E(Y)}{\Gamma(X)\Gamma(Y)}$$

$$E_{sym}(XY) = \frac{1}{N}\sum_{i=1}^{N} X(x_i, y_i) Y(2x_m - x_i, 2y_m - y_i) \qquad (12)$$

$$x_m = \frac{x_i - x_1}{mx_1 - x_1}(mx_2 - mx_1) + mx_1, \quad y_m = \frac{y_i - y_1}{my_1 - y_1}(my_2 - my_1) + my_1$$

The point $(x_m,y_m)$ belongs to the segment $[m_1,m_2]$, and we have used parametric representation for the computation. The expectations $E(X)$ and $E(Y)$ and the standard deviations $\Gamma(X)$ and $\Gamma(Y)$ are unchanged. Finally, if the symmetric correlation score is too low the face hypothesis is rejected.

## Filtering Using Image Models

The last filtering techniques are using eye and face template matching techniques. Both techniques are based on statistical correlations (Eq 3). In order to be robust to the non-linear changes caused by various lighting conditions, we have modified the measure of correlations [Mariani].

The size of the eyes templates is 70x26 pixels, and the eyes coordinates are (10,13) and (60,13) respectively. The size of the face template is 20x20 pixels and the eyes coordinates are (5,5) and (15,5) respectively.

**Figure 7: 2 Eyes Template and Face Template**

Therefore, given a face hypothesis $f_{ij} = \{(x_i,y_i),(x_j,y_j)\}$, and given a template (eyes or face) with eyes coordinates $(x_{left},y_{left})$ and $(x_{right},y_{right})$, we normalize the region of the input image in scale and rotation by setting the points $(x_i,y_i)$ to $(x_{left},y_{left})$ and $(x_j,y_j)$ to $(x_{right},y_{right})$ (rotation and scaling of the input image), **and by** cropping the portion of the image enclosed in the rectangle defining the template.

Then, given a template $T$ and an image $F$, we propose the following robust correlation: let $T=(T_{left}, T_{right})$ and $F=(F_{left}, F_{right})$, the left and right parts of $T$ and $F$ respectively, and let $\rho(X,Y)$ the coefficient of correlation defined in Eq. (3), we have:

$$\rho_{temp}(T,F) = \max(\rho(T_{left}, F_{left}), \rho(T_{right}, F_{right})) \quad (13)$$

For human faces in near frontal positions, this measure is more robust to complex lighting conditions than the direct correlation [Mariani]. Finally, the faces hypothesis $f_{ij}$ for which the eyes or face template matching scores are too low are discarded

## Selecting the Best Face

At the previous step, we have obtained several possible face locations. Our aim is now to select the best one, according to a given criterium. This face hypothesis is the most suitable for its recognition. Given the set $F = \{f_1,...,f_k\}$ of face hypothesis obtained at the previous step, the best face $f^*$ is the one that maximizes the following cost function

$$f^* = \arg\max_{i=1}^{k}(1 - |1 - \gamma(f_i)|) \quad (14)$$

where the cost function $\gamma(.)$ is defined as a linear combination of four scores obtained at the previous steps: $\alpha(f_{ij}) = \alpha(x_i,y_i)+\alpha(x_j,y_j)$, the total eye contour correlation cost (cf. Eq 6), $S(f)$ the eyeballs similarity (cf. Eq 11), $\rho_f(f)$ the face template and $\rho_e(f)$ the eye template correlation score (cf. Eq 13). We have

$$\gamma(f) = a\alpha(f)+bS(f)+c\rho_f(f)+d\rho_e(f) \quad (15)$$

The parameters $(a,b,c,d)$ have been obtained by supervised learning of 500 examples, using the least mean square technique. Given a training set of faces $\{f_1,...,f_k\}$, the cost associated to the best face $f^*$ was fixed to 1 and 0 for all the others, satisfying $\gamma(f^*) > \gamma(f_i)$, $i=1..k$, $f_i \neq f^*$. $(a,b,c,d)$ were found by minimizing the error function

$$E = \frac{1}{2}\sum_{i=1}^{k}\left(\gamma(fi) - d(fi)\right)^2 \; where \; d(fi) = \begin{cases} 1 \; if \; fi = f* \\ 0 \; otherwise \end{cases} \quad (16)$$

with respect to *(a,b,c,d)*. At the end, if the score associated to *f**, *1-|1-γ(f*)|* is too low, the hypothesis is rejected and nothing is detected within this frame.

**Figure 8: Face Validation and Selection**

## *Face Tracking*

In our context, the face tracking is reduced to its simplest. Given the face hypothesis detected in the previous frame, $f = \{(x_1,y_1),(x_2,y_2)\}$, where $(x_1,y_1)$ is the center of the left eye, and $(x_2,y_2)$ is the center of the right eye, we research in the current frame the face *f'*, by applying the eye validation, face extraction and best face selection, only in a small neighborhood around these two points, ie by exploring the *set* $F = \{f_{ij} = ((x_i,y_i),(x_j,y_j)) \, / \, (x_i,y_i) \in d(x_1,y_1,\varepsilon), (x_j,y_j) \in d(x_1,y_1,\varepsilon)\}$, where $d(x,y,\varepsilon)$ is the disc centered in *(x,y)* and having a ray $\varepsilon$. A satisfactory value for $\varepsilon$ is 15 pixels for a 640x480 image, which allows small motion between two frames. If the face was not detected at the previous frame, the complete face detection is applied at the current frame. This simple tracking system has proved to be very efficient in our system.

## **Robust Face Recognition**

The face recognition techniques proposed in the litterature belong to two broad categories [Brunelli]: the template matching techniques, like the *eigenfaces* [Turk] based on a principal component analysis..., and the feature matching techniques like the elastic graph attributed with gabor wavelets extracted from the image around each vertex of the graph [Manjunath].

The technique we propose here, uses *a priori* knowledge about the face location performances, and combines a face template matching with feature matching techniques, unified under the tangent distance formalism [Simard]. More precisely, a face selection is realized using a face template matching, very robust to lighting conditions, changes of expressions and moderate changes of poses. A feature-based verification technique is then applied to the K best selected faces, providing the final face similarity.

The two techniques were tested independently on MV2TS and ORL databases (neutral lighting conditions), and for the lighting conditions, we used our database of 40 persons under 16 lighting conditions. The system recognizes daily more than 40 persons in an uncontrolled lighting environment and with two months apart.

In the first section, we present the tangent distance theory. In the second section, we describe the *a priori* knowledge on the face location performances, and its encoding in the tangent distance formalism. In the third section, we propose the face template matching technique, relying on a description of each person as a multitude of small synthetic face prototypes, all generated automically during the registration, from a single face image. In the fourth section, we detail the feature-based matching technique, and in the fifth section, the combination of the two techniques is explained. Finally, the integration of the face similarity over a number of frames in the video, is provided in the sixth section. It makes an optimal use of the face location system to achieve the best recognition score within a time interval. To conclude, we present the results and performances of our system, and the future optimization.


## Tangent Distance

The tangent distance was introduced by Simard el al. [Simard], and has been applied successfully in the handwritten character recognition community [Keysers] where the authors define this technique extended tangent distance. They encode a 10x10 pixels binary handwritten character with many allowable variations, and subsequently train a neural network to recognize a noisy character. Therefore, the tangent distance measure is robust in compensating for little transformations of the character. In our case, we have extended this technique for the face recognition, to compensate for geometric transformations created by an inaccurate face location, changes of facial expressions and moderate changes of pose, and to be robust to photometric transformations created by lighting conditions. Another work [Vascolensos] applies geometric transformations on the original image, namely rotation and scaling, in the tangent distance framework. We redefine and extend the geometric and photometric transformations defining a tangent space suitable for a human face.

Let an image $I$, and let $t(I,\alpha)$ a transformation of this image which depends on the L-dimensional parameter-vector $\alpha$. This transformation can be geometric, modifying the pixels' position or photometric, changing the pixels' intensity, or both. Pratically, a synthetic image can be derived from the original image by applying a linear combination of these elementary transformations. Let $M_I$, the set of all the synthesized images derived from the original image,

$$M_I = \left\{ I + \sum_{l=1}^{L} \alpha_l . T_l(I) : \alpha = \{\alpha_1, \alpha_2, ... \alpha_L\} \in \Re^L \right\} \quad (17)$$

$M_I$ is defined as the tangent subspace to the manifold $M=\{t(I,\alpha) : \alpha \in \Re^L\}$, and the vectors $\{T_1(I), T_2(I), ... T_L(I)\}$ span the tangent subspace.

The single sided tangent distance $D(I,\mu)$, between an image $I$ and a reference image $\mu$ is defined as the minimum distance between $\mu$ and the tangent subspace $M_I$,

$$D(I,\mu) = \min_{\alpha} \left\{ \left\| I + \sum_{l=1}^{L} \alpha_l T_l(I) - \mu \right\|^2 \right\} \quad (18)$$

The tangent vectors $\{T_1(I), T_2(I), ... T_L(I)\}$ can be computed using simple finite difference between the original image $I$, and a small transformation of $I$. We have defined the tangent vectors as geometric and photometric masks, along with translation, rotation and scaling, directly expressed in term of eyes' location error realized by the face location system.


*A priori Knowledge Encoding of Rotation, Translation and Scaling*

Given a face image $I$, within an observed frame, where the eyes have been located at the position $(x_1, y_1)$ and $(x_2, y_2)$ , the traditional approach is to crop the region of the frame containing the face, and to normalize it in rotation and scaling, by setting the left and right eyes at a fix position. This face image is then fed to the face registration or face matching algorithm.

The weakness of this technique is that it relies on the accuracy of the eyes detection. A little displacement of an eye position from its true location, and we have a translation, rotation and scaling problem between the registered and the observed faces.

To be more robust to this problem, we use, during the registration of a given face, multiple eyes location hypothesis defined from the two eyes positions provided by the face location system. Here, we use a priori knowledge on the error in eyes' position accuracy.

We have an error of 8% of detected interocular distance, ie for two detected eyes position $(x_1,y_1)$ and $(x_2,y_2)$, distant from 50 pixels, the real eyes are respectively within a disk centered in $(x_1,y_1)$ and $(x_2,y_2)$ of 4 pixels. We take 5 possible positions for each eye, leading to 25 hypothesis of geometrical normalization. From these 25 hypothesis, we derive 25 normalized images, each being rescaled to 75x75 pixels. We have therefore stored faces that are slightly rotated, scaled and translated. Each of these 25 images are processed for template registration and features are extracted for feature-based registration. For the template registration, we synthesize a multitude of small face prototypes and store them. For the feature-based technique, we extract gabor wavelets graph for each image, and store them.

The following image illustrates the case for 9 hypothesis for each eye, leading to 81 hypothesis of normalization.

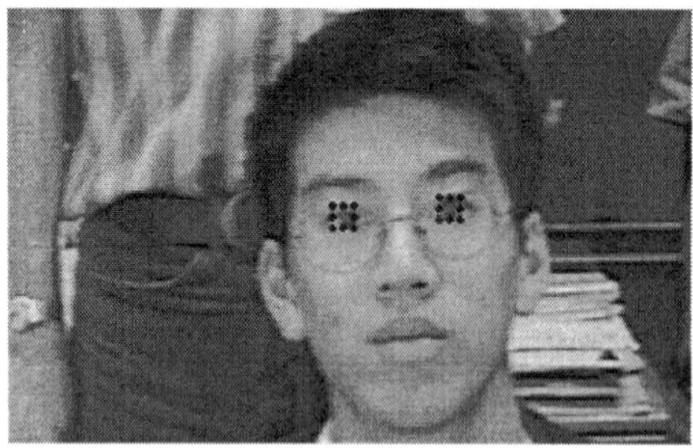

**Figure 9: 9 Possible Position for Each Eye**

## *Face Prototyping for Template-Based Matching*

Several masks are generated for face prototype modeling. Two different nonlinear transforms namely, photometric transforms and geometric transforms are encoded into these generated masks. During the image registration, these masks are used to compose realistic facial prototypes.

## Photometric Transforms

A Photometric transform modifies the grey level of a pixel using a nonlinear function, and may depend on the pixel position. Linear transformations are not modeled as classical image normalization (histogram equalization,…) processes exist to cancel their negative effect. Described below is the set of lighting masks used in the process. These masks approximate real lighting conditions and are proved to be effective for face recognition applications. We use three different types of masks, but it is straightforward to extend their number.

### *Mask1: Logarithmic function on grey-levels*

The purpose of applying this mask is to obtain a brighter image from the original image. A lookup table is formed to accomplish this task. The entries of the lookup table are calculated as follows:

$$L(w) = 255 \left( \frac{\log(v) - \log(k_{min})}{\log(255) - \log(k_{min})} \right), v = k_{min} + \frac{w(255 - k_{min})}{255} \quad (19)$$

where $w$, is the grey level of the image ranging within $[0,255]$, $v$ is the transformed grey level ranging within $[k_{min},255]$, $k_{min} \geq 0$, and $L(w)$ is the output grey level ranging within $[0,255]$.

### *Mask2: Exponential function on grey-levels*

The purpose of applying this mask on grey levels is to obtain a darker image from the original image. This is accomplished by forming a look up table and the entries of the table are calculated as follows:

$$L(w) = 255 \left( \frac{\exp\left( \frac{w * k_{max}}{255} \right) - 1}{\exp(k_{max}) - 1} \right) \quad (20)$$

where $w \in [0,255]$, $k_{max} > 0$, and $L(w) \in [0,255]$.

 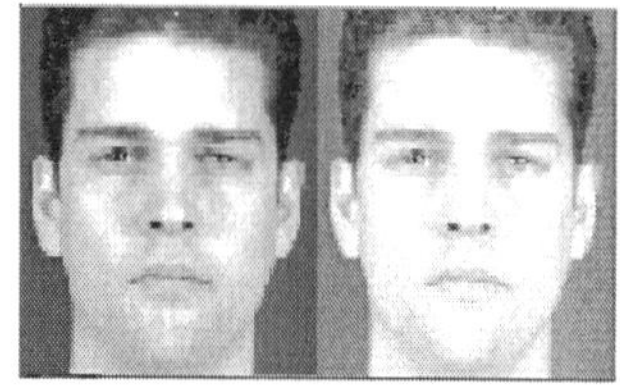

**Figure 10: The input image and the resulting image after exponential lut (kmax=4) and logarithmic lut (kmin=32)**

### Mask3: Generation of Vertical and Horizontal shadow masks

As the basic idea behind the generation of both vertical and horizontal masks is the same, we describe only the approach adopted for generating vertical shadow for the $x$ abscissa. This function modifies the grey level value of a pixel depending on its spatial position in the image. The process is carried out line by line.

Let the width of the image be $X$, and $\lambda$ a real coefficient where $0 < \lambda < 1$. Let $m = \lambda * X$. Then we can define the function $f(x)$ for $x \in [0,X]$ as follows:

$$f(x) = \begin{cases} \dfrac{x}{m} & \text{if } x \in [0,m] \\[2mm] 1 + \dfrac{(x-m)}{(X-m)} & \text{if } x \in ]m, X] \end{cases} \qquad (21)$$

Given a pixel $p=(x,y)$ whose grey level is $v$, we can calculate the corresponding pixel value $w$ at position $(x,y)$ as $w=v*f(x)$. By doing so, we can generate an image whose first $m$ pixels are darker and the pixels beyond $m$ are brighter. Horizontal shadow masks are generated in a similar fashion by taking into account the $y$ coordinates, and the height of the image $Y$. At then end, the output image is normalized between [0,255]. The following images illustrate the vertical shadow process for 5 values of $\lambda$.

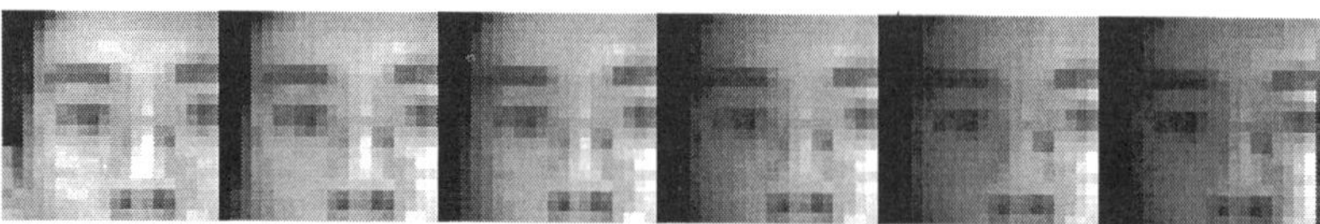

**Figure 11: Vertical Shadows**

## Geometric Transform

When a face is captured for its recognition, the pose variation may affect the recognition performance. As a mean to solve this difficulty, face warping algorithms have been proposed [Bai][Beymer], as well as pose-dependent face recognition [Huang], once the face pose is estimated. In our case, we propose to encode the geometric transformations at the registration time. Indeed, we apply to the captured frontal face, several geometrical masks that have been elaborated offline using 500 images of 25 persons. We have employed the optical flow estimation between images [Bai].

Given an observed face with fixed eyes position $(x_1,y_1)$ and $(x_2,y_2)$, the synthesis of a frontal face is done by computing the optical flow between a face and its mirror image about the vertical axis. We established these masks on 75x75 pixels face images, where the eyes are aligned horizontally at a fixed position. By multiscale dynamic programming, we established the translation that each pixel of the original image has to undergo in order to reproduce optimally the mirror image. Half of this optical flow produces the frontal face.


### *Optical Flow Estimation*

Given an image $L$, and its mirror image $M$, we can represent the $i^{th}$ row of each image as a vector of $N$ pixels where $l = \{p_1,..p_N\}$ and $m = \{q_1,...,q_N\}$, respectively. Transformation of $l$ into $m$ is optimized by minimizing the overall stretching and maximizing the grey level correlation. This is achieved by dynamic programming [bellmann].

Let $H = \{H_1,...H_N\}$, where $H_i$ is a set of potential pixels associated to the pixel $p_i$, and $x(p_i)$ is the abscissa of the pixel $p_i$ in the line $l$ and $\delta$ is a fixed threshold:

$$H_i = \left\{(p_i q) : q \in M, |x(p_i) - x(q)| < \delta\right\} \quad (22)$$

Let $T = \{T_1,...,T_{N-1}\}$ where $T_i$ represents the set of transitions between the two hypothesis sets $H_i$ and $H_{i+1}$: $T_i = H_i \times H_{i+1}$. The weight associated with to the hypothesis $H_{ij} = (p_i,q_j)$ depends on the grey value between the two pixels $p_i$ and $q_j$:

$$w(\text{Hij}) = \lambda |g(p_i) - g(q_j)| \quad (23)$$

where $\lambda$ is a constant and g(.) is the grey level of a given pixel. The cost associated with the transition $t(H_{ij},H_{i+1,k})$ can be expressed as

$$w(t(H_{ij}, H_{i+1,k})) = \left| x(p_i) - x(q_j) - x(p_{i+1}) + x(q_k) \right| \quad (24)$$

By constructing the directed graph (*{start,end}* u *H,T*), and by computing the shortest path linking the starting point *start* to the ending point *end*, we obtain the optimal set of pixels' translation that transform the line *l* into the line *m*. The cost function linking two nodes in this graph, (ie two hypothesis $H_{ij}$ and $H_{i+1k}$) is a tradeoff between the grey level similarity and the allowable line stretching.

$$c(H_{ij}, H_{i+1,k}) = \gamma(w(H_{ij})) + (1-\gamma)(w(t(H_{ij}, H_{i+1,k}))) \quad (25)$$

*Multiresolution Optical Flow Estimation*

This technique is insufficient because each line is matched individually. A multiresolution technique can overcome these drawbacks, by extending constraints across several adjacent lines. The fact that two adjacent lines roughly must undergo the same warp allows the correction of local errors. We employ an iterative algorithm which starts with large bands and large translation hypothesis. During each iteration, the width of the band and the allowed translations are reduced. This is carried out until the band and the magnitude of the translation hypothesis are only a few pixels. The continuity constraint of the optical flow is strengthened by band overlapping, with each band contributing equally.

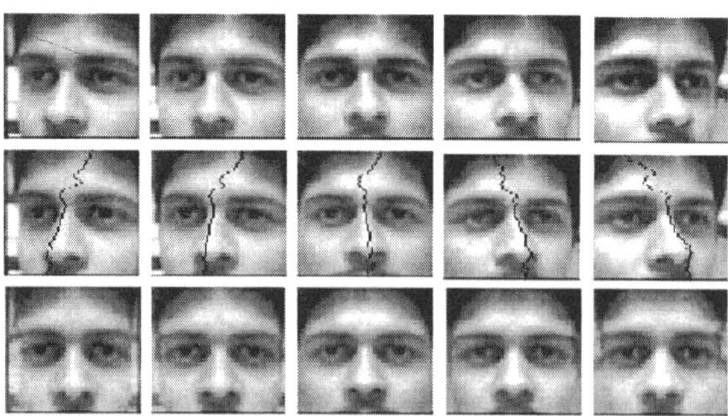

**Figure 12:The first row represents 5 original images, the second row represents the nose axis, established by reverse half optical flow applied to the vertical line passing through the center of the image, and the last row shows the synthetic frontal faces obtained.**

Prototypes Synthesis

Referring to the definition of the tangent distance, the geometric and photometric masks are used to generate a multitude of artificial face prototypes. Concretely, given an input face image, we have obtained 25 75x75 pixels hypothesis of normalized faces, using the *a priori* knowledge about the performance of the eyes detector. Then, for each normalized face we apply the 3 lighting conditions masks, and then we apply 4 morphing masks to these 75 obtained prototypes. A single input face is then represented by 225 prototypes for its registration. To add robustness to our system, we use 5 input frames for which the eyes detection has been very good. As the user moves in front of the camera, these input faces are all different. A person is then represented by 1125 synthetic prototypes. Each prototype is then subsampled to a 15x15 pixels, where the grey level of each pixel of the smaller prototype is the minimum value of its corresponding 5x5 window in the 75x75 pixels prototype.

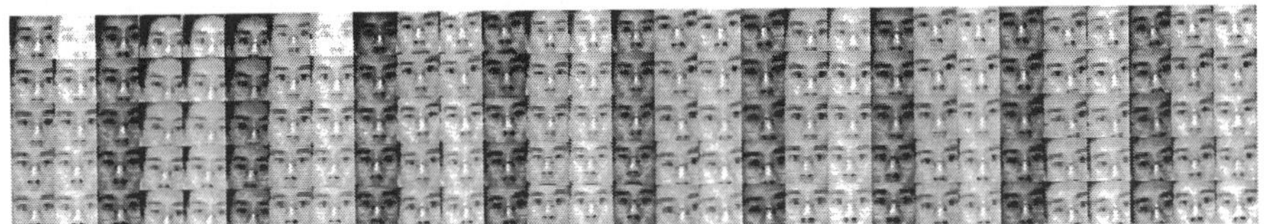

**Figure 13: Some Synthetic Face Prototypes**

Face Template Similarity Based on Tangent Distance

let $p = \{f_1, f_2, ..., f_N\}$ the face cluster containing $N=1125$ face prototypes. The similarity between an observed face $f$ and the cluster $p$ is given by:

$$d_T(f,p) = \min_{i=1}^{N} d_f(f,f_i)$$

$$d_f(f,f_k) = \frac{1}{R}\sum_{i=1}^{R} \partial\big(|f(i) - f_k(i)|\big), \quad \partial(x) = \begin{cases} 0 & if \quad x < T \\ 1 & if \quad x \geq T \end{cases} \quad (26)$$

The face $f$ obtained after the eyes detection, is normalized to 75x75 pixels and then subsampled to $R=15\text{x}15$ pixels. The grey levels are then normalized between [0,1], as well as for each prototype of the face cluster. This technique has demonstrated robustness, outperforming statistical correlation. Here, we count the number of pixels that have different grey levels. Two pixels are different if their grey level difference exceeds the threshold T. This similarity is within [0,1] and the lower, the better.

The minimum filter that we have used for the subsampling outperformed the mean, the median, the maximum, and interquantile filters. The reason is that it reinforces the facial features (eyes, nose, eyebrows) over the skin, as these components are darker. By taking the minimum within a 5x5 window, we actually dilates the darker pixels to the brighter pixels, the eyes, the nostrils and the mouth become larger, and the face similarity becomes more discriminative. Moreover, this operation cancels the facial expressions.

To speed up the computation over the cluster, and over the database, the face similarity df() is stopped as soon as the number of mismatched pixels exceeds a given threshold.

## *Face Representation Using Gabor Wavelets*

With wavelets, multiscale representation of an image can be achieved. This is realized by decomposing an image at various scales and orientations. Features detected by Gabor wavelets are known to be less sensitive to transformations such as local distortions, translation and rotation. In our approach, Gabor responses extracted at predefined set of feature points are used to validate the accuracy of the face matching process. Normalized images, prior to geometric and photometric transformations are subjected to Gabor response extraction.

### Feature point selection

As eye area seems to be more invariant to facial expressions and gestures, we selected more points in the eye area. Three points across the base of the nose were also selected. The positions of the eyes are set at fixed coordinates and the relative position of the nose is determined intuitively using anthropometric standards. We finally represent a face with 14 fiducial points are illustrated in the Figure 14.

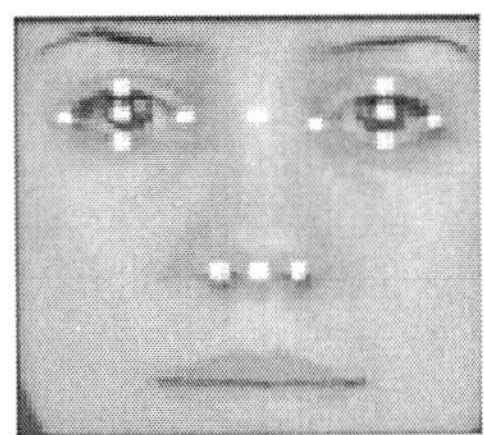

**Figure 14: Selected Fiducial Points**

## Gabor Filter Responses

The 2-D complex valued Gabor kernel used for retrieving multi-scale and multi-orientation features is given by:

$$\psi_k(p) = \frac{k^2}{\sigma^2}\exp\left(-\frac{k^2 p^2}{2\sigma^2}\right)\left[\exp(ikp) - \exp\left(-\frac{\sigma^2}{2}\right)\right] \quad (27)$$

where $p$ is the point coordinates relative to the center, $\sigma$ is the ratio of window width to wavelength, and $k$ controls the width of the gaussian window, and the wavelength and orientation of the oscillatory part. The first term in the brackets determines the oscillatory part and the second term compensates for the DC-value of the kernel, making the filter insensitive to changes of illuminations.

The Gabor kernels are generated for 3 spatial frequencies ($\pi/2,\pi/4,\pi/8$) and 6 orientations ($0,\pi/6,\pi/3,\pi/2,2\pi/3,5\pi/6$), for $\sigma=\pi$, and $k=\pi$, resulting in 18 kernels. Gabor response at each feature point $f_i$ is evaluated by convolving the image with these kernels. Hence, we can represent a feature vector of a point as a collection of Gabor coefficients. $f_i = [f_{i1},f_{i2}....f_{i18}]^T$ where $f_{ij}$ corresponds to the Gabor feature $j$ evaluated at the $i^{th}$ point.

## Feature-Based Face Similarity Distance Based on Tangent Distance

Given an input face, we generated 25 face hypothesis. Moreover, we use 5 frames to register a person, leading to 125 face hypothesis. For each of these 125 face images, we have extracted 14 points attributed with gabor wavelets feature vectors. According to the tangent distance definition, we define the feature-based face similarity between a face representation $f$ and a cluster $p$ = $\{f_1,f_2,...,f_N\}$, N=125, as

$$dw(f,p) = \min_{i=1}^{N} dg(f,fi)$$

$$dg(f,g) = \frac{1}{14}\sum_{i=1}^{14}\frac{1-\cos(f(i),g(i))}{2} \qquad (28)$$

Indeed, the similarity between the feature vectors $f(i)$ and $g(i)$, of the $i^{th}$ feature point, is determined by their normalized inner product (cos), varying between [-1,1], the higher, the better. We have transformed it ((1-cos)/2) so that the value varies within [0,1], with the convention the lower the better. The final similarity between two faces $f$ and $g$, $dg(f,g)$ is calculated by taking the average of all the similarities between the corresponding feature points.

## Template-Based and Feature-Based Face Recognition

We propose a two-fold algorithm to achieve the face recognition task, combining in an optimum manner the two techniques. After extensive experiments on MV2TS and ORL databases, both acquired on neutral lighting conditions and without face template synthesis, the template matching based on 15x15 pixels, was consistently retrieving within the K best faces, one or several occurences of the same candidate, and this with a probability exceeding 86% for the first match, 97% for K=16 and 99.3% for K=31, having 1180 images in MV2TS, 4 images per person, 295 persons, and 400 in ORL database, 10 images per person, 40 persons. These estimations were conducted automatically using the straightforward face template matching measure (cf. Eq 26).

Similar tests were conducted using the gabor wavelets-based face similarity. The template-matching was more consistent on the K best, but the feature-based technique was more able to discriminate the correct face among the K best. Therefore, we have combined the template-based matching and feature-based matching in a hierachical manner. We first select the K best faces using the template matching technique, then we use the feature-based technique on this small set to determine the correct person.

Tests on the standard databases MV2TS and ORL have shown little improvements using this method, as the two techniques fail almost for the same faces. The real improvement has been observed on our database, containing 40 persons under 16 lighting conditions. Gabor wavelets have been introduced to confirm and to reinforce the validity of the selected faces. The overall face similarity, combining the two techniques is given as:

$$S(f,g) = \begin{cases} 1 & if \quad dt(f,g) \succ Th1 \\ 1 & if \quad dw(f,g) \succ Th2 \\ (dt(f,g) + dw(f,g))/2 & otherwise \end{cases} \qquad (29)$$

The feature-based test dw() is realized only on a small subset of the database, obtained using the face template matching, dt(). The overall measure S() varies between [0,1], and if S exceeds a given threshold, the person is not recognized.

In our system, we went further, once again generalizing the use of the tangent distance: we take several frames to recognize a person, and excellent performances have been obtained, with 40 persons in an uncontrolled environment, where light changes are common.

Currently, we use 5 frames per person for the recognition, and the overall face similarity is calculated by averaging the scores. These 5 frames are selected carefully by the face location system. More precisely, the system has two stacks, one for face hypothesis that it judges *excellent* (5 frames), and one that it judges *good* (10 frames). The 5 frames are sent to the recognizer when 5 face hypothesis are *excellent*, or when the stack *good* is full: at that time, it selects the 5 best faces among the good one, to achieve the recognition. A face hypothesis is judge *good* when the face score (Eq. 14) exceeds $Th_{good}$, and excellent when the face score exceeds $Th_{exc}$, with $Th_{exc} > Th_{good}$.

## Results and Performances

We conducted several experiments to test the performances of the system. We registered 40 persons, and tested the system with 16 lighting conditions, and with slightly changes of poses.

Classical systems based on Principal Component Analysis failed dramatically with a recognition rate of 37%. This is because the lighting conditions modify the intensity of the image in a nonlinear way, and a PCA or correlation techniques are very sensitive to these nonlinearities. Moreover, the exact image alignment resulting from a perfect geometric normalization of the face, given the eyes positions, is not guaranteed as eyes' position may be imprecise. This image alignment also affects the PCA and correlation techniques.

Techniques based on gabor wavelets extracted at specific points are more robust to the lighting conditions, as they are localized and the DC component is cancelled. However, we found that the image quality of the acquired face, affects the magnitude of the wavelets, and because the components are non-orthogonal, if affects the similarity measure in a meaningful way. One reason is that gabor wavelets may be viewed as derivatives of a gaussian, ie edge detectors in given direction and with a standard deviation of a given width. Operations like scaling an image (zoom in/zoom out), affects the quality of the image. As the faces detected are of various size, large variations of the scaling factors used during the face normalization, are responsible for important transformation of the face edge map, and therefore variations of the gabor responses for the same face. These variations are especially important between a zoom in and a zoom out of the image. This reduction of performances is compensated by the superior robustness of the template-based matching technique against the scaling operation.

Concretely, our system recognizes daily 40 persons with a registration time greater than one month, with very different lighting conditions, and different head poses. The system is based on an enumeration of possible face appeareances of a single face, and the more appearances, the better the performance. The recognition scores are 97.5% for the top one, and 99% for the top five. These scores are very good thanks to the fact that we use 5 frames to recognize a person and because we use a very strict parameterization of the face locator, ensuring very good face located. When a face is mis-recognized, usually in second or third position, the top 3 scores are almost equal, and usually not good enough. By fixing a rejection threshold of 0.20, the system has an acceptable false acceptance rate, for an very low false recognition rate. Usually, when two faces are similar, the probability that the score is below 0.15 has been estimated at 95%.

## Conclusion

We have proposed an integrated system of face location and recognition, robust to the lighting conditions. The face location is based on an eye extraction algorithm, validated by a face model. The face recognition, major contribution in this paper, is based on the tangent distance, where we enumerate during the registration process, all the appearances a face may have. This is realized using *a priori* knowledge about the accuracy of the face locator, and using synthetic masks that reproduce lighting conditions and head pose variations. 225 face templates are generated from a single face image, and 5 faces are used for registration, resulting in 1125 face templates, subsampled to 15x15 pixels. Similarly, we store 25 gabor wavelets graphs extracted from a single face image, and applying this to 5 faces, we obtain 125 gabor wavelets graphs. Face similarity combines, in hierarchical manner, a template-based face selection and a feature-based verification. The system has proven, after extensive experiments on 40 persons daily, to be very robust to lighting conditions, facial expressions and head movement. It is currently implemented to the mobile robot JIJO-II, which evolves in an uncontrolled indoor environment. In the future, we use a compressed version of a face-template cluster (1125 images), by training an auto-associative memory (RBF neural neural). This will lead to a much faster face selection.

# References


Takacs B. and Wechsler H. *Detection of Faces and Facial Landmarks Using Iconic Filter Banks*. Pattern Recognition, 30(1):1623-1636,1997.

Keysers D. et al. *Experiments with an Extended Tangent Distance*,15th International Conference on Pattern Recognition,Vol. 2, pp. 38-42, 2000.

Simard P. et al. *Transformation Invariance in Pattern Recognition -Tangent Distance and Tangent Propagation*. In G. Orr and K. R. Muller editors, Neural Networks: tricks of the trade, vol 1524 of Lecture Notes in Computer Science, Springer, Heidelberg, pp 239-274, 1998.

Bai Y. et al. *Face Warping Using a Single Image*. In T. Tan, Shi Y, Gao W. editors, Advances in Multimodal Interfaces - ICMI 2000, vol 1948 of Lecture Notes in Computer Science, Springer, pp 176-183, 2000.

Wiskott L. et al. *Face Recognition by Elastic Bunch Graph Matching*. Proc. IEEE International Conference on Image Processing. Vol. 1 pp. 129-132, 1997.

Dahmen J. et al. *Invariant Image Object Recognition using Mixture Densities*. Proc 15th International Conference on Pattern Recognition. Vol. 2, pp. 614-617, 2000.

Asoh H et al. JIJO-II Project. *Learning and Integrated Information processing of Office Conversant Mobile Robot*. http://www.etl.go.jp/~7440/index-e.html.

Sun Q.B. et al. *Face Detection Based on Color and Local Symmetry Information*. Proc. 3rd International Conference on Automatic Face and Gesture Recognition. pp 130-135. Apr 14-16, 1998. Nara, Japan.

Jordao L et al. *Active Face and Feature Tracking*. 10th International Conference on Image Analysis and Processing. pp 572-576, Sept. 27-29, 1999. Venice, Italy.

Huang W. and Mariani R. *Face Detection and Precise Eyes Location.* Proc 15th International Conference on Pattern Recognition. Vol. 4, pp. 722-727, 2000.

Sirohey S.A, *Human Face Segmentation and Identification.* Technical Report, CS-TR-3176, Univ. of Maryland, 1993.

Manjunath B.S. et al. *A Feature-Based Approach to Face Recognition.* Proc. IEEE Computer Soc. Conf. Computer Vision and Pattern Recognition, pp 373-378, 1992.

Moghaddam B. and Pentland A. *Probabilistic Visual Learning for Object Detection.* Proc. 5th International Conference on Computer Vision, June 1995.

Osuna E et al. *Training Support Vector Machines: An Application to Face Detection.* Computer Vision and Pattern Recognition, 1997.

Brunelli R and Poggio T. *Face Recognition: Features Versus Templates.* IEEE Trans. Pattern Analysis and Machine Intelligence, vol 15, no 10,  pp 1042-1052, Oct 1993.

Rowley H. et al. *Neural Network-Based Face Detection.* IEEE Trans. Pattern Analysis and Machine Intelligence, 1998.

Sung K. and Poggio T. *Example-Based Learning for View-Based Human Face Detection.* Technical Report, MIT, 1994.

Feraud R. et al. *A Fast and Accurate Face Detector Based on Neural Networks.* IEEE Trans. Pattern Analysis and Machine Intelligence, vol 23, no 1,  pp 42-53, Jan 2001.

Huang J. et al. *Detection of Human Faces Using Decision Trees.* Proc. 2nd International Conference on Automatic Face and Gesture Recognition. pp 248-252, 1996.

Elagin E. et al. *Automatic Pose Estimation System for Human Faces Based on Bunch Graph Matching Technology.* Proc. 3rd International Conference on Automatic Face and Gesture Recognition. pp 136-141, 1998.

Mariani R. *A Face Location Algorithm Robust to Complex Lighting Conditions.* To appear in 2nd Audio and Video-Based Biometric Person Authentication, Sweden, 2001.

Hotta K. et al. *Scale Invariant Face Detection Method using Higher-Order Local Autocorrelation Features Extracted from Log-Polar Image.* Proc. 3rd International Conference on Automatic Face and Gesture Recognition. pp 70-75, 1998.

Deriche R. *Using Canny's Criteria to Derive a Recursively Implemented Optimal Edge Detector.* International Journal of Computer Vision, 1(2):167-187, May 1987.

Vascolensos N and A. Lippman. *Multiresolution Tangent Distance for Affine Invariant Classification.* In M.I. Jordan, M.J. Kearns, and S.A. Solla Editors. Advances in Neural Inf. Proc. Systems. Vol 10. MIT Press, pp 843-849, 1998.

Beymer D and Poggio T. *Face Recognition From One Example View.* 5th International Conference on Computer Vision, pp 500-507, 1995.

Huang J et al. *Face Pose Discrimination Using Support Vector Machine (SVM)*. Proc 14th International Conference on Pattern Recognition. Vol. 2, pp. 154-156, 1998.

Bellmann. *Dynamic Programming*. Princeton University Press, 1957.

Turk M and Pentland A. *Eigenfaces for Recognition*. Journal of Cognitive Neuroscience, vol 3, no 1, pp 71-86, 1991

# Recognizing Action Units for Facial Expression Analysis *


Ying-li Tian [1]    Takeo Kanade[1]  and Jeffrey F. Cohn[1,2]

[1] Robotics Institute, Carnegie Mellon University
[2] Department of Psychology, University of Pittsburgh
Email: {yltian, tk}@cs.cmu.edu    jeffcohn@pitt.edu


## Abstract


*Most automatic expression analysis systems attempt to recognize a small set of prototypic expressions, such as happiness, anger, surprise, and fear. Such prototypic expressions, however, occur rather infrequently. Human emotions and intentions are more often communicated by changes in one or a few discrete facial features. In this paper, we develop an Automatic Face Analysis (AFA) system to analyze facial expressions based on both permanent facial features (brows, eyes, mouth) and transient facial features (deepening of facial furrows) in a nearly frontal-view face image sequence. The AFA system recognizes fine-grained changes in facial expression into action units (AUs) of the Facial Action Coding System (FACS), instead of a few prototypic expressions. Multi-state face and facial component models are proposed for tracking and modeling the various facial features, including lips, eyes, brows, cheeks, and furrows. During tracking, detailed parametric descriptions of the facial features are extracted. With these parameters as the inputs, a group of action units(neutral expression, 6 upper face AUs, and 10 lower face AUs) are recognized whether they occur alone or in combinations. The system has achieved average recognition rates of 96.4% (95.4% if neutral expressions are excluded) for upper face AUs and 96.7% (95.6% with neutral expressions excluded) for lower face AUs. The generalizability of the system has been tested by using independent image databases collected and FACS-coded for ground-truth by different research teams.*


---

## 1. Introduction

Facial expression is one of the most powerful, natural, and immediate means for human beings to communicate their emotions and intentions. The face can express emotion sooner than people verbalize or even realize their feelings. In the past decade, much progress has been made to build computer systems to understand and use this natural form of human communication [4, 3, 8, 10, 16, 18, 24, 26, 28, 32, 37, 38, 36, 40]. Most such systems attempt to recognize a small set of prototypic emotional expressions, i.e. joy, surprise, anger, sadness, fear, and disgust. This practice may follow from the work of Darwin [9] and more recently Ekman [14, 12] and Izard et al. [19] who proposed that basic emotions have corresponding prototypic facial expressions. In everyday life, however, such prototypic expressions occur relatively infrequently. Instead, emotion more often is communicated by subtle changes in one or a few discrete facial features, such as a tightening of the lips in anger or obliquely lowering the lip corns in sadness [7]. Change in isolated features, especially in the area of the eyebrows or eyelids, is typical of paralinguistic displays; for instance, raising the brows signals greeting [11]. To capture such subtlety of human emotion and paralinguistic communication, automated recognition of fine-grained changes in facial expression is needed.

### 1.1. Facial Action Coding System

Ekman and Friesen [13] developed the Facial Action Coding System (FACS) for describing facial expressions by action units (AUs). Of 44 FACS AUs that they defined, 30 AUs are anatomically related to the contractions of specific facial muscles: 12 are for upper face, and 18 are for lower face. AUs can occur either singly or in combination. When AUs occur in combination they may be *additive*, in which the combination does not change the appearance of the constituent AUs, or *non-additive*, in which the appearance of the constituents does change. Although the number of atomic action units is relatively small, more than 7,000 different AU combinations have been observed [30]. FACS provides descriptive power necessary to describe the details of facial expression.

Commonly occurring AUs and some of the additive and non-additive AU combinations are shown in Tables 1 and 2. As an example of a non-additive effect, AU 4 appears differently depending on whether it occurs alone or in combination with AU 1 (as in AU 1+4). When AU 4 occurs alone, the brows are drawn together and lowered. In AU 1+4, the brows are drawn together but are raised due to the action of AU 1. AU 1+2 is another example of non-additive combinations. When AU 2 occurs alone, it not only raises the outer brow, but also often pulls up the inner brow which results in a very similar appearance to AU 1+2. These effects of the non-additive AU combinations increase the difficulties of AU recognition.

## Table 1. Upper face action units and some combinations

| *NEUTRAL* | AU 1 | AU 2 | AU 4 |
|---|---|---|---|
| Eyes, brow, and cheek are relaxed. | Inner portion of the brows is raised. | Outer portion of the brows is raised. | Brows lowered and drawn together |
| AU 5 | AU 6 | AU 7 | AU 1+2 |
| Upper eyelids are raised. | Cheeks are raised. | Lower eyelids are raised. | Inner and outer portions of the brows are raised. |
| AU 1+4 | AU 4+5 | AU 1+2+4 | AU 1+2+5 |
| Medial portion of the brows is raised and pulled together. | Brows lowered and drawn together and upper eyelids are raised. | Brows are pulled together and upward. | Brows and upper eyelids are raised. |
| AU 1+6 | AU 6+7 | AU 1+2+5+6+7 | |
| Inner portion of brows and cheeks are raised. | Lower eyelids cheeks are raised. | Brows, eyelids, and cheeks are raised. | |

**Table 2. Lower face action units and some combinations. Single AU 23 and AU 24 are not included in this table because our database happens to contain only occurences of their combination, but not individual ones.**

| *NEUTRAL* | AU 9 | AU 10 | AU 20 |
|---|---|---|---|
| | | | |
| Lips relaxed and closed. | The infraorbital triangle and center of the upper lip are pulled upwards. Nasal root wrinkling is present. | The infraorbital triangle is pushed upwards. Upper lip is raised. Causes angular bend in shape of upper lip. Nasal root wrinkle is absent. | The lips and the lower portion of the nasolabial furrow are pulled pulled back laterally. The mouth is elongated. |
| AU 12 | AU15 | AU 17 | AU 25 |
| | | | |
| Lip corners are pulled obliquely. | The corners of the lips are pulled down. | The chin boss is pushed upwards. | Lips are relaxed and parted. |
| AU 26 | AU 27 | AU 23+24 | AU 9+17 |
| | | | |
| Lips are relaxed and parted; mandible is lowered. | Mouth stretched open and the mandible pulled downwards. | Lips tightened, narrowed, and pressed together. | |
| AU9+25 | AU9+17+23+24 | AU10+17 | AU 10+25 |
| | | | |
| AU 10+15+17 | AU 12+25 | AU12+26 | AU 15+17 |
| | | | |
| AU 17+23+24 | AU 20+25 | | |
| | | | |

## 1.2. Automated Facial Expression Analysis

Most approaches to automated facial expression analysis so far attempt to recognize a small set of prototypic emotional expressions. Suwa *et al.* [31] presented an early attempt to analyze facial expressions by tracking the motion of twenty identified spots on an image sequence. Essa and Pentland [16] developed a dynamic parametric model based on a 3D geometric mesh face model to recognize 5 prototypic expressions. Mase [26] manually selected facial regions that corresponded to facial muscles and computed motion within these regions using optical flow. The work by Yacoob and Davis [37] used optical flow like Mase's work, but tracked the motion of the surface regions of facial features (brows, eyes, nose, and mouth) instead of that of the underlying muscle groups. Zhang [40] investigated the use of two types of facial features: the geometric positions of 34 fiducial points on a face and a set of multi-scale, multi-orientation Gabor wavelet coefficients at these points for facial expression recognition.

Automatic recognition of FACS action units (AU) is a difficult problem, and relatively little work has been reported. AUs have no quantitative definitions and, as noted, can appear in complex combinations. Mase [26] and Essa [16] described patterns of optical flow that corresponded to several AUs, but did not attempt to recognize them. Bartlett et al. [2] and Donato et al. [10] reported some of the most extensive experimental results of upper and lower face AU recognition. They both used image sequences that were free of head motion, manually aligned faces using three coordinates, rotated the images so that the eyes were in horizontal, scaled the images, and, finally, cropped a window of 60x90 pixels. Their system was trained and tested using the leave-one-out cross-validation procedure, and the mean classification accuracy was calculated across all of the test cases. Bartlett *et al.* [2] recognized 6 single upper face AUs (AU 1, AU 2, AU 4, AU 5, AU 6, and AU 7) but no AUs occurring in combinations. They achieved 90.9% accuracy by combining holistic spatial analysis and optical flow with local feature analysis in a hybrid system. Donato *et al.* [10] compared several techniques for recognizing action units. These techniques included optical flow, principal component analysis, independent component analysis, local feature analysis, and Gabor wavelet representation. The best performances were obtained by using Gabor wavelet representation and independent component analysis with which a 95.5% average recognition rate was reported for 6 single upper face AUs (AU 1, AU 2, AU 4, AU 5, AU 6, and AU 7) and 2 lower face AUs and 4 AU combinations (AU 17, AU 18, AU 9+25, AU 10+25, AU 16+25, AU 20+25). For analysis purpose, they treated each combination as if it were a separate new AU.

The authors' group has developed a few version of the facial expression analysis system. Cohn *et al.* [8] and Lien *et al.* [24] used dense-flow, feature-point tracking, and edge extraction to recognize 4 upper face AUs and 2 combinations (AU 4, AU 5, AU 6, AU 7, AU 1+2, and AU 1+4) and 4 lower face AUs and 5 combinations (AU 12, AU 25, AU 26, AU 27, AU 12+25, AU 20+25±16, AU

15+17, AU 17+23+24, and AU 9+17±25). Again each AU combination was regarded as a separate new AU. The average recognition rate ranged from 80% to 92% depending on the method used and AUs recognized.

These previous versions have several limitations. 1) They require manual marking of 38 to 52 feature points around face landmarks in the initial input frame. A more automated system is desirable. 2) The initial input image is aligned with a standard face image by affine transformation, which assumes that any rigid head motion is in-plane. 3) The extraction of dense flow is relatively slow, which limits its usefulness for large databases and real-time applications. 4) Lip and eye feature tracking is not reliable because of the aperture problem and when features undergo a large amount of change in appearance, such as open to tightly closed mouth or eyes. 5) While they used three separate feature extraction modules, they were not integrated for the purpose of AU recognition. By integrating their outputs, it is likely that even higher accuracy could be achieved. 6) A separate hidden Markov model is necessary for each single AU and each AU combination. Because FACS consists of 44 AUs and potential combinations numbering in the thousands, a more efficient approach will be needed.

The current AFA system addresses many of these limitations. 1) Degree of manual preprocessing is reduced by using automatic face detection [29]. Templates of face components are quickly adjusted in the first frame and then tracked automatically. 2) No image alignment is necessary, and in-plane and limited out-of-plane head motion can be handled. 3) To decrease processing time, the system uses a more efficient facial feature tracker instead of a computationally intensive dense-flow extractor. Processing now requires less than 1 second per frame pair. 4) To increase the robustness and accuracy of the feature extraction, multi-state face-component models are devised. Facial feature tracking can cope with a large change of appearance and limited out-of-plane head motion. 5) Extracted features are represented and normalized based on an explicit face model that is invariant to image scale and in-plane head motion. 6) More AUs are recognized, and they are recognized whether they occur alone or in combinations. Instead of one HMM for each AU or AU combination, the current system employs two Artificial Neural Networks (one for the upper face and one for the lower face) for AU recognition. It recognizes 16 of the 30 AUs that have a specific anatomic basis and occur frequently in emotion and paralinguistic communication.

## 2. Multi-State Feature-based AU Recognition

An automated facial expression analysis system must solve two problems: facial feature extraction and facial expression classification. In this paper, we describe our multi-state feature-based AU recognition system, which explicitly analyzes appearance changes in localized facial features in a nearly frontal image sequence. Since each AU is associated with a specific set of facial muscles, we believe that accurate geometrical modeling and tracking of facial features will lead to better recognition results. Furthermore, the knowledge of exact facial feature positions could be useful for the area-based [37], holistic analysis [2], and optical flow based [24] classifiers.

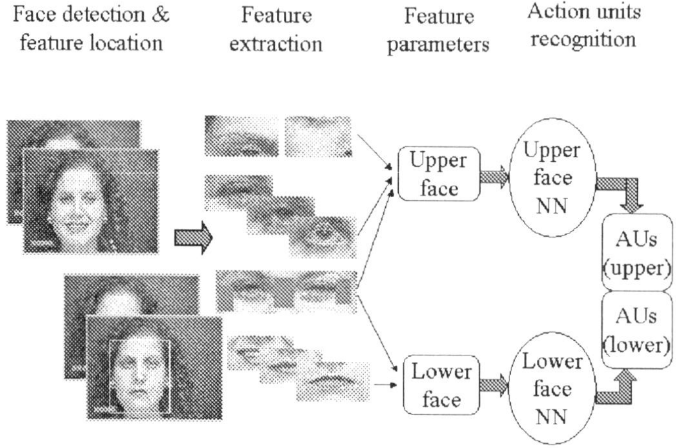


**Figure 1. Feature-based Automatic Facial Action Analysis (AFA) system.**

Figure 1 depicts the overall structure of the AFA system. Given an image sequence, the region of the face and approximate location of individual face features are detected automatically in the initial frame [29]. The contours of the face features and components then are adjusted manually in the initial frame. Both permanent (e.g., brows, eyes, lips) and transient (lines and furrows) face feature changes are automatically detected and tracked in the image sequence. Informed by FACS AUs, we group the facial features into separate collections of feature parameters because the facial actions in the upper and lower face are relatively independent for AU recognition [13]. In the upper face, 15 parameters describe shape, motion, eye state, motion of brow and cheek, and furrows. In the lower face, 9 parameters describe shape, motion, lip state, and furrows. These parameters are geometrically normalized to compensate for image scale and in-plane head motion.

The facial feature parameters are fed to two neural-network based classifiers. One recognizes 6 upper face AUs (AU 1, AU 2, AU 4, AU 5, AU 6, AU 7) and *NEUTRAL*, and the other recognizes 10 lower face AUs (AU 9, AU 10, AU 12, AU 15, AU 17, AU 20, AU 25, AU 26, AU 27, AU 23+24) and *NEUTRAL*. These classifiers are trained to respond to the designated AUs whether they occur singly or in combination. When AUs occur in combination, multiple output nodes could be excited. For the upper face, we have achieved an average recognition rate of 96.4% for 50 sample sequences of 14 subjects performing 7 AUs (including $NEUTRAL$) singly or in combination. For the lower face, our system has achieved an average recognition rate of 96.7% for 63 sample sequences of 32 subjects performing 11 AUs (including $NEUTRAL$) singly or in combination. The generalizability of AFA has been tested further on an independent database recorded under different conditions and ground-truth coded by an independent laboratory. A 93.3% average recognition rate has been achieved for 122 sample sequences of 21 subjects for neutral expression and 16 AUs whether they occurred individually or in combinations.

## 3. Facial Feature Extraction

Contraction of the facial muscles produces changes in the direction and magnitude of the motion on the skin surface and in the appearance of permanent and transient facial features. Examples of permanent features are the lips, eyes, and any furrows that have become permanent with age. Transient features include facial lines and furrows that are not present at rest but appear with facial expressions. Even in a frontal face, the appearance and location of the facial features can change dramatically. For example, the eyes look qualitatively different when open and closed. Different components require different extraction and detection methods. Multi-state models of facial components have been introduced to detect and track both transient and permanent features in an image sequence.

### 3.1. Multi-State Face Component Models

To detect and track changes of facial components in near frontal images, we develop multi-state facial component models. The models are illustrated in Table 3, which includes both permanent (i.e. lips, eyes, brows, and cheeks) and transient components (i.e. furrows). A three-state lip model describes lip state: open, closed, and tightly closed. A two-state model (open or closed) is used for each of the eyes. Each brow and cheek has a one-state model. Transient facial features, such as nasolabial furrows, have two states: present and absent.

### 3.2. Permanent Features

**Lips:** A three-state lip model represents open, closed and tightly closed lips. A different lip contour template is prepared for each lip state. The open and closed lip contours are modeled by two parabolic arcs, which are described by six parameters: the lip center position (xc, yc), the lip shape ($h1$, $h2$ and $w$), and the lip orientation ($\theta$). For tightly closed lips, the dark mouth line connecting the lip corners represents the position, orientation, and shape.

Tracking of lip features uses color, shape, and motion. In the first frame, the approximate position of the lip template is detected automatically. It then is adjusted manually by moving four key points. A Gaussian mixture model represents the color distribution of the pixels inside of the lip template [27]. The details of our lip tracking algorithm have been presented in [33].

**Eyes:** Most eye trackers developed so far are for open eyes and simply track

**Table 3. Multi-state facial component models of a frontal face**

| Component | State | Description/Feature |
|---|---|---|
| Lip | Open | 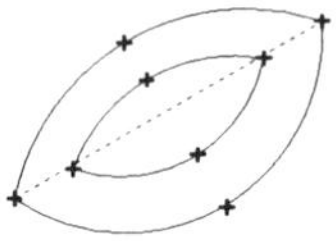 |
| | Closed | 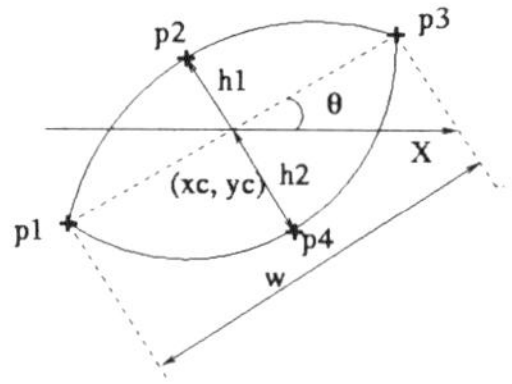 |
| | Tightly closed |  |
| Eye | Open | 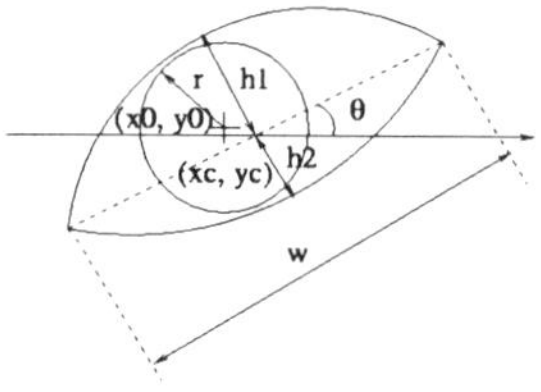 |
| | Closed |  |
| Brow | Present | 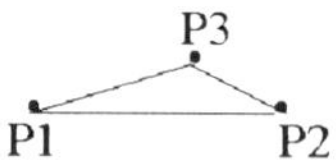 |
| Cheek | Present | 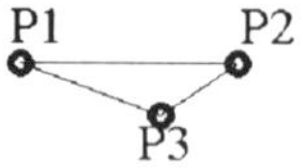 |
| Furrow | Present | 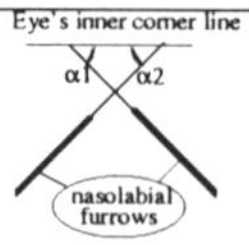 |
| | Absent | |

the eye locations [23, 39]. To recognize facial AUs, however, we need to detect whether the eyes are open or closed, the degree of eye opening, and the location and radius of the iris. For an open eye, the eye template (Table 3), is composed of a circle with three parameters $(x_0, y_0, r)$ to model the iris and two parabolic arcs with six parameters $(x_c, y_c, h_1, h_2, w, \theta)$ to model the boundaries of the eye. This template is the same as Yuille's [39] except for the two points located at the center of the whites of the eyes. For a closed eye, the template is reduced to 4 parameters: two for the position of each of the eye corners.

The open-eye template is adjusted manually in the first frame by moving 6 points for each eye. We found that the outer corners are more difficult to track than the inner corners; for this reason, the inner corners of the eyes are tracked first. The outer corners then are located on the line that connects the inner corners at a distance of the eye width as estimated in the first frame.

The iris provides important information about the eye state. Part of the iris is normally visible if the eye is open. Intensity and edge information are used to detect the iris. We have observed that the eyelid edge is noisy even in a good quality image. However, the lower part of the iris is almost always visible, and its edge is relatively clear if the eye is open. Thus, we use a half circle mask to filter the iris edge (Figure 2). The radius of the iris circle template $r_0$ is determined in the first frame, since it is stable except for large out-of-plane head motion. The radius of the circle is increased or decreased slightly $(\delta r)$ from $r_0$ so that it can vary between minimum radius $(r_0 - \delta r)$ and maximum radius $(r_0 + \delta r)$. The system determines that the iris is found when the following two conditions are satisfied. One is that the edges in the mask are at their maximum. The other is that the change in the average intensity is less than a threshold. Once the iris is located, the eye is determined to be open and the iris center is the iris mask center $(x_0, y_0)$. The eyelid contours then are tracked. For a closed eye, a line connecting the inner and outer corners of the eye is used as the eye boundary. The details of our eye-tracking algorithm have been presented in [34].

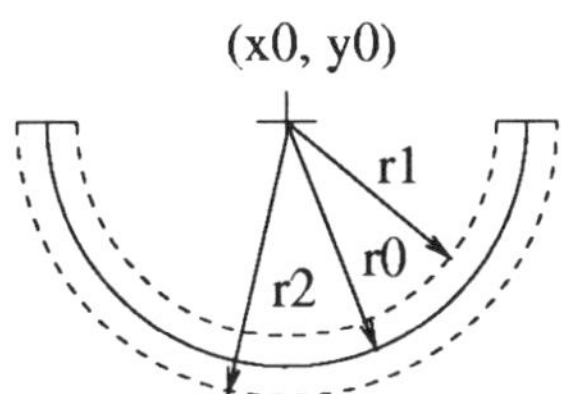


**Figure 2. Half circle iris mask.** $(x_0, y_0)$ **is the iris center;** $r_0$ **is the iris radius;** $r_1$ **is the minimum radius of the mask;** $r_2$ **is the maximum radius of the mask.**

**Brow and cheek:** Features in the brow and cheek areas are also important for expression analysis. Each left or right brow has one model – a triangular template with six parameters $(x1, y1)$, $(x2, y2)$, and $(x3, y3)$. Each cheek has also a similar six parameter down-ward triangular template model. Both brow and cheek templates are tracked using Lucas-Kanade algorithm [25].

### 3.3. Transient Features

In addition to permanent features that move and change their shape and positions, facial motion also produces transient features that provide crucial information for recognition of certain AUs. Wrinkles and furrows appear perpendicular to the direction of the motion of the activated muscles. Contraction of the *corrugator* muscle, for instance, produces vertical furrows between the brows, which is coded in FACS as AU 4, while contraction of the medial portion of the *frontalis* muscle (AU 1) causes horizontal wrinkling in the center of the forehead.

Some of these transient features may become permanent with age. Permanent crows-feet wrinkles around the outside corners of the eyes, which are characteristic of AU 6, are common in adults but not in children. When wrinkles and furrows become permanent, contraction of the corresponding muscles produces only changes in their appearance, such as deepening or lengthening. The presence or absence of the furrows in a face image can be determined by edge feature analysis [22, 24], or by eigen-image analysis [21, 35]. Terzopoulos and Waters [32] detected the nasolabial furrows for driving a face animator, but with artificial markers. Kwon and Lobo [22] detected furrows using snakes to classify pictures of people into different age groups. Our previous system [24] detected horizontal, vertical, and diagonal edges using a complex face template.

In our current system, we detect wrinkles in the nasolabial region, the nasal root, and the areas lateral to the outer corners of the eyes (Figure 3). These areas are located using the tracked locations of the corresponding permanent features. We classify each of the wrinkles into one of two states: present and absent. Compared with the neutral frame, the wrinkle state is classified as present if wrinkles appear, deepen, or lengthen. Otherwise, it is absent.

We use a Canny edge detector to quantify the amount and orientation of furrows [6]. For nasal root wrinkles and crows-feet wrinkles, we compare the number of edge pixels $E$ in the wrinkle areas of the current frame with the number of edge pixels $E_0$ of the first frame. If the ratio $E/E_0$ is larger than a threshold, the furrows are determined to be present. Otherwise, the furrows are absent. For nasolabial furrows, the existence of vertical to diagonal connected edges is used for classification. If the connected edge pixels are larger than a threshold, the nasolabial furrow is determined to be present and is modeled as a line. The orientation of the furrow is represented as the angle between the furrow line and line connecting the eye inner corners. This angle changes according to different AUs. For example, the nasolabial furrow angle of AU 9 or AU 10 is larger than that of AU 12.

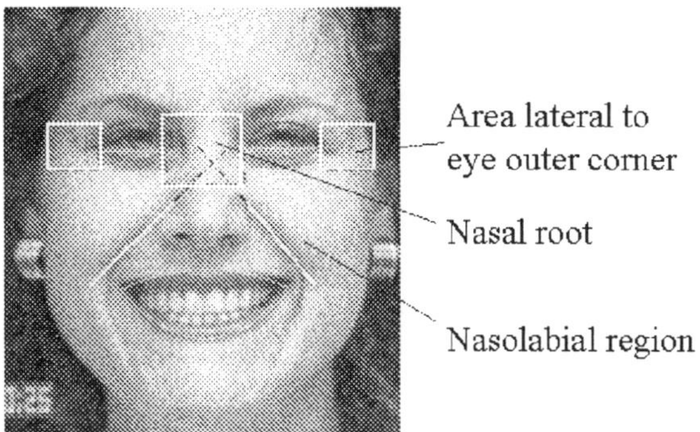


**Figure 3. The areas for nasolabial furrows, nasal root, and outer eye corners.**

### 3.4. Examples of Feature Extraction

**Permanent Features:** Figure 4 shows the results of tracking permanent features for the same subject with different expressions. In Figure 4 (a), (b) and (d), the lips are tracked as they change in state from open to closed and tightly closed. The iris position and eye boundaries are tracked while the eye changes from widely opened to tightly closed and blink (Figure 4 (b), (c), and (d)). Notice that the semi-circular iris model tracks the iris even when the iris is only partially visible. Figures 5 and 6 show examples of tracking in subjects who vary in age, sex, skin color, and in amount of out-plane head motion. Difficulty occurs in eye tracking when the eye becomes extremely narrow. For example, in Figure 5 (a), the left eye in the last image is mistakenly determined to be closed because the iris was too small to be detected. In these examples, face size varies between $90 \times 80$ and $220 \times 200$ pixels. For display purpose, images have been cropped to reduce space. Additional results can be found at http://www.cs.cmu.edu/~face.

**Transient Features:** Figure 7 shows the results of nasolabial furrow detection for different subjects and AUs. The nasolabial furrow angles systematically vary between AU 9 and AU 12 (Figure 7 (a) and (b)). For some images, the nasolabial furrow is detected only on one side. In the first image of Figure 7 (d), only the left nasolabial furrow exists, and it is correctly detected. In the middle image of Figure 7 (b), the right nasolabial furrow is missed because the length of the detected edges is less than threshold. The results of nasal root and crows-feet wrinkle detection are shown in Figure 8. Generally, the crows-feet wrinkles are present for AU 6, and the nasal root wrinkles appear for AU 9.

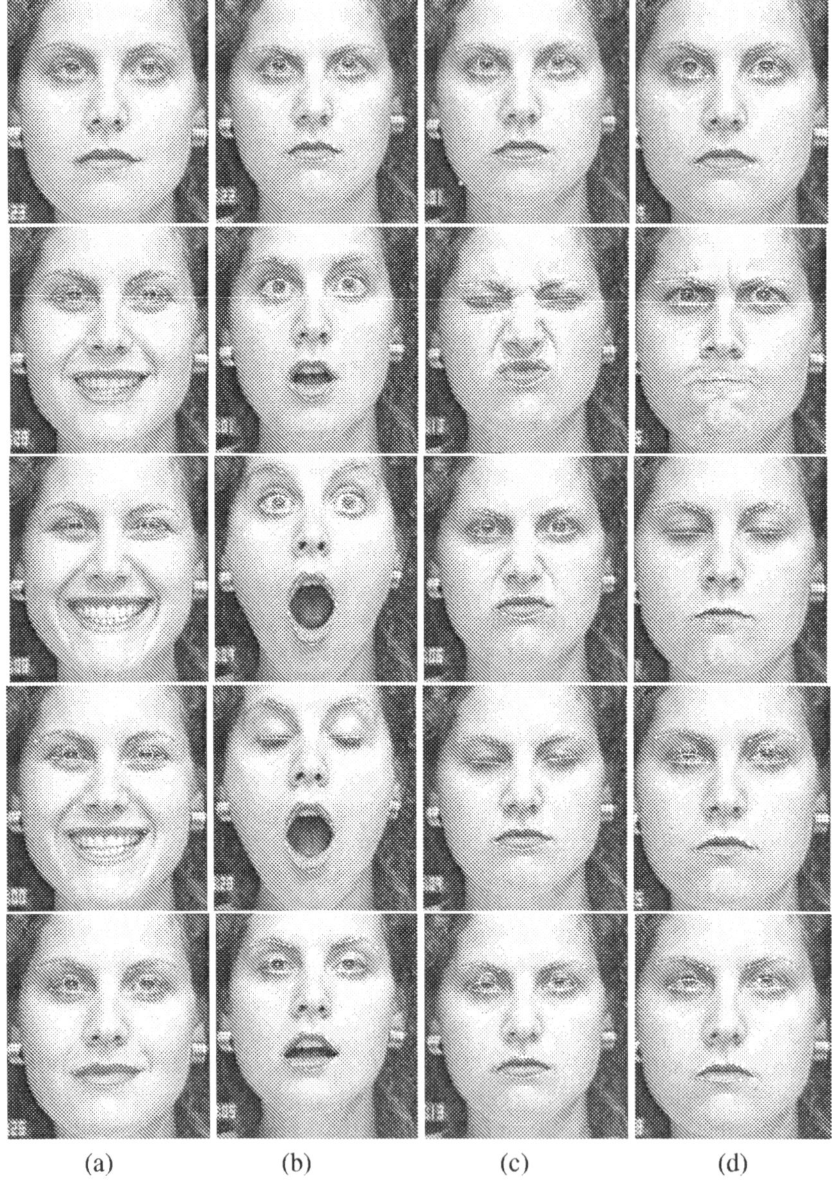

(a)    (b)    (c)    (d)

**Figure 4. Permanent feature tracking results for different expressions of same subject. (a) Happy, (b) Surprise, (c) Disgust, (d) Anger. Note appearance changes in eye and mouth states. In this and the following figures, images have been cropped for display purpose. Face size varies between 90×80 and 220×200 pixels.**

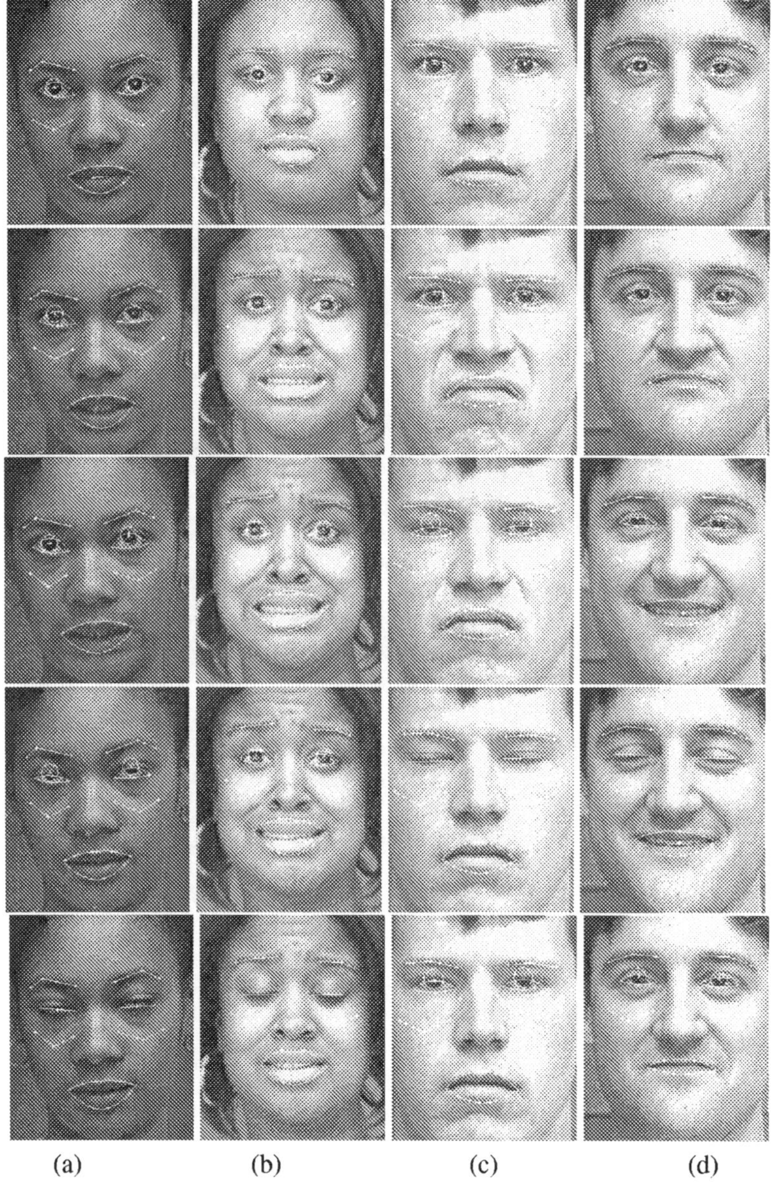

(a)       (b)       (c)       (d)

**Figure 5. Permanent feature tracking results for different subjects (a), (b), (c), (d).**

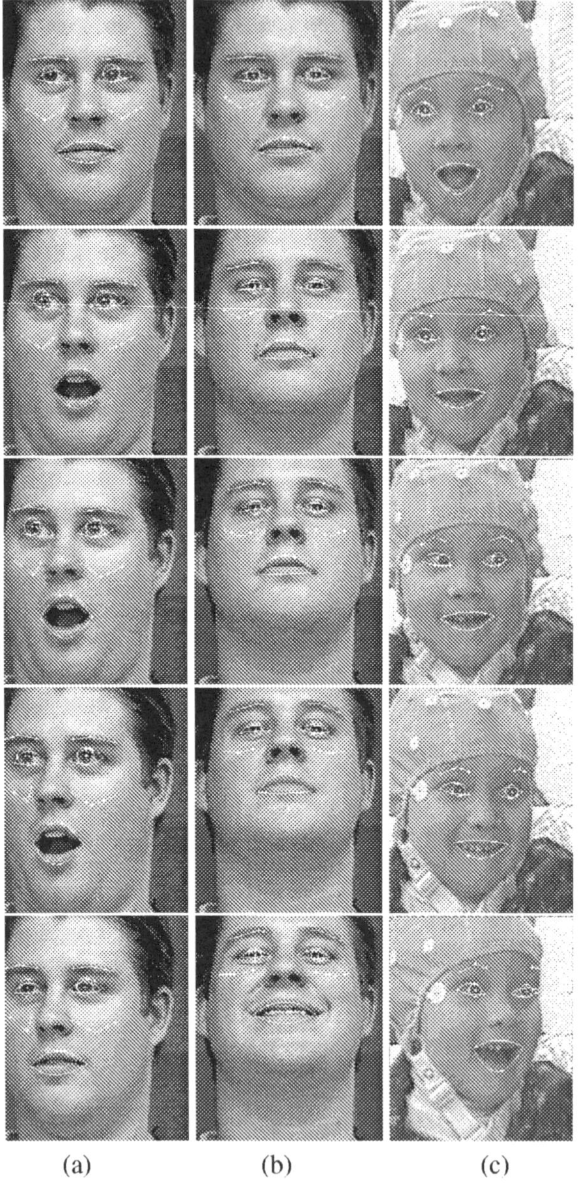

(a)          (b)          (c)

**Figure 6. Permanent feature tracking results with head motions. (a) Head yaw, (b) Head pitch, (c) Head up and left with background motion.**

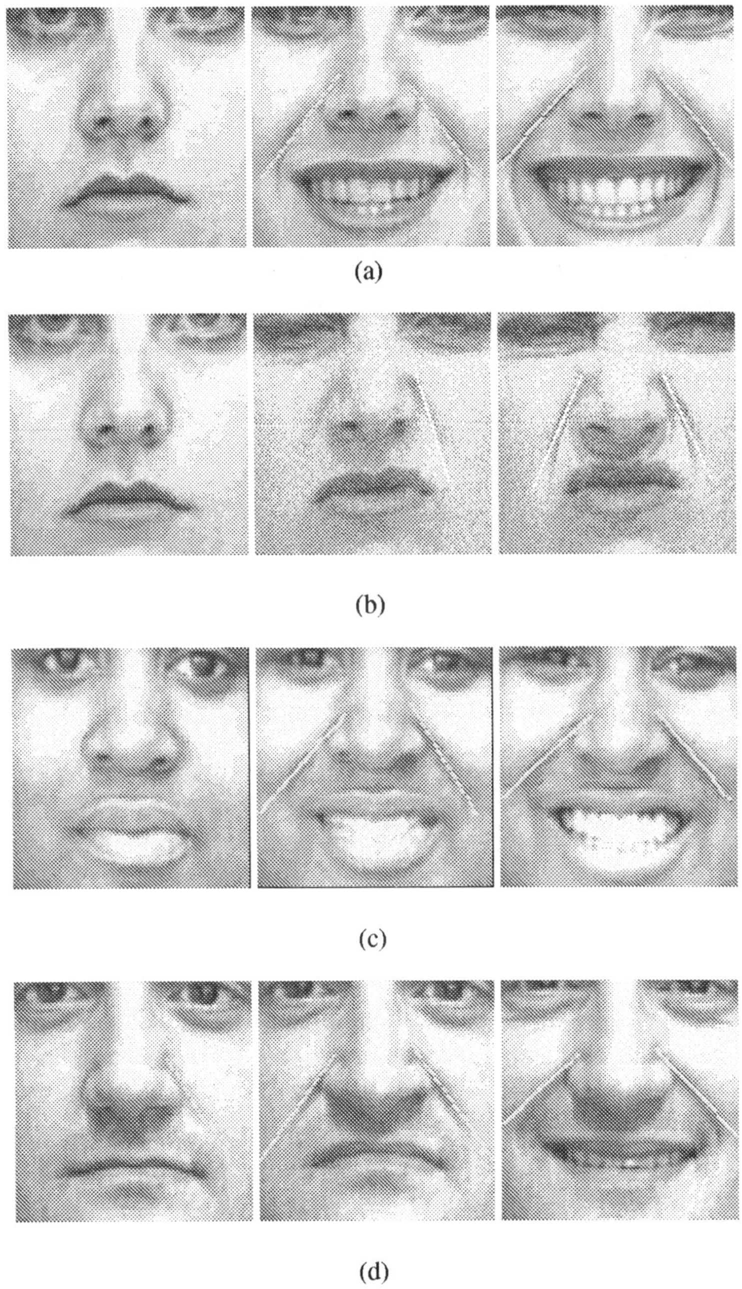

(a)

(b)

(c)

(d)

**Figure 7. Nasolabial furrow detection results.**

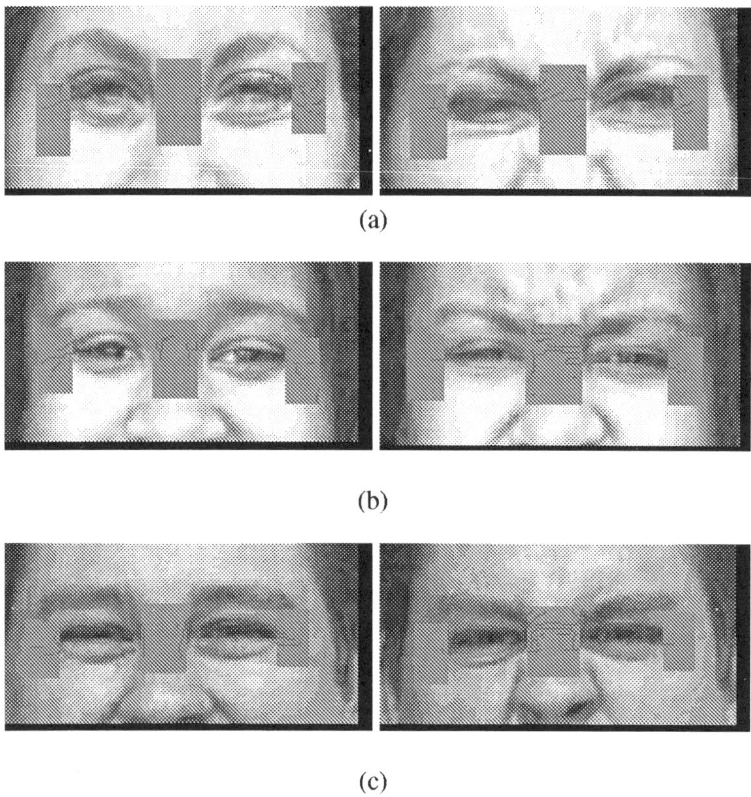

(a)

(b)

(c)

Figure 8. Nasal root and crows-feet wrinkle detection. For the left image of (a), (b), and (c), crows-feet wrinkles are present. For the right image of (a), (b), and (c), the nasal root wrinkles appear.

## 4. Facial Feature Representation and AU recognition by Neural Networks

We transform the extracted features into a set of parameters for AU recognition. We first define a face coordinate system. Because the inner corners of the eyes are most reliably detected and their relative position is unaffected by muscle contraction, we define the $x$-axis as the line connecting two inner corners of eyes and the $y$-axis as perpendicular to it. We split the facial features into two groups (upper face and lower face) of parameters because facial actions in the upper face have little interaction with facial motion in lower face, and vice versa [13].

**Upper Face Features:**  We represent the upper face features by 15 parameters, which are defined in Table 4. Of these, 12 parameters describe the motion and shape of the eyes, brows, and cheeks, 2 parameters describe the state of the crows-feet wrinkles, and 1 parameter describes the distance between the brows. To remove the effects of variation in planar head motion and scale between image sequences in face size, all parameters are computed as ratios of their current values to that in the initial frame. Figure 9 shows the coordinate system and the parameter definitions.

### Table 4. Upper face feature representation for AU recognition

| Permanent features (Left and right) | | | Other features |
|---|---|---|---|
| Inner brow motion $(r_{binner})$ | Outer brow motion $(r_{bouter})$ | Eye height $(r_{eheight})$ | Distance of brows $(D_{brow})$ |
| $r_{binner}$ $=\frac{bi-bi_0}{bi_0}.$ If $r_{binner} > 0$, Inner brow move up. | $r_{bouter}$ $=\frac{bo-bo_0}{bo_0}.$ If $r_{bouter} > 0$, Outer brow move up. | $r_{eheight}$ $=\frac{(h1+h2)-(h1_0+h2_0)}{(h1_0+h2_0)}.$ If $r_{eheight} > 0$, Eye height increases. | $D_{brow}$ $=\frac{D-D_0}{D_0}.$ If $D_{brow} < 0$ Two brows drawn together. |
| Eye top lid motion $(r_{top})$ | Eye bottom lid motion $(r_{btm})$ | Cheek motion $(r_{cheek})$ | crows-feet wrinkles $W_{left/right}$ |
| $r_{top}$ $=\frac{h1-h1_0}{h1_0}.$ If $r_{top} > 0$, Eye top lid move up. | $r_{btm}$ $=-\frac{h2-h2_0}{h2_0}.$ If $r_{btm} > 0$, Eye bottom lid move up. | $r_{cheek}$ $=-\frac{c-c_0}{c_0}.$ If $r_{cheek} > 0$, Cheek move up. | If $W_{left/right} = 1$, Left/right crows feet wrinkle present. |

**Lower Face Features:**  Nine parameters represent the lower face features ( Table 5 and Figure 10). Of these, 6 parameters describe lip shape, state and motion,

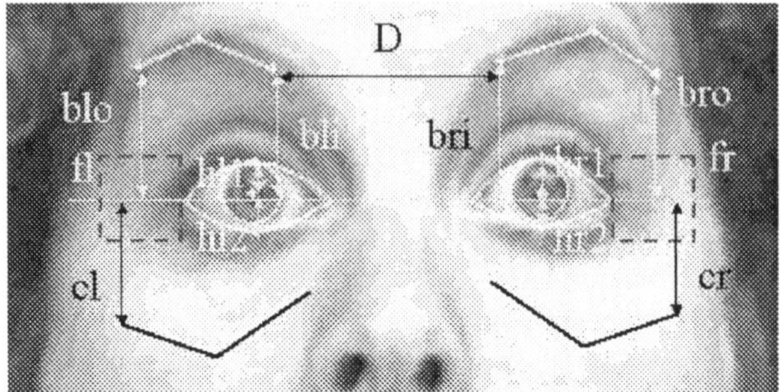

**Figure 9. Upper face features.** $hl(hl1 + hl2)$ **and** $hr(hr1 + hr2)$ **are the height of left eye and right eye;** $D$ **is the distance between brows;** $cl$ **and** $cr$ **are the motion of left cheek and right cheek.** $bli$ **and** $bri$ **are the motion of the inner part of left brow and right brow.** $blo$ **and** $bro$ **are the motion of the outer part of left brow and right brow.** $fl$ **and** $fr$ **are the left and right crows-feet wrinkle areas.**

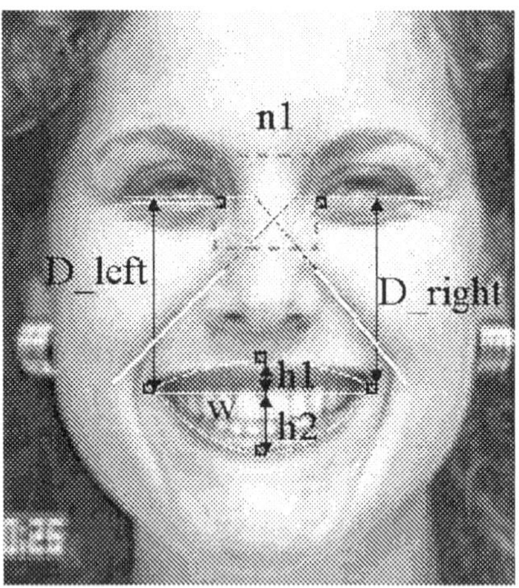

**Figure 10. Lower face features.** $h1$ **and** $h2$ **are the top and bottom lip heights;** $w$ **is the lip width;** $D_{left}$ **is the distance between the left lip corner and eye inner corners line;** $D_{right}$ **is the distance between the right lip corner and eye inner corners line;** $n1$ **is the nasal root area.**

## Table 5. Lower face feature representation for AUs recognition

| Permanent features | | |
|---|---|---|
| Lip height $(r_{height})$ | Lip width $(r_{width})$ | Left lip corner motion $(r_{left})$ |
| $r_{height}$ $=\dfrac{(h1+h2)-(h1_0+h2_0)}{(h1_0+h2_0)}$. If $r_{height} > 0$, lip height increases. | $r_{width}$ $=\dfrac{w-w_0}{w_0}$. If $r_{width} > 0$, lip width increases. | $r_{left}$ $=-\dfrac{D_{left}-D_{left0}}{D_{left0}}$. If $r_{left} > 0$, left lip corner moves up. |
| Right lip corner $(r_{right})$ | Top lip motion $(r_{top})$ | Bottom lip motion $(r_{btm})$ |
| $r_{right}$ $=-\dfrac{D_{right}-D_{right0}}{D_{right0}}$. If $r_{right} > 0$, right lip corner moves up. | $r_{top}$ $=-\dfrac{D_{top}-D_{top0}}{D_{top0}}$. If $r_{top} > 0$, top lip moves up. | $r_{btm}$ $=-\dfrac{D_{btm}-D_{btm0}}{D_{btm0}}$. If $r_{btm} > 0$, bottom lip moves up. |
| Transient features | | |
| Left nasolibial furrow angle $(Ang_{left})$ | Right nasolibial furrow angle $(Ang_{right})$ | State of nasal root wrinkles $(S_{nosew})$ |
| Left nasolibial furrow present with angle $Ang_{left}$. | Left nasolibial furrow present with angle $Ang_{right}$. | If $S_{nosew} = 1$, nasal root wrinkles present. |

and 3 describe the furrows in the nasolabial and nasal root regions. These parameters are normalized by using the ratios of the current feature values to that of the neutral frame.

**AU Recognition by Neural Networks:** We use three-layer neural networks with one hidden layer to recognize AUs by a standard back-propagation method [29]. Separate networks are used for the upper- and lower face. For AU recognition in the upper face, the inputs are the 15 parameters shown in Table 4. The outputs are the 6 single AUs (AU 1, AU 2, AU 4, AU 5, AU 6, and AU7) and $NEUTRAL$. In the lower face, the inputs are the 7 parameters shown in Table 5 and the outputs are 10 single AUs ( AU 9, AU 10, AU 12, AU 15, AU 17, AU 20, AU 23+24, AU 25, AU 26, and AU 27) and $NEUTRAL$. These networks are trained to respond to the designated AUs whether they occur singly or in combination. When AUs occur in combination, multiple output nodes are excited.

## 5. Experimental Evaluations

We conducted three experiments to evaluate the performance of our system. The first is AU recognition in the upper face when image data contain only single AUs. The second is AU recognition in the upper and lower face when image data contain both single AUs and combinations. The third experiment evaluates the generalizability of our system by using completely disjointed databases for training and testing, while image data contain both single AUs and combinations. Finally, we compared the performance of our system with that of other AU recognition systems.

### 5.1. Facial Expression Image Databases

Two databases were used to evaluate our system: the Cohn-Kanade AU-Coded Face Expression Image Database [20] and Ekman-Hager Facial Action Exemplars [15].

**Cohn-Kanade AU-Coded Face Expression Image Database:** We have been developing a large-scale database for promoting quantitative study of facial expression analysis [20]. The database currently contains a recording of the facial behavior of 210 adults who are 18 to 50 years old; 69% female and 31% male; and 81% Caucasian, 13% African, and 6% other groups. Over 90% of the subjects had no prior experience in FACS. Subjects were instructed by an experimenter to perform single AUs and AU combinations. Subjects' facial behavior was recorded in an observation room. Image sequences with in-plane and limited out-of-plane motion were included.

The image sequences began with a neutral face and were digitized into 640x480 pixel arrays with either 8-bit gray-scale or 24-bit color values. To date, 1,917 image sequences of 182 subjects have been FACS coded by certified FACS coders for either the entire sequence or target AUs. Approximately 15% of these sequences were coded by two independent certified FACS coders to validate the accuracy of the coding. Inter-observer agreement was quantified with coefficient kappa, which is the proportion of agreement above what would be expected to occur by chance [17]. The mean kappas for inter-observer agreement were 0.82 for target AUs and 0.75 for frame-by-frame coding.

**Ekman-Hager Facial Action Exemplars:** This database was provided by Ekman at the Human Interaction Laboratory, University of California, San Francisco, and contains images that were collected by Hager, Methvin, and Irwin. Bartlett et al. [2] and Donato et al. [10] used this database to train and test their AU recognition systems. The Ekman-Hager database includes 24 Caucasian subjects (12 males and 12 females). Each image sequence consists of 6 to 8 frames that were sampled from a longer image sequence. Image sequences begin with a neutral expression (or weak facial actions) and end with stronger facial actions. AUs were coded for each frame. Sequences containing rigid head motion detectable by a human observer were excluded. Some of the image sequences contain large lighting changes between frames, and we normalized intensity to keep the average intensity constant throughout the image sequence.

## 5.2. Upper Face AU Recognition for Image Data Containing Only Single AUs

In the first experiment, we used a neural network-based recognizer having the structure shown in Figure 11. The inputs to the network were the upper face feature parameters shown in Table 4. The outputs were the same set of 6 single AUs (AU 1, AU 2, AU 4, AU 5, AU 6, AU 7); these are the same set that were used by Bartlett and Donato. In addition, we included an output node for $NEUTRAL$. The output node that showed the highest value was interpreted as the recognized AU. We tested various numbers of hidden units and found that 6 hidden units gave the best performance.

From the Ekman-Hager database, we selected image sequences in which only a single AU occurred in the upper face. 99 image sequences from 23 subjects met this criterion. These 99 image sequences we used are the superset of the 80 image sequences used by Bartlett and Donato. The initial and final two frames in each image sequence were used. As shown in Table 6, the image sequences were assigned to training and testing sets in two ways. In $S1$, the sequences were randomly selected, so the same subject was allowed to appear in both training and testing sets. In $S2$, no subject could appear in both training and testing sets; testing was performed done with novel faces.

Table 7 shows the recognition results with the $S1$ testing set. The average recognition rate was 88.5% when samples of $NEUTRAL$ were excluded (Recognizing neutral faces is easier), and 92.3% when samples of $NEUTRAL$ were included. For the $S2$ test set (i.e. novel faces), the recognition rate remained virtually identical: 89.4% ($NEUTRAL$ exclusive) and 92.9% ($NEUTRAL$ inclusive), which is shown in Table 8.

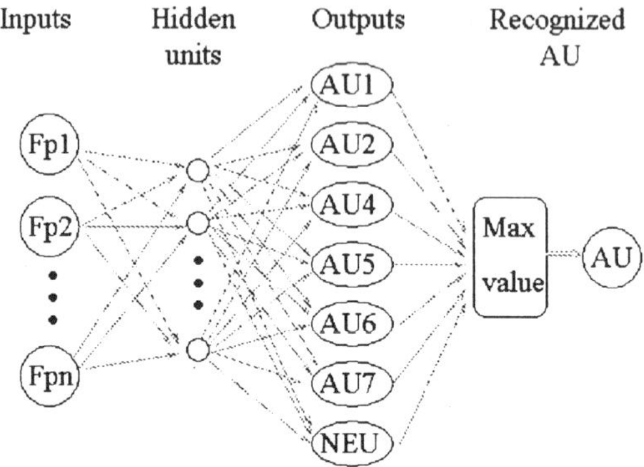


**Figure 11. Neural network-based recognizer for single AUs in the upper face. The inputs are the feature parameters, and the output is one label out of 6 single AUs and** $NEUTRAL$**.**

**Table 6. Details of training and testing data from Ekman-Hager Database that are used for single AU recognition in the upper face. In** $S1$**, some subjects appear in both training and testing sets. In** $S2$**, no subject appears in both training and testing sets.**

| Data Set | | number of Sequences | Single AUs | | | | | | | |
|---|---|---|---|---|---|---|---|---|---|---|
| | | | AU1 | AU2 | AU4 | AU5 | AU6 | AU7 | $NEUTRAL$ | Total |
| $S1$ | $Train$ | 47 | 14 | 12 | 16 | 22 | 12 | 18 | 47 | 141 |
| | $Test$ | 52 | 14 | 12 | 20 | 24 | 14 | 20 | 52 | 156 |
| $S2$ | $Train$ | 50 | 18 | 14 | 14 | 18 | 22 | 16 | 50 | 152 |
| | $Test$ | 49 | 10 | 10 | 22 | 28 | 4 | 22 | 49 | 145 |

**Table 7. AU recognition for single AUs on $S1$ training and testing sets in experiment 1. A same subject could appear in both training and testing sets. The numbers in bold are results excluding** *NEUTRAL.*

| | | Recognition outputs | | | | | | |
|---|---|---|---|---|---|---|---|---|
| | | AU 1 | AU 2 | AU 4 | AU 5 | AU 6 | AU 7 | *NEUTRAL* |
| H | **AU1** | **12** | **2** | **0** | **0** | **0** | **0** | 0 |
| u | **AU2** | **3** | **9** | **0** | **0** | **0** | **0** | 0 |
| m | **AU4** | **0** | **0** | **20** | **0** | **0** | **0** | 0 |
| a | **AU5** | **0** | **0** | **0** | **22** | **0** | **0** | 2 |
| n | **AU6** | **0** | **0** | **0** | **0** | **12** | **2** | 0 |
| | **AU7** | **0** | **0** | **0** | **0** | **2** | **17** | 1 |
| | *NEUTRAL* | 0 | 0 | 0 | 0 | 0 | 0 | 52 |
| Recognition Rate | | **88.5%** (excluding *NEUTRAL*) | | | | | | |
| | | 92.3% (including *NEUTRAL*) | | | | | | |

**Table 8. AU recognition for single AUs on $S2$ train and testing sets in experiment 1. No subject appears in both training and testing sets. The numbers in bold are results excluding** *NEUTRAL.*

| | | Recognition outputs | | | | | | |
|---|---|---|---|---|---|---|---|---|
| | | AU 1 | AU 2 | AU 4 | AU 5 | AU 6 | AU 7 | *NEUTRAL* |
| H | **AU1** | **10** | **0** | **0** | **0** | **0** | **0** | 0 |
| u | **AU2** | **2** | **7** | **0** | **0** | **0** | **0** | 1 |
| m | **AU4** | **0** | **0** | **20** | **0** | **0** | **0** | 2 |
| a | **AU5** | **0** | **0** | **0** | **26** | **0** | **0** | 2 |
| n | **AU6** | **0** | **0** | **0** | **0** | **4** | **0** | 2 |
| | **AU7** | **0** | **0** | **0** | **0** | **0** | **21** | 1 |
| | *NEUTRAL* | 0 | 0 | 0 | 0 | 0 | 0 | 49 |
| Recognition Rate | | **89.4%** (excluding *NEUTRAL*) | | | | | | |
| | | 92.9% (including *NEUTRAL*) | | | | | | |

### 5.3. Upper and Lower Face AU Recognition for Image Sequences Containing Both Single AUs and Combinations

Because AUs can occur either singly or in combinations, an AU recognition system must have the ability to recognize them however they occur. All previous AU recognition systems [2, 10, 24] were trained and tested on single AUs only. In these systems, even when AU combinations were included, each combination was treated as if it were a separate AU. Because potential AU combinations number in the thousands, this method of separately treating AU combinations is impractical. In our second experiment, we trained a neural network to recognize AUs singly and in combinations by allowing multiple output units of the networks to fire when the input consists of AU combinations.

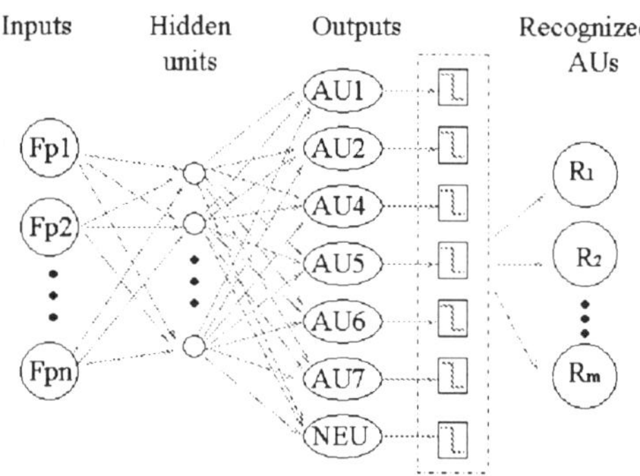


**Figure 12. Neural network-based recognizer for AU combinations in the upper face.**

**Upper Face AUs:** The neural network-based recognition system for AU combination is shown in Figure 12. The network has a similar structure to that used in experiment 1, where the output nodes correspond to 6 single AUs plus $NEUTRAL$. However, the network for recognizing AU combinations is trained so that when an AU combination is presented, multiple output nodes that correspond to the component AUs are excited. In training, all of the output nodes that correspond to the input AU components are set to have the same value. For example, when a training input is AU 1+2+4, the output values are trained to be 1.0 for AU 1, AU 2, and AU 4; 0.0 for the remaining AUs and $NEUTRAL$. At the run time, AUs whose output nodes show values higher than the threshold are considered to be recognized.

A total of 236 image sequences of 23 subjects from the Ekman-Hager database (99 image sequences containing only single AUs and 137 image sequences containing AU combinations) were used for recognition of AUs in the upper face. We split them into training (186 sequences) and testing (50 sequences) sets by subjects (9 subjects for training and 14 subjects for testing) to ensure that the same subjects did not appear in both training and testing. Testing, therefore, was done with "novel faces". From experiments, we have found that it was necessary to increase the number of hidden units from 6 to 12 to obtain optimized performance.

Because input sequences could contain one or more AUs, several outcomes were possible. *Correct* denotes that the recognized results were completely identical to the input samples. *Partially correct* denotes that some but not all of the AUs were recognized (*Missing AUs*) or that AUs that did not occur were misrecognized in addition to the one(s) that did (*Extra AUs*). If none of the AUs that occurred were recognized, the result was *Incorrect*.

Using Equations (1) and (2), we calculated recognition- and false-alarm rates for input samples and input AU components, respectively. Human FACS coders typically use the latter to calculate percentage agreement. We believe, however, that the recognition rates based on input samples are the more conservative measures.

$$Recognition\ rate =$$
$$\begin{cases} \dfrac{Total\ number\ of\ correctly\ recognized\ \textbf{samples}}{Total\ number\ of\ \textbf{samples}} & \text{based on input } \textbf{samples} \\[2em] \dfrac{Total\ number\ of\ correctly\ recognized\ \textbf{AUs}}{Total\ number\ of\ \textbf{AUs}} & \text{based on } \textbf{AU components} \end{cases} \quad (1)$$

$$False\ alarm\ rate =$$
$$\begin{cases} \dfrac{Total\ number\ of\ recognized\ \textbf{samples}\ with\ extra\ AUs}{Total\ number\ of\ \textbf{samples}} & \text{based on input } \textbf{samples} \\[2em] \dfrac{Total\ number\ of\ extra\ \textbf{AUs}}{Total\ number\ of\ \textbf{AUs}} & \text{based on } \textbf{AU components} \end{cases} \quad (2)$$

Table 9 shows a summary of the AU combination recognition results of 50 test image sequences of 14 subjects from the Ekman-Hager database. For input samples, we achieved average recognition and false alarm rates of 88% and 6.7% respectively when $NEUTRAL$ was included, and 82% and 12% respectively when $NEUTRAL$ was excluded. AU component-wise, an average recognition rate of 96.4% and a false alarm rate of 6.3% were achieved when $NEUTRAL$ was included and a recognition rate of 95.4% and a false alarm rate of 8.2% was obtained when $NEUTRAL$ was excluded.

Recognition rates in experiment 2 were slightly higher than those in experiment 1. There are two possible reasons. One is that in the neural network used in experiment 2, multiple output nodes could be excited to allow for recognition of AUs occurring in combinations. Another reason maybe that a larger training data set was used in experiment 2.

**Table 9. Upper face AU recognition with AU combinations in experiment 2. The numbers in bold face are results excluding** *NEUTRAL.* **The** *Missing AUs* **column shows the AUs that are missed. The** *Extra AUs* **column lists the extra AUs that are mis-recognized. The recognized AU with "*" indicates that it includes both** *Missing AUs* **and** *Extra AUs.*

| Actual AUs | Samples | Recognized AUs | | | Incorrect |
| --- | --- | --- | --- | --- | --- |
| | | Correct | Partially correct | | |
| | | | Missing AUs | Extra AUs | |
| AU 1 | 8 | 4 | - | 4(AU 1 + AU 2) | - |
| AU 2 | 4 | - | - | 2(AU 1 + AU 2)<br>2(AU 1 + AU 2 + AU 4) | - |
| AU 4 | 8 | 8 | - | - | - |
| AU 5 | 8 | 8 | - | - | - |
| AU 6 | 8 | 8 | - | - | - |
| AU 7 | 4 | 2 | - | 2(AU 6 + AU 7) | - |
| AU 1+2 | 16 | 16 | - | - | - |
| AU 1+2+4 | 8 | 8 | - | - | - |
| AU 1+2+5 | 4 | 2 | 2(AU 1 + AU 2 + AU 4)* | | - |
| AU 1+4 | 4 | 4 | - | - | - |
| AU 1+6 | 4 | 2 | 2(AU 1) | - | - |
| AU 4+5 | 8 | 6 | 2(AU 4) | - | - |
| AU 6+7 | 16 | 14 | 2(AU 6) | - | - |
| *NEUTRAL* | 50 | 50 | - | - | - |
| With respect to samples | Total | **100** | **82** | 18 | |
| | | 150 | 132 | | |
| | Recognition rate | 82% (excluding *NEUTRAL*) | | | |
| | | 88% (including *NEUTRAL*) | | | |
| | False alarm | 12% (excluding *NEUTRAL*) | | | |
| | | 6.7% (including *NEUTRAL*) | | | |
| With respect to AU components | Total | **172** | **164** | 8 | 14 | - |
| | | 222 | 214 | | | |
| | Recognition rate | **95.4%** (excluding *NEUTRAL*) | | | |
| | | 96.4% (including *NEUTRAL*) | | | |
| | False alarm | **8.2%** (excluding *NEUTRAL*) | | | |
| | | 6.3% (including *NEUTRAL*) | | | |

**Lower Face AUs:** The same structure of the neural network-based recognition scheme as shown in Figure 12 was used, except that the input feature parameters and the output component AUs now are those for the lower face. The inputs were the lower face feature parameters shown in Table 5. The outputs of the neural network were the 11 single AUs (AU 9, AU 10, AU 12, AU 15, AU 17, AU 20, AU 25, AU 26, AU 27, AU23+24, and *NEUTRAL*) (see Table 2). Note that AU 23+24 is modeled as a single unit, instead of as AU 23 and AU 24 separately, because they almost always occurred together in our data. Use of 12 hidden units achieved the best performance in this experiment.

A total of 463 image sequences from the Cohn-Kanade AU-Coded Face Expression Image Database were used for lower face AU recognition. Of these, 400 image sequences were used as the training data and 63 sequences were used as the testing data. The test data set included 10 single AUs, *NEUTRAL*, and 11 AU combinations (such as AU 12+25, AU 15+17+23, AU 9+17+23+24, and AU 17+20+26) from 32 subjects; none of these subjects appeared in training dataset. Some of the image sequences contained limited planar and out-of-plane head motions.

Table 10 shows a summary of the AU recognition results for the lower face when image sequences contain both single AUs and AU combinations. As above, we report the recognition and false alarm rates based on both number of input samples and number of AU components (see equations (1) and (2)). With respect to the input samples, an average recognition rate of 95.8% was achieved with a false alarm rate of 4.2% when *NEUTRAL* was included and a recognition rate of 93.7% and a false alarm rate of 6.4% when *NEUTRAL* was excluded. With respect to AU components, an average recognition rate of 96.7% was achieved with a false alarm rate of 2.9% when *NEUTRAL* was included, and a recognition rate of 95.6% with a false alarm rate of 3.9% was obtained when *NEUTRAL* was excluded.

**Major Causes of the Misidentifications:** Most of the misidentifications come from confusions between similar AUs: AU1 and AU2, AU6 and AU7, and AU25 and AU26. The confusions between AU 1 and AU 2 were caused by the strong correlation between them. The action of AU 2, which raises the outer portion of the brow, tends to pull the inner brow up as well (see Table 1). Both AU 6 and AU 7 raise the lower eyelids and are often confused by human AU coders as well [8]. All the mistakes of AU 26 were due to confusion with AU 25. AU 25 and AU 26 contain parted lips but differ only with respect to motion of the jaw, but jaw motion was not detected or used in the current system.

### 5.4. Generalizability between Databases

To evaluate the generalizability of our system, we trained the system on one database and tested it on another independent image database that was collected and FACS coded for ground-truth by a different research team. One was Cohn-

## Table 10. Lower face AU recognition results in experiment 2.

| Actual AUs | Samples | Correct | Partially correct<br>Missing AUs | Partially correct<br>Extra AUs | Incorrect |
|---|---|---|---|---|---|
| AU 9 | 2 | 2 | - | - | - |
| AU 10 | 4 | 4 | - | - | - |
| AU 12 | 4 | 4 | - | - | - |
| AU 15 | 2 | 2 | - | - | - |
| AU 17 | 6 | 6 | - | - | - |
| AU 20 | 4 | 4 | - | - | - |
| AU 25 | 30 | 30 | - | - | - |
| AU 26 | 12 | 9 | - | - | 3(AU 25) |
| AU 27 | 8 | 8 | - | - | - |
| AU 23+24 | 0 | - | - | - | - |
| AU 9+17 | 12 | 12 | - | - | - |
| AU 9+17+23+24 | 2 | 2 | - | - | - |
| AU 9+25 | 2 | 2 | - | - | - |
| AU 10+17 | 4 | 1 | 1(AU 17)<br>2(AU 10 + AU 12)* | - | - |
| AU 10+15+17 | 2 | 2 | - | - | - |
| AU 10+25 | 2 | 2 | - | - | - |
| AU 12+25 | 8 | 8 | - | - | - |
| AU 12+26 | 2 | - | 2(AU 12 + AU 25)* | - | - |
| AU 15+17 | 8 | 8 | - | - | - |
| AU 17+23+24 | 4 | 4 | - | - | - |
| AU 20+25 | 8 | 8 | - | - | - |
| *NEUTRAL* | 63 | 63 | - | - | - |
| With respect to samples — Total No. of input samples | 126<br>189 | 118<br>181 | 8 | | |
| With respect to samples — Recognition rate of samples | 93.7% (excluding *NEUTRAL*)<br>95.8% (including *NEUTRAL*) | | | | |
| With respect to samples — False alarm of samples | 6.4% (excluding *NEUTRAL*)<br>4.2% (including *NEUTRAL*) | | | | |
| With respect to AU components — Total No. of AUs | 180<br>243 | 172<br>235 | 5 | 7 | 3 |
| With respect to AU components — Recognition rate of AUs | 95.6% (excluding *NEUTRAL*)<br>96.7% (including *NEUTRAL*) | | | | |
| With respect to AU components — False alarm of AUs | 3.9% (excluding *NEUTRAL*)<br>2.9% (including *NEUTRAL*) | | | | |

Kanade database and the other was the Ekman-Hager database. This procedure ensured a more rigorous test of generalizability than more usual methods which divide a single database into training and testing sets. Table 11 summarizes the generalizability of our system.

For upper face AU recognition, the network was trained on 186 image sequences of 9 subjects from the Ekman-Hager database and tested on 72 image sequences of 7 subjects from the Cohn-Kanade database. Of the 72 image sequences, 55 consisted of single AUs (AU 1, AU 2, AU 4, AU 5, AU 6, and AU 7) and the others contained AU combinations such as AU 1+2, AU 1+2+4, and AU 6+7. We achieved a recognition rate of 93.2% and a false alarm of 2% (when samples of $NEUTRAL$ were included), which is only slightly (3-4%) lower than the case Ekman-Hager database was used for both training and testing.

**Table 11. Generalizability to independent databases. The numbers in bold are results from independent databases.**

| | | Test databases | | Train |
|---|---|---|---|---|
| | | Cohn-Kanade | Ekman-Hager | databases |
| Recognition Rate | upper face | **93.2%** | 96.4% (Table 9) | Ekman-Hager |
| | lower face | 96.7% (Table 10 ) | **93.4%** | Cohn-Kanade |

For lower face AU recognition, the network was trained on 400 image sequences of 46 subjects from the Cohn-Kanade database and tested on 50 image sequences of 14 subjects from the Ekman-Hager database. Of the 50 image sequences, half contained AU combinations, such as AU 10+17, AU 10+25, AU 12+25, AU 15+17, and AU 20+25. No instances of AU 23+24 were available in the Ekman-Hager database. We achieved a recognition rate of 93.4% (when samples of $NEUTRAL$ were included). These results were again only slightly lower than those of using the same database. The system showed high generalizability.

## 5.5. Comparison With Other AU Recognition Systems

We compare the current AFA system's performance with that of Cohn et al. [8], Lien et al. [24], Bartlett et al. [2], and Donato et al. [10]. The comparisons are summarized in Table 12. When performing comparison of recognition results in general, it is important to keep in mind differences in experimental procedures between systems. For example, scoring methods may be either by dividing the dataset into training and testing sets [8, 24] or by using a leave-one-out cross-validation procedure [2, 10]. Even when the same dataset is used, the particular AUs that were recognized or the specific image sequence that were used for evaluation are not necessarily the same. Therefore, minor differences in recognition

**Table 12. Comparison with other AU recognition systems. In the fourth column, "*No*" means that no AU combination was recognized. "*Yes/Yes*" means that AU combinations were recognized and AUs in combination were recognizable individually. "*Yes/No*" means that AU combinations were recognized but each AU combination was treated as if it were a separate new AU.**

| Systems | Methods | Recognition rates | Treatment of AU combinations | AUs to be recognized | Databases |
|---|---|---|---|---|---|
| Current AFA system | Feature-based | 88.5% (old faces) | *No* | AU 1, 2, 4, AU 5, 6, 7. | Ekman-Hager |
| | | 89.4% (novel faces) | | | |
| | | 95.4% | *Yes/Yes* | | |
| | | 95.6% | *Yes/Yes* | AU 9,10,12,15, AU17,20,25,26, AU27,23+24. | Cohn-Kanade |
| Bartlett et al. [2] | Feature-based | 85.3% (old faces) | *No* | AU 1, 2, 4, AU 5, 6, 7. | Ekman-Hager |
| | | 57% (novel faces) | | | |
| | Optic-flow | 84.5% | | | |
| | Hybrid | 90.9% | | | |
| Donato et al. [10] | ICA or Gabor wavelet | 96.9% | *No* | AU 1, 2, 4, AU 5, 6, 7. | Ekman-Hager |
| | Others | 70.3%-85.6% | | | |
| | ICA or Gabor | 95.5% | *Yes/No* | AU17,18,9+25 | |
| | Others | 70.3%-85.6% | | AU10+25,16+25 | |
| Cohn et al.[8] | Feature-Tracking | 89% | *Yes/No* | AU1+2,1+4, 4, AU 5, 6, 7. | Cohn-Kanade (Subset) |
| | | 82.3% | *Yes/No* | AU12,6+12+25, AU20+25,15+17, AU17+23+24,9+17. AU 25, 26, 27 | |
| Lien et al.[24] | Dense-flow | 91% | *Yes/No* | AU 1+2,1+4, AU 4. | Cohn-Kanade (Subset) |
| | Edge-detection | 87.3% | | | |
| | Feature-Tracking | 89% | *Yes/No* | AU1+2,1+4, 4, AU 5, 6, 7. | |
| | Dense-flow | 92.3% | *Yes/No* | AU12,6+12+25, AU20+25,15+17, AU17+23+24,9+17. | |
| | Feature-Tracking | 88% | *Yes/No* | AU12,6+12+25, AU20+25,15+17, AU17+23+24,9+17. AU 25, 26, 27 | |
| | Edge-detection | 80.5% | *Yes/No* | AU9+17,12+25. | |

rates between systems are not meaningful.

In Table 12, the systems were compared along several characteristics: feature extraction methods, recognition rates, treatment of AU combinations, AUs recognized, and databases used. The terms "old faces" and "novel faces" in the third column requires some explanation. "Old faces" means that in obtaining the recognition rates some subjects appear in both training and testing sets. "Novel faces" means no same subject appears in both training and testing sets; this is obviously a little more difficult case than "Old faces". In the fourth column, the terms "$No$", "$Yes/Yes$", and "$Yes/No$" are used to describe how the AU combinations are treated. "$No$" means that no AU combination was recognized. "$Yes/Yes$" means that AU combinations were recognized and AUs in combination were recognizable individually. "$Yes/No$" means that AU combinations were recognized but each AU combination was treated as if it were a separate new AU. Our current AFA system, while being able to recognize a larger number of AUs and AU combinations, shows the best or near the best recognition rates even for the tests with "novel faces" or in tests where independent different databases are used for training and testing.

## 6. Conclusion

Automatically recognizing facial expressions is important to understand human emotion and paralinguistic communication, to design multimodal user interfaces, and to relate applications such as human identification. The facial action coding system (FACS) developed by Ekman and Friesen [13] is considered to be one of the best and accepted foundations for recognizing facial expressions. Our feature-based automatic face analysis (AFA) system has shown improvement in AU recognition over previous systems.

It has been reported [2, 5, 40] that template based methods (including image decomposition with image kernels such as Gabors, Eigenfaces, and Independent Component Images) outperform explicit parameterization of facial features. Our comparison indicates that a feature-based method performs just as well as the best template based method and in more complex data. It may be premature to conclude that one or the other approach is superior. Recovering FACS-AUs from video using automatic computer vision techniques is not an easy task, and numerous challenges remain [20]. We feel that further efforts will be required for combining both approaches in order to achieve the optimal performance, and that tests with a substantially large database are called for [1].

## Acknowledgements

The authors would like to thank Paul Ekman, at the Human Interaction Laboratory, University of California, San Francisco for providing the Ekman-Hager database. The authors also thank Zara Ambadar, Bethany Peters, and Michelle Lemenager for processing the images. The authors appreciate the helpful comments and suggestions of Marian Bartlett, Simon Baker, Karen Schmidt, and anonymous reviewers. This work was supported by the NIMH grant R01 MH51435.

# References

[1] *Facial Expression Coding Project.* Cooperation and competition between Carnegie Mellon University and University of California, San Diego (Unpublished), 2000.

[2] M. Bartlett, J. Hager, P.Ekman, and T. Sejnowski. Measuring facial expressions by computer image analysis. *Psychophysiology*, 36:253–264, 1999.

[3] M. J. Black and Y. Yacoob. Trcking and recognizing rigid and non-rigid facial motions using local parametric models of image motion. In *Proc. Of International conference on Computer Vision*, pages 374–381, 1995.

[4] M. J. Black and Y. Yacoob. Recognizing facial expressions in image sequences using local parameterized models of image motion. *International Journal of Computer Vision*, 25(1):23–48, October 1997.

[5] R. Brunelli and T. Poggio. Face recognition: Features versus templates. *IEEE Trans. on Pattern Analysis and Machine Intelligence*, 15(10):1042–1052, Oct. 1993.

[6] J. Canny. A computational approach to edge detection. *IEEE Trans. Pattern Analysis Mach. Intell.*, 8(6), 1986.

[7] J. M. Carroll and J. Russell. Facial expression in hollywood's portrayal of emotion. *Journal of Personality and Social Psychology.*, 72:164–176, 1997.

[8] J. F. Cohn, A. J. Zlochower, J. Lien, and T. Kanade. Automated face analysis by feature point tracking has high concurrent validity with manual facs coding. *Psychophysiology*, 36:35–43, 1999.

[9] C. Darwin. *The Expression of Emotions in Man and Animals.* John Murray, reprinted by University of Chicago Press, 1965, 1872.

[10] G. Donato, M. S. Bartlett, J. C. Hager, P. Ekman, and T. J. Sejnowski. Classifying facial actions. *IEEE Transaction on Pattern Analysis and Machine Intelligence*, 21(10):974–989, Oct. 1999.

[11] Eihl-Eihesfeldt. *Human ethology.* NY: Aldine de Gruvter, 1989.

[12] P. Ekman. Facial expression and emotion. *American Psychologist*, 48:384–392, 1993.

[13] P. Ekman and W. Friesen. *The Facial Action Coding System: A Technique For The Measurement of Facial Movement.* Consulting Psychologists Press, Inc., San Francisco, CA, 1978.

[14] P. Ekman and W. V. Friesen. *Pictures of facial affect.* Palo Alto, CA: Consulting Psychologist., 1976.

[15] P. Ekman, J. Hager, C. H. Methvin, and W. Irwin. *Ekman-Hager Facial Action Exemplars.* Unpublished data, Human Interaction Laboratory, University of California, San Francisco.

[16] I. Essa and A. Pentland. Coding, analysis, interpretation, and recognition of facial expressions. *IEEE Trans. on Pattern Analysis and Machine Intell.*, 19(7):757–763, July 1997.

[17] J. Fleiss. *Statistical Methods for Rates and Proportions.* NY: Wiley, 1981.

[18] K. Fukui and O. Yamaguchi. Facial feature point extraction method based on combination of shape extraction and pattern matching. *Systems and Computers in Japan*, 29(6):49–58, 1998.

[19] C. Izard, L. Dougherty, and E. A. Hembree. A system for identifying affect expressions by holistic judgments. In *Unpublished Manuscript, University of Delaware*, 1983.

[20] T. Kanade, J. Cohn, and Y. Tian. Comprehensive database for facial expression analysis. In *Proceedings of International Conference on Face and Gesture Recognition*, pages 46–53, March, 2000.

[21] M. Kirby and L. Sirovich. Application of the k-1 procedure for the characterization of human faces. *IEEE Transc. On Pattern Analysis and Machine Intelligence*, 12(1):103–108, Jan. 1990.

[22] Y. Kwon and N. Lobo. Age classification from facial images. In *Proc. IEEE Conf. Computer Vision and Pattern Recognition*, pages 762–767, 1994.

[23] K. Lam and H. Yan. Locating and extracting the eye in human face images. *Pattern Recognition*, 29(5):771–779, 1996.

[24] J.-J. J. Lien, T. Kanade, J. F. Cohn, and C. C. Li. Detection, tracking, and classification of action units in facial expression. *Journal of Robotics and Autonomous System*, 31:131–146, 2000.

[25] B. Lucas and T. Kanade. An interative image registration technique with an application in stereo vision. In *The 7th International Joint Conference on Artificial Intelligence*, pages 674–679, 1981.

[26] K. Mase. Recognition of facial expression from optical flow. *IEICE Transactions*, E. 74(10):3474–3483, October 1991.

[27] R. R. Rao. *Audio-Visal Interaction in Multimedia*. PHD Thesis, Electrical Engineering, Georgia Institute of Technology, 1998.

[28] M. Rosenblum, Y. Yacoob, and L. S. Davis. Human expression recognition from motion using a radial basis function network archtecture. *IEEE Transactions On Neural Network*, 7(5):1121–1138, 1996.

[29] H. A. Rowley, S. Baluja, and T. Kanade. Neural network-based face detection. *IEEE Transactions On Pattern Analysis and Machine intelligence*, 20(1):23–38, January 1998.

[30] K. Scherer and P. Ekman. *Handbook of methods in nonverbal behavior research*. Cambridge University Press, Cambridge, UK, 1982.

[31] M. Suwa, N. Sugie, and K. Fujimora. A preliminary note on pattern recognition of human emotional expression. In *International Joint Conference on Pattern Recognition*, pages 408–410, 1978.

[32] D. Terzopoulos and K. Waters. Analysis of facial images using physical and anatomical models. In *IEEE International Conference on Computer Vision*, pages 727–732, 1990.

[33] Y. Tian, T. Kanade, and J. Cohn. Robust lip tracking by combining shape, color and motion. In *Proc. Of ACCV'2000*, pages 1040–1045, 2000.

[34] Y. Tian, T. Kanade, and J. Cohn. Dual-state parametric eye tracking. In *Proceedings of International Conference on Face and Gesture Recognition*, pages 110–115, March, 2000.

[35] M. Turk and A. Pentland. Face recognition using eigenfaces. In *Proc. IEEE Conf. Computer Vision and Pattern Recognition*, pages 586–591, 1991.

[36] Y. Yacoob and M. J. Black. Parameterized modeling and recognition of activities. In *Proc. 6th IEEE Int. Conf. on Computer Vision*, pages 120–127, Bombay, India, 1998.

[37] Y. Yacoob and L. Davis. Recognizing human facial expression from long image sequences using optical flow. *IEEE Trans. on Pattern Analysis and Machine Intell.*, 18(6):636–642, June 1996.

[38] Y. Yacoob, H.-M. Lam, and L. Davis. Recognizing faces showing expressions. In *Proc. Int. Workshop on Automatic Face- and Gesture-Recognition*, pages 278–283, Zurich, Switserland, 1995.

[39] A. Yuille, P. Haallinan, and D. S. Cohen. Feature extraction from faces using deformable templates. *International Journal of Computer Vision*, 8(2):99–111, 1992.

[40] Z. Zhang. Feature-based facial expression recognition: Sensitivity analysis and experiments with a multi-layer perceptron. *International Journal of Pattern Recognition and Artificial Intelligence*, 13(6):893–911, 1999.

# View Synthesis under Perspective Projection[*]


G C Feng[+], P C Yuen[++] and J H Lai[+]

[+]*Department of Mathematics*
*Zhongshan University, Guangzhou, China*

[++]*Department of Computer Science*
*Hong Kong Baptist University, Hong Kong*

*Email: mcsfgc@zsu.edu.cn*


## Abstract


*This paper addresses the issue on generating a 2D view of a 3D object from its other 2D views. Linear Combination method is the typical approach to this problem. However, a 2D view cannot be represented by a linear combination of other 2D views under perspective projection. Instead, we have presented a solution under perspective projection. The proposed method also applies to construction of virtual frontal view face image and the results are encouraging.*


---


* Extracted from International Journal of Pattern Recognition and Artificial Intelligence, Vol. 14, No. 5, pp. 649-661. Copyright World Scientific Publishing Company

# 1. Introduction

Generating 2D views of a 3D object from different perspective angles is an important part in human computer communication. The straightforward method is to construct a 3D object image using a 3D scanner [4,5], and so, any 2D views of that object can be easily obtained. However, this approach requires a very expensive 3D scanner, which may not be affordable in daily applications. The second approach constructs 2D views based on the other 2D views of the object. This approach is relatively complicate but requires only a few 2D views of an object.

Ullman and Basri [2,3] first proposed that any 2D views of a 3D object can be represented by a linear combination of a set of 2D views under scaled orthographic projection (SOP). After that, Poggio [6] provided a detailed mathematical description on the Ullman and Basri's method. Poggio showed that any 2D views of a 3D object can be represented by a linear combination of six 2D views. If the x and the y coordinates of a view are separately considered, 3 views are sufficient. In linear algebra, the result is strikingly succinct, but it is very useful in image synthesis and pattern matching. It tells us that only the coefficients of the linear combination are determined suitably, the shape or pattern of a new view of the 3D object can be synthesized. This result is also employed in face image reconstruction in face recognition [8,10].

As it is well known, scaled orthographic projection serves to approximate perspective projection (PP) by assuming that all points on a 3-D object are roughly the same distance from the camera [7]. SOP assumed that the distance between the camera and object ($d_{cf}$) is large comparing with the size of the object in depth ($s_f$). That is, $s_f \ll d_{cf}$.

There are some advantages for using SOP instead of PP. First of all, the mathematical model of SOP is simpler than that of PP. In turn, the computations involved are less complicated. Second, the intrinsic parameters of camera, such as focal length are not required in SOP. Third, if distance between the camera and face is large comparing with the size of an object (say 100 times or larger), SOP provides a very good approximation to PP. Owing to these advantages, many systems [8, 10] have been developed based on SOP. However, in human computer communication applications, distance between the human face and the camera is likely equal to the distance between the computer operator and the desktop computer. Feng and Yuen [9] have reported the relation between the error and the distance between camera and object.

This paper follows the second approach, in which, the new 2D view is generated from other views. The contributions of this paper include,

- We mathematically prove that, under perspective projection, a new view cannot be generated by a linear combination of the other views.
- A new method under true perspective projection is developed. Experimental results show that accuracy of the proposed method is better than the existing approach. Moreover, two 2D views are sufficient for generating other 2D views. Especially, when an object has bilateral symmetry, the new view can be synthesized from a single view. The result is applied in synthesizing the virtual frontal face.

This paper is organized as follows. Section 2 defines the notation to be used in this paper while Section 3 proves that linear combination does not exist under perspective projection. The proposed method is reported in Section 4. Experimental results are presented in section 5 while Section 6 gives the conclusions of this paper.

## 2. Notations

There are two configurations to capture different views of an object (Figure 1). The first configuration assumes that object is fixed while camera rotates around the object as in shown Figure 1(a). In the second configuration, camera is fixed while the object rotates around its center as shown in Figure 1(b). Basically, 2D views obtained in these two configurations are the same. In this paper, we adopt the second configuration.

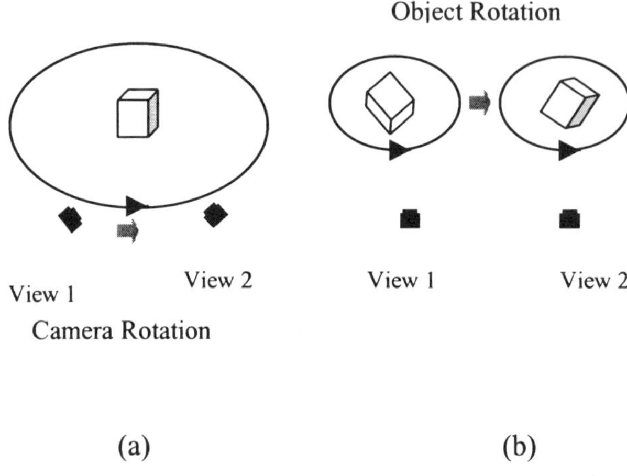



Figure 1. Two models for two configurations

We set the center of the object rotation as coordinate origin, optical axis of the camera as z-axis. The coordinate system is shown figure 2.

We denote the camera focal length as $f$ (which is usually assumed to be unity), the distance between camera and object as $D$, rotation matrix for $i$-th view as $\boldsymbol{R^i}$,

$$R^i = \begin{pmatrix} r^i_{11} & r^i_{12} & r^i_{13} \\ r^i_{21} & r^i_{22} & r^i_{23} \\ r^i_{31} & r^i_{32} & r^i_{33} \end{pmatrix}$$

$\boldsymbol{P}$ is a point on the object and its coordinates are $(X,\ Y,\ Z)^T$. $\boldsymbol{I(\xi,\ \eta)}$ is the 2D view image. The $i$th view of the point $\boldsymbol{P}$ with rotation matrix $R^i$ is denoted as $\boldsymbol{P^i(X^i,Y^i,Z^i)}$ and its corresponding image is $\boldsymbol{I^i(\xi^i,\ \eta^i)}$.

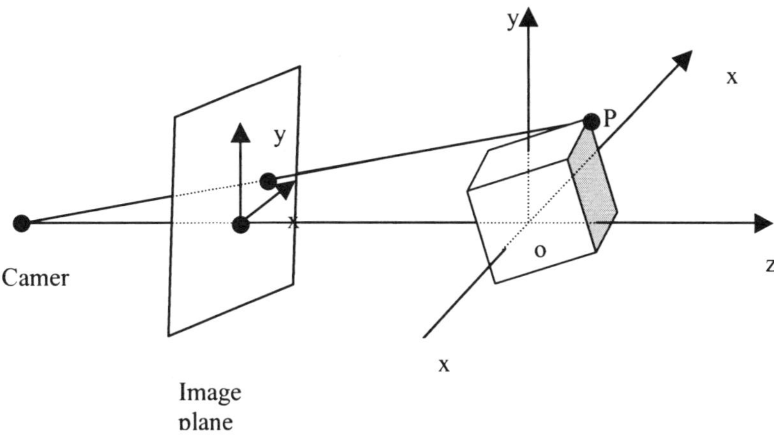


Figure 2. The coordinate system

## 3. Linear Combination does not exist under Perspective Projection

In this section, we prove that a new 2D view cannot be a linear combination of the other 2D views under perspective projection. Under perspective projection, each 2D image point is represented by,

$$\begin{cases} \xi = f \dfrac{X}{Z+D} \\ \eta = f \dfrac{Y}{Z+D} \end{cases} \quad (1)$$

The relation between point P(X,Y,Z), $\boldsymbol{P}^{i}(X^{i},Y^{i},Z^{i})$ and rotation matrix $R^{i}$ is as follows.

$$\begin{pmatrix} X^i \\ Y^i \\ Z^i \end{pmatrix} = R^i \begin{pmatrix} X \\ Y \\ Z \end{pmatrix} = \begin{pmatrix} r_{11}^i X + r_{12}^i Y + r_{13}^i Z \\ r_{21}^i X + r_{22}^i Y + r_{23}^i Z \\ r_{31}^i X + r_{32}^i Y + r_{33}^i Z \end{pmatrix} \qquad (2)$$

and its corresponding image $I^i(\xi^i, \eta^i)$ becomes,

$$\begin{cases} \xi^i = f \dfrac{r_{11}^i X + r_{12}^i Y + r_{13}^i Z}{r_{31}^i X + r_{32}^i Y + r_{33}^i Z + D} \\[2em] \eta^i = f \dfrac{r_{21}^i X + r_{22}^i Y + r_{23}^i Z}{r_{31}^i X + r_{32}^i Y + r_{33}^i Z + D} \end{cases} \qquad (3)$$

In deriving the proof, we need following proposition.

Proposition 1

*The rational function* $\dfrac{1}{x-a}$ *can't be decomposed into the linear combination of*

*rational functions* $\dfrac{1}{x-a_i}$ ( $a_i{\neq}a$, $i=1,2$ ...,$n$).

**Proof:**

If the rational function $\dfrac{1}{x-a}$ can be decomposed into the linear combination of

rational functions $\dfrac{1}{x-a_i}$ ( $a_i{\neq}a$, $i=1,2$ ...,$n$), there exist $k_i$ ($i=1,2,$ ...,$n$) such that

$$\frac{1}{x-a} \equiv \sum_{i=1}^{n} \frac{k_i}{x-a_i}$$

This is

$$\prod_{j=1}^{n}(x-a_j) \equiv \sum_{i=1}^{n} k_i(x-a)\prod_{\substack{j=1\\j\neq i}}^{n}(x-a_j)$$

This expression is identity for all $x$. Let $x=a_i$, we can get the $k_i=0$ ($i=1, 2,...,n$). It is obvious contradiction. So the rational function 1/(x-a) cannot be decomposed into linear combination of different rational functions.

Based on proposition 1, we can extend more general conclusion as follows.

Proposition 2

*The rational function* $\dfrac{ax+by+cz}{dx+ey+fz+g}$ *($d\neq0$ $e\neq0$) can't be decomposed into the*

*linear combination of rational functions* $\dfrac{a_i x+b_i y+c_i z}{d_i x+e_i y+f_i z+g_i}$ *($i=1,2,...,n$).*

*where* $d_i : e_i : f_i : g_i \neq d : e : f : g(i=1,2,...,n)$

The basic idea for the proof of the proposition is similar as proposition 1. Here we omit the tedious process.

From proposition 2, equation (3) cannot be decomposed as a linear combination of rational function. In turn, a new 2D view ($\xi$, $\eta$) cannot be represented by a set of linear combination of the other 2D views $I^i(\xi^i, \eta^i)$.

This result also shows that even if given the camera distance $D$ (calibrate camera), it does not exist a linear combination among views.

## 4. Proposed Method

In view of the limitation on existing methods, we propose to a new solution under perspective projection.

Let $w = Z/(Z+D)$, and replace $\xi$, $\eta$ and $w$ in equation (3), we have

$$\begin{cases} \xi^i = f \dfrac{r_{11}^i \xi + r_{12}^i \eta + r_{13}^i w}{r_{31}^i \xi + r_{32}^i \eta + r_{33}^i w + (1-w)} \\[4mm] \eta^i = f \dfrac{r_{21}^i \xi + r_{22}^i \eta + r_{23}^i w}{r_{31}^i \xi + r_{32}^i \eta + r_{33}^i w + (1-w)} \end{cases} \tag{4}$$

For the uncalibrated system, $D$ is an unknown parameter relative to camera position, so the parameter $w$ is unknown.  Eliminating the unknown $w$, we get a new equation involving images $I^i(\xi^i, \eta^i)$ and $I(\xi, \eta)$ which is shown as follows,

$$(r_{11}^i r_{23}^i - r_{13}^i r_{21}^i)\xi + (r_{12}^i r_{23}^i - r_{13}^i r_{22}^i)\eta - r_{23}^i \xi^i + r_{13}^i \eta^i$$

$$- (r_{21}^i(1-r_{33}^i) + r_{23}^i r_{31}^i)\xi\xi^i + (r_{13}^i r_{31}^i + r_{11}^i(1-r_{33}^i))\xi\eta^i$$

$$- (r_{23}^i r_{32}^i + r_{22}^i(1-r_{33}^i))\eta\xi^i + (r_{13}^i r_{32}^i + r_{12}^i(1-r_{33}^i))\eta\eta^i = 0$$

The expression can be simplified as

$$a_1^i \xi + b_1^i \eta - c^i \xi^i - d^i \eta^i + a_2^i \xi\xi^i + a_3^i \xi\eta^i + b_2^i \eta\xi^i + b_3^i \eta\eta^i = 0 \tag{5}$$

or

$$(a_1^i + a_2^i \xi^i + a_3^i \eta^i)\xi + (b_1^i + b_2^i \xi^i + b_3^i \eta^i)\eta = c^i \xi^i + d^i \eta^i \tag{6}$$

where

$$a_1^i = r_{11}^i r_{23}^i - r_{13}^i r_{21}^i, \quad a_2^i = -(r_{21}^i(1-r_{33}^i) + r_{23}^i r_{31}^i), \quad a_3^i = r_{13}^i r_{31}^i + r_{11}^i(1-r_{33}^i)$$

$$b_1^i = r_{12}^i r_{23}^i - r_{13}^i r_{22}^i, \quad b_2^i = -(r_{23}^i r_{32}^i + r_{22}^i(1-r_{33}^i)), \quad b_3^i = r_{13}^i r_{32}^i + r_{12}^i(1-r_{33}^i)$$

$$c^i = r_{23}^i, \quad d^i = -r_{13}^i$$

Equation (6) has 7 independent unknown parameters. We can get their solution by given image of 7-pair points. We observed that equation (6) can be reformulated as follows.

$$p_i^T \mathbf{F}\, p = 0$$

where $p_i=(\xi', \eta', 1)^T$, $p=(\xi\ \eta, 1)^T$ and $\mathbf{F} = \begin{pmatrix} a_2^i & b_2^i & -c^i \\ a_3^i & b_3^i & -d^i \\ a_1^i & b_1^i & 0 \end{pmatrix}$ are fundamental

matrix. The equation (6) is unanimous with Longuet-Higgins equation [1, 13]. The advantage is that we can derive directly the shape of new views by rotation matrix **R**.

This expression elucidate the relation between image $I'(\xi', \eta')$ and $I(\xi\ \eta)$. Unfortunately, image $I(\xi\ \eta)$ cannot be determined uniquely from the equation (6). But if we consider two views: view 1 $I^1(\xi', \eta')$ and view 2 $I^2(\xi', \eta')$, the $I(\xi\ \eta)$ can be uniquely determined. From equation (6), we have

$$\begin{cases} (a_1^1 + a_2^1\xi^1 + a_3^1\eta^1)\xi + (b_1^1 + b_2^1\xi^1 + b_3^1\eta^1)\eta = c^1\xi^1 + d^1\eta^1 \\ (a_1^2 + a_2^2\xi^2 + a_3^2\eta^2)\xi + (b_1^2 + b_2^2\xi^2 + b_3^2\eta^2)\eta = c^2\xi^2 + d^2\eta^2 \end{cases} \tag{7}$$

So $I(\xi\ \eta)$ can be found with $I^1(\xi', \eta')$ and $I^2(\xi', \eta')$ and if $\Delta \neq 0$, their relation is as follows,

$$\begin{cases} \xi = \dfrac{\Delta_1}{\Delta} \\ \eta = \dfrac{\Delta_2}{\Delta} \end{cases} \qquad (8)$$

where

$$\Delta_1 = \begin{vmatrix} c^1\xi^1 + d^1\eta^1 & b_1^1 + b_2^1\xi^1 + b_3^1\eta^1 \\ c^2\xi^2 + d^2\eta^2 & b_1^2 + b_2^2\xi^2 + b_3^2\eta^2 \end{vmatrix}$$

$$\Delta_2 = \begin{vmatrix} a_1^1 + a_2^1\xi^1 + a_3^1\eta^1 & c^1\xi^1 + d^1\eta^1 \\ a_1^2 + a_2^2\xi^2 + a_3^2\eta^2 & c^2\xi^2 + d^2\eta^2 \end{vmatrix}$$

$$\Delta = \begin{vmatrix} a_1^1 + a_2^1\xi^1 + a_3^1\eta^1 & b_1^1 + b_2^1\xi^1 + b_3^1\eta^1 \\ a_1^2 + a_2^2\xi^2 + a_3^2\eta^2 & b_1^2 + b_2^2\xi^2 + b_3^2\eta^2 \end{vmatrix}$$

In conclusion, given two 2D views and 7 corresponding points, the shape of the new view can be generated by equation (8). The parameters in equation (8) can be determined by the equation (7).

This result also shows that if the orientations of the two 2D views are given, a new 2D view can also be generated from the two 2D views. This is particular important in face recognition. It is found that the performance of a recognition system on a fixed view is very good and the system can be very simple. Along this direction, given any view, if we can synthesize a predefined view, e.g. frontal-view face image, the orientation problem in face recognition can be solved.

We have shown that, under perspective transform, the shape of new views can be synthesized by two given 2D views. The second step in the view synthesis is the texture mapping. In this paper, we adopt the triangulation texture mapping[11] using affine transform. The detailed process for mapping $i$th triangle from on oriented real image to on virtual image is as follows.

Assume $A(x_1,y_1)$, $B(x_2,y_2)$, $C(x_3,y_3)$ are the vertices of a triangle on oriented real image, and $A'(u_1,v_1)$, $B'(u_2,v_2)$, $C'(u_3,v_3)$ is a corresponding vertices of the triangle on virtual image. The spatial transformation on the triangular facet defines an affine relationship between each point in the input and output images as

$$\begin{pmatrix} u \\ v \\ 1 \end{pmatrix} = \begin{pmatrix} a_{11} & a_{12} & a_{13} \\ a_{21} & a_{22} & a_{23} \end{pmatrix} \begin{pmatrix} x \\ y \\ 1 \end{pmatrix}$$

The three pairs of points can determine the unknown parameters $a_{ij}$, therefore the texture on each point on virtual image is employed the relationship

$T(u,v)=T(x,y)$

where $T(u,v)$ represents gray level on the point.

## 5. Experimental Results

Two experiments are presented in this section. The first experiment evaluates the error introduced when using linear combination method under perspective projection. The second experiment applies the proposed method in construction of a frontal-view face image from a single input image.

### 5.1 Experiment 1: Error in Linear Combination Method

The objective of this section is to demonstrate the error introduced in linear combination when the distance between camera and object is small comparing with depth of an object. A computer-generated cube is used in this experiment. The simulated experiment setting is shown in Figure 3(a). The corners of the cube are marked as point correspondence. The cube is then rotated in different pose and three 2D view images are captured as shown in Figures 3(c) – 3(e). Using the linear combination method to construct the 2D view as shown in Figure 3(b), the result is shown in Figure 3(f). Overlapping the target view in Figure 3(b) onto generated view Figure 3(f), the resultant image is shown in

Figure 3(g). It can be seen that the generated view using linear combination method is highly distorted in shape. Using the proposed solution with figure 3(c) and 3(d) as the input 2D views, the generated view is shown in Figure 3(h). It can be seen that the proposed method provides exact construction in shape.

To measure the error introduced in the linear combination method, we define the error function as follows.

$$E = \frac{\sum_{j=1}^{N} d(I_j, \hat{I}_j)}{N \max_{1 \le j \le n} d(I_j, o)}$$

where $d(I_j, \hat{I}_j)$ is a distance between the real image $I_j$ and the synthesized image $\hat{I}_j$. The point $o$ is the center of image and $N$ is number of points used in synthesis process. Figure 4 shows the error introduced by linear combination method with different separations between the camera and the object. The x-axis represents the ratio of the object size and distance between camera and the object. The y-axis is the percentage error. Figure 4 shows that the error increases when the distance between camera and the object decreases. This result is consistent with the theory of scaled orthographic projection image model.

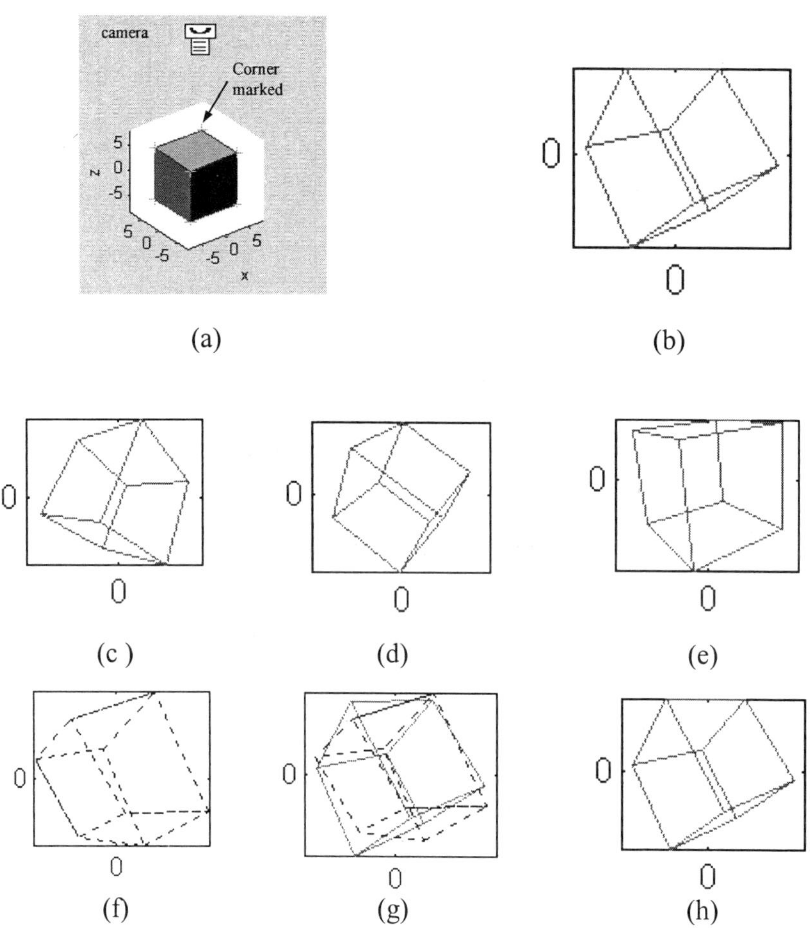


Figure 3. Testing cube

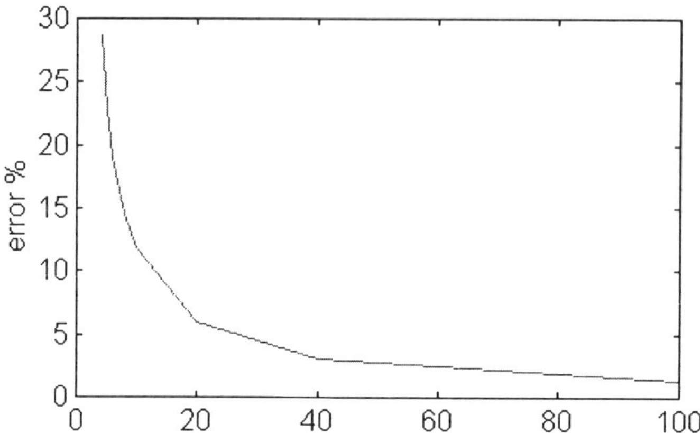

Figure 4. The error introduced by the linear combination method.

## 5.2 Experiment 2: Frontal face image synthesis

The objective of this experiment is to apply the proposed method to construct a virtual frontal view face image for face recognition. If a virtual frontal view face image can be generated from an unknown input, the training and recognition parts in a face recognition system will be simplified. In constructing the virtual frontal view image, we make use of the fact that human face has good symmetry in vertical direction, and therefore, its mirror image indeed constructs a new view. After rotation, the point corresponding to $P(X,Y,Z)$ on mirror image is presented as follows

$$\begin{pmatrix} \tilde{X}^i \\ \tilde{Y}^i \\ \tilde{Z}^i \end{pmatrix} = \tilde{R}^i \begin{pmatrix} X \\ Y \\ Z \end{pmatrix}$$

where point $(\tilde{X}^i, \tilde{Y}^i, \tilde{Z}^i)^T$ is the coordinate for mirror image  under Euclidean

coordinate system, $\tilde{R}^i = \begin{pmatrix} r_{11}^i & -r_{12}^i & -r_{13}^i \\ -r_{21}^i & r_{22}^i & r_{23}^i \\ -r_{31}^i & r_{32}^i & r_{33}^i \end{pmatrix}$ is corresponding rotation matrix.

From the assumption, we can simplify equations (7) as

$$\begin{cases} (a_1^1 + a_2^1\xi^1 + a_3^1\eta^1)\xi + (b_1^1 + b_2^1\xi^1 + b_3^1\eta^1)\eta = c^1\xi^1 + d^1\eta^1 \\ (a_1^1 - a_2^1\xi^2 + a_3^1\eta^2)\xi + (-b_1^1 + b_2^1\xi^2 - b_3^1\eta^2)\eta = c^1\xi^2 - d^1\eta^2 \end{cases}$$

To implement the experiment, we manually located for 7 pair-points on an oriented face and a reference face. To construct the texture in the virtual view, we select 30 extra points on the oriented view. Those points can mesh into 58 triangle as shown in Figure 5. Figure 6 shows the results. Figure 6(a) is frontal view target image. Figures 6(b) and (d) are given image and its mirror image respectively. Figure 6(c) is synthesized without  mirror texture rendering. It is obvious that there exists serious distortion on left face. Figure 6(e) shows the result by making use of mirror texture rending. We can see the virtual face is similar with the frontal reference face. Figures 7 shows more experimental results for same person in different head poses, while Figure 8 shows the virtual faces for the different persons in variety poses.

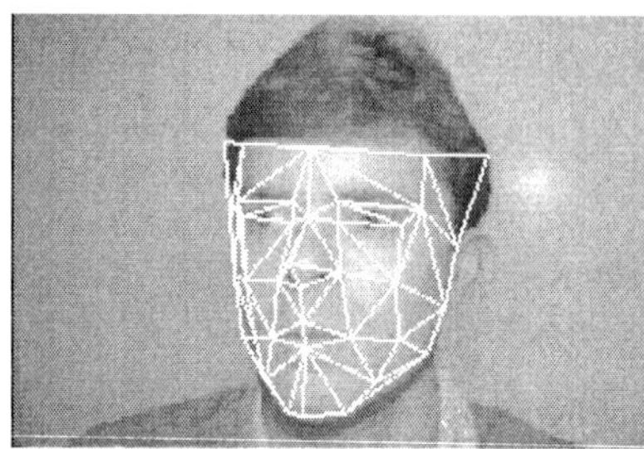

Figure 5. Selected points and mesh triangles on oriented face

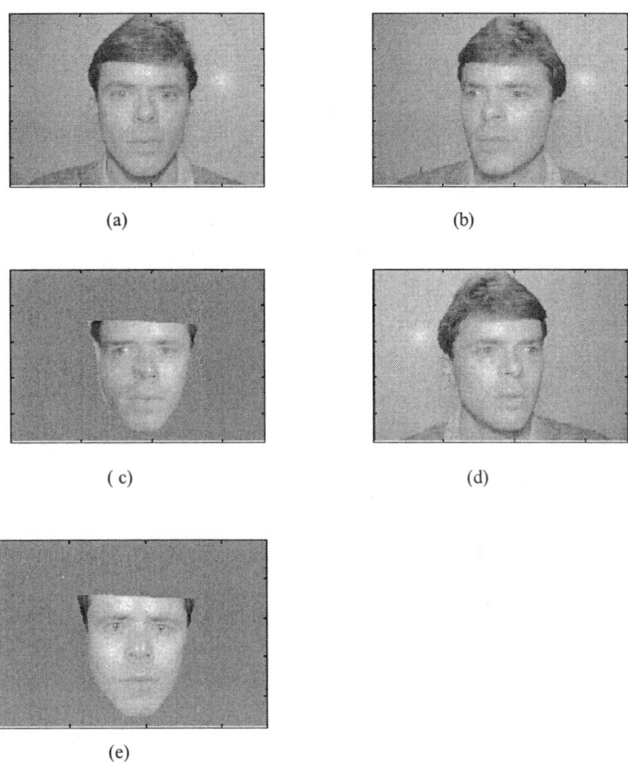

Figure 6. Synthesized virtual face from an oriented view and its mirror.

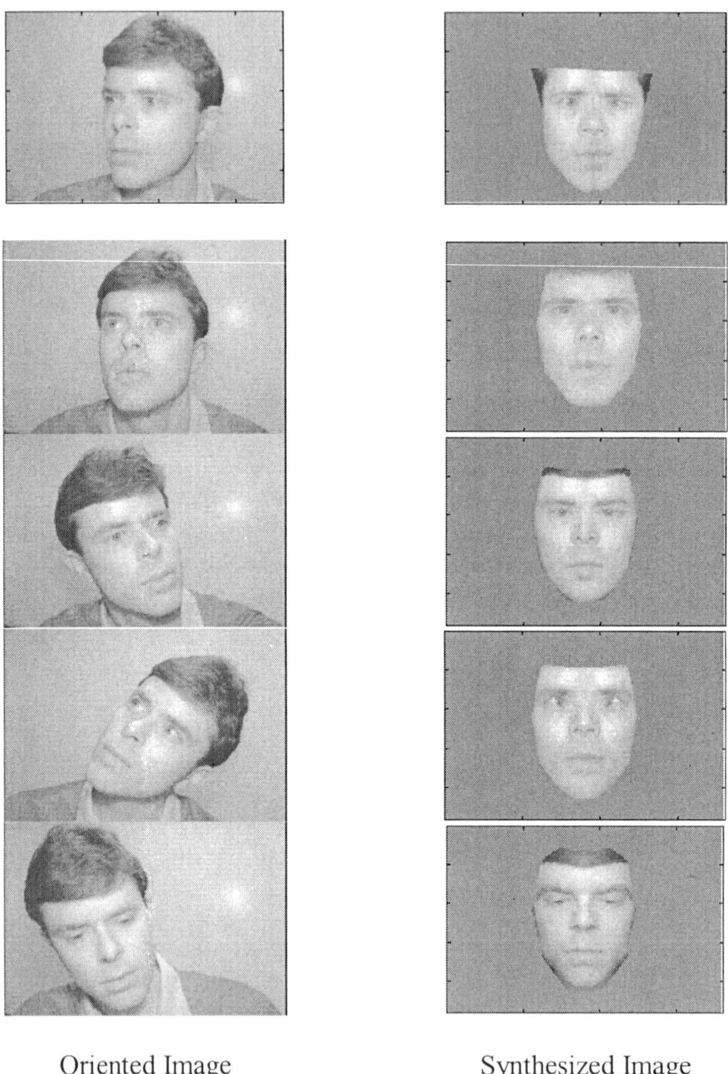

Oriented Image                    Synthesized Image

Figure 7: Other examples on generating virtual frontal-view image.

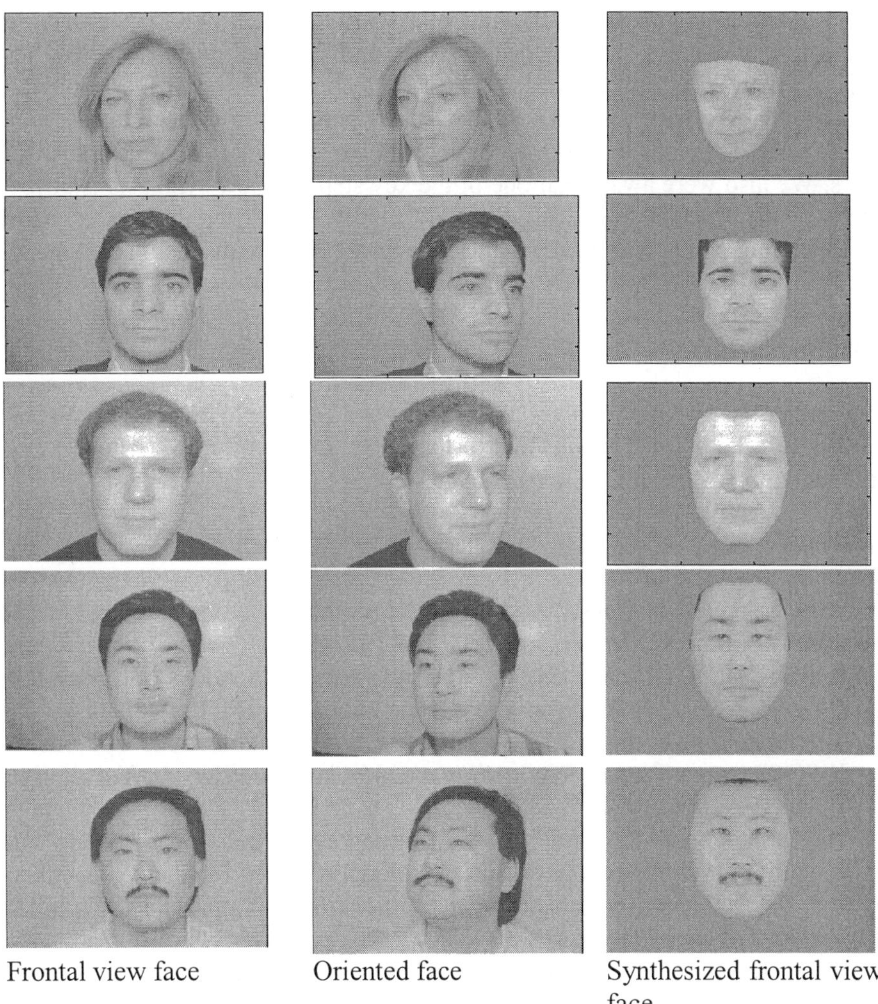

Frontal view face    Oriented face    Synthesized frontal view face

Figure 8: Other examples on generating virtual frontal view image.

## 6. Conclusions

A new solution on generating 2D view of a 3D object from two 2D views under perspective projection has been presented and reported in this paper. The proposed method is also applied on the face reconstruction and the results are encouraging. We have also proved that, under perspective projection, 2D view of a 3D object cannot be represented by a linear combination of the other 2D views. We also were aware that one of the key steps in view synthesis is how to automatically locate the corresponding points on different views. More corresponding points will make synthesized image more realistic and convinced.

## Acknowledgements

This project was supported by the Faculty of Science, Hong Kong Baptist University. The authors would like to thank Dr. D. Beymer of AI Laboratory, MIT for supplying with face image database.

## References

1.  H. C. Longuest-Higgins, "A computer algorithm for reconstructing a scene from two project", *Nature*, Vol. 293, 133-135, 1981
2.  R. Basri and S. Ullman, "Recognition by linear combinations of models", *A. I. Memo*, No. 1152, Artificial Intelligence Laboratory, MIT, 1990
3.  S. Ullman and R. Basri, "Recognition by linear combinations of models", *IEEE Trans. on Pattern Recognition and Machine Intelligence*, Vol. 13, No. 10, pp.992-1006, 1991
4.  T. Kurihara and K. Arai, "A transformation method for modeling and animation of the human face from photographs". In N. Magnenat-Thalmann and D. Thalmann, editors, *Computer Animation'91*, pp. 45-58, Springer-Verlag, Tokyo, 1991
5.  K. Waters and D. Terzopoulos, "Modeling and animating faces using scanned data", *Journal of Visualization and Computer Animation*, Vol. 2, No.4, pp.123-128, 1991

6.  T. Poggio, "3D object recognition and matching: on a result of Basri and Ullman", *in  "Spatial vision in humans and robots"*, edited by L. Harris and M. Jenkin, pp.203-210, Cambridge University Press,1993

7.  T. D. Alter, "3D pose from three points using weak-perspective", *IEEE Trans. on Pattern Recognition and Machine Intelligence*, Vol. 16, No.8, pp. 802-808, 1994.

8.  T. Vetter and T.Poggio, "Linear object classes and image synthesis from a single example image", *IEEE Trans. on Pattern Recognition and Machine Intelligence*, Vol. 19, No.7, pp.733-742, 1997

9.  G. C. Feng, P. C. Yuen and D. Q. Dai, "A Novel Method for Face Orientation Determination in Human Face", 1st international. Workshop on Computer Vision, Pattern Recognition and Image Processing(CVPRIP'98) in 1998 Joint Conference On Information Sciences(JCIS'98), Carolina, USA, Oct. 23-28, 1998

10. D. Beymer , A. Shashua and  T. Poggio, "Example based image analysis and synthesis", *A.I Memo,* No. 1431, Artificial Intelligence Laboratory, MIT, 1993

11. G. Wolberg, *Digital Image Worping*, IEEE Computer Society Press, 1990

12. S. M. Seitz and C. R. Dyer, View morphing, In *Proc. SIGGRAPH'96*, pp.21-30, 1996

13. O. Faugeras, Three-Dimensional ComputerVision, A Geometric Viewpoint, MIT Press, Cambridge, MA, 1993.

# Part II  Single Modality Systems

# Sign Language Recognition

Wen Gao, Chunli Wang

*University of Science and Technology*
*China*

## 1. Introduction

Hand gesture recognition that can contribute to a natural man-machine interface is still a challenging task. Closely related to the field of gesture recognition is that of sign language recognition. Sign language, a kind of structured gesture, is one of the most natural ways of exchanging information for the hearing impaired. It is a kind of visual language via hand and arm movements accompanying facial expression and lip motion. The facial expression and lip motion are less important than hand gestures in sign language, but they may help to understand some signs. This has spawned interest in developing systems that can accept sign language as one of the input modalities for human-computer interaction, as well as supporting the communication between the deaf and hearing society. In fact, a new field of sign language engineering is emerging that attempts to make use of advanced computer technology in order to enhance the system capability to serve all people in our society through powerful and friendly human-computer interface. Our aim of recognizing sign language is to provide an efficient and accurate mechanism to transcribe human sign language into text or speech.

In a system, capturing gestures is the first step of sign language recognition. There are two approaches to get the data of gestures. The first one is the vision-based approach, which utilizes cameras to capture the images of hand gestures. Hand gesture features are subsequently extracted from the images. In order to obtain the features of hand gestures robustly, a special glove with areas painted on it to indicate the positions of the fingers is often used. A glove, for example, bright points on edges of fingers or color block on regions of fingers could be used. The vision-based approach has the advantage that the signer does not have to wear any complex powered input devices. The disadvantages of this approach are its instability and impreciseness due to poor illuminant conditions and limited computing power in popular computers. Furthermore, the vision-based approach has a difficult time performing the task of large vocabulary sign language recognition, because many technical issues on image understanding are still open or need to improve. The second class of approaches is wear-device based. On the contrary, this class measures hand gestures using direct devices such as datagloves and position-trackers. The advantage of this approach is that it captures gesture data robustly and extracts features for further recognition in real-time using less computing power. The disadvantage is that the signer has to wear the device, and the device might be expensive. For our purse of fostering the sign language recognizer, not on data capturing technology, we decided to use the dataglove to capture gesture data in our first stage of system implementation, and to consider the camera-based input in our future system implementation.

Some basic definitions used through out this chapter are first given below. A Posture is specific configuration of hand flexion observed at some time instance. A gesture is a sequence of postures connected by motions over a short time span.

## 2. Previous work

Attempts to automatically recognize sign language began to appear at the end of 80's. Charaphayan and Marble [1] investigated a way using image processing to understand American Sign Language (ASL). This system can recognize correctly 27 of the 31 ASL symbols. Starner[2] reported a correct rate for 40 signs achieved 91.3% based on the image. The signers wear color gloves. By imposing a strict grammar on this system, the accuracy rates in excess of 99% were possible with real-time performance. Fels and Hinton[3][4] developed a system using a VPL DataGlove Mark II with a Polhemus tracker attached for position and orientation tracking as input devices. The system focused on a gesture-to-speech interface. The neural network was employed for classifying hand gestures. Takahashi and Kishino[5] investigated a system for understanding the Japanese kana manual alphabets corresponding to 46 signs using a VPL dataGlove. Their system could correctly recognize 30 of the 46 signs. Y. Nam and K.Y. Wohn[6] used three–

dimensional data as input to HMMs for continuous recognition of a very small set of gestures. They introduced the concept of movement primes, which make up sequences of more complex movements. R.H.Liang and M.Ouhyoung[7] used HMM for continuous recognition of Tainwan Sign language with a vocabulary between 71 and 250 signs based Dataglove as input devices. Kisti Grobel and Marcell Assan [8] used HMMs to recognize isolated signs with 91.3% accuracy out of a 262-sign vocabulary. They extracted the features from video recordings of signers wearing colored gloves. C.Vogler and D.Metaxas[9] used HMMs for continuous ASL recognition with a vocabulary of 53 signs and a completely unconstrained sentence structure. C.Vogler and D.Metaxas[10][11] described an approach to continuous, whole-sentence ASL recognition that uses phonemes instead of whole signs as the basic units. They experimented with 22 words and achieved similar recognition rates with phoneme-based and word-based approaches. Wen Gao[12] proposed a Chinese Sign language recognition system with a vocabulary of 1064 signs. The recognition accuracy is about 93.2%.

By reviewing of foregoing research work we know that most researches on continuous sign language recognition were made on small test vocabulary. C. Vogler and D. Metaxas[14] pointed that the major challenge to sign language recognition is how to develop approaches that scale well with increasing vocabulary size. He used parallel HMMs (PaHMMs) to solve the problem. PaHMMs process multi streams independently. He ran several experiments with 22 sign vocabulary and demonstrated that PaHMMs could improve the robustness of HMM-based recognition even at a small scale. When streams are not frame synchronous, the complexity that the decoding algorithm requires may increase considerably. Results in speech recognition have indicated that allowing asynchrony among streams does not give any signification performance improvement.

## 3. Chinese Sign Language

Chinese Sign Language (CSL) is classified into two categories. One is hand gesture in which each gesture corresponds to a Chinese phrase. Some meaning is expressed by the transformation of the hand shape, orientation and position. The CSL dictionary contains about 5500 conventional Chinese phrases. The advantages of gestures include visualization, simpleness, and understandability. But gestures cannot express all Chinese phrases, especially the virtual words, terms, and the abstract words. The other category is the fingerspelling language in which each posture corresponds to a phonetic alphabet. There are 30 Bopomofo(Fig.1), by which any Chinese phrase can be spelled according to its pronunciation. Usually, hand gestures blended with finger-alphabet are used for communication among the hearing impaired in the daily life. The vocabulary can include all Chinese words. It is obvious that it is impossible to build HMM for every word. In this case, we must find a set of gestures that can be combined to form any word. So, the concept of etyma is proposed, which is similar to the phoneme in spoken language. In order to be consistent with the spoken language, we use the term "phoneme" instead of "etyma" in this chapter.

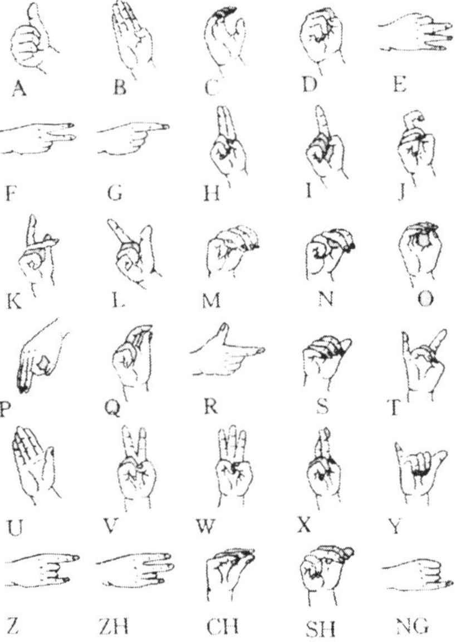

**Figure 1. Bopomofo**

A phoneme here is defined to be the smallest contrastive unit in a language, that is, a unit that has some meaning and distinguishes one sign from another. In CSL, an example of such a phoneme would be the "Room"(Fig.2(a)), which can form "Classroom" with another phoneme "Education"(Fig.2(b)). The Chinese idiom "zuo-jing-guan-tian"(Fig.2(c)) consists of four phonemes. The Bopomofo are considered as phonemes, which can facilitate the CSL recognition when finger-alphabet is blended with gestures. Unlike the phonemes in spoken language, no explicit definition of the etyma exits in the CSL linguistics. Based on extensive and thorough analysis of CSL signs, we find all the units that form all the signs in the CSL dictionary, and then unite those that cannot be distinguished in terms of their gesture effects, such as finger alphabet "V" and the gesture "two". Finally, about 2400 phonemes are explicitly defined for CSL.

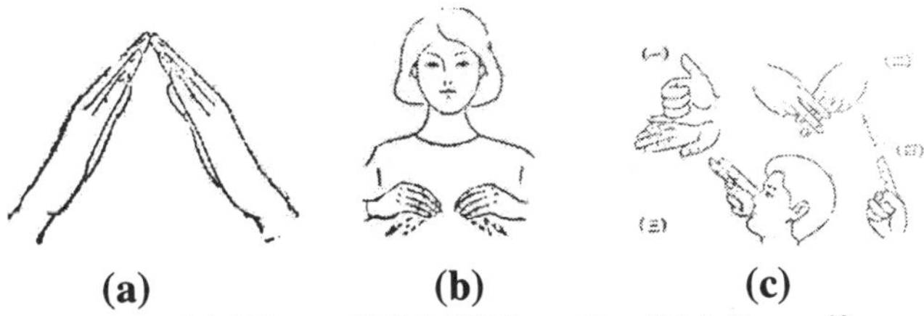

**(a)**                    **(b)**                    **(c)**

**Figure 2. Phonemes:(a)"Room" (b) "Education"(c) "zuo-jing-guan-tian"**

## 4. Feature Extraction

To calculate all gesture data from the left hand, right hand and body parts in a well-defined space, we need to consider the modeling of the relative 3D motion of three receivers working with a transmitter. The geometrical relationships between the transmitter and receivers are shown in Fig.3.

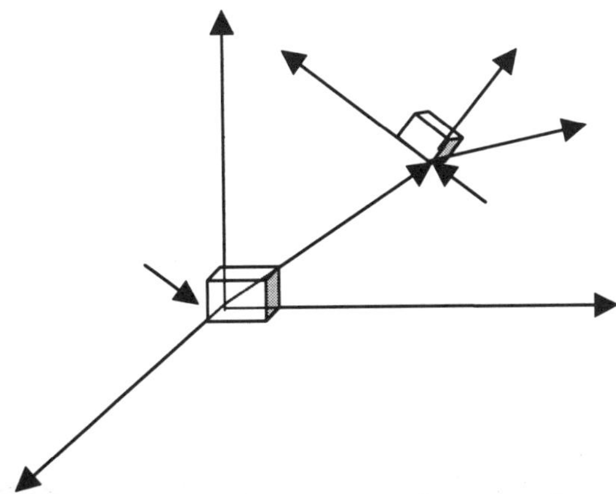

**Figure 3.  The geometrical relationships between the transmitter and receivers.**

The timely motion of the transmitter will be also considered. 3D motion of receivers can be viewed as the rigid motion. It is well known that 3D displacement of a rigid object in the Cartesian coordinates can be modeled by an affine transformation as the following,

$$X' = R(X - S) \tag{1}$$

where $R$ is a 3×3 rotation matrix,

$$R = \begin{pmatrix} 1 & 0 & 0 \\ 0 & \cos\alpha & -\sin\alpha \\ 0 & \sin\alpha & \cos\alpha \end{pmatrix} \begin{pmatrix} \cos\beta & 0 & \sin\beta \\ 0 & 1 & 0 \\ -\sin\beta & 0 & \cos\beta \end{pmatrix} \begin{pmatrix} \cos\gamma & -\sin\gamma & 0 \\ \sin\gamma & \cos\gamma & 0 \\ 0 & 0 & 1 \end{pmatrix} \tag{2}$$

$$= \begin{pmatrix} \cos\beta\cos\gamma & \cos\beta\sin\gamma & -\sin\beta \\ \sin\alpha\sin\beta\cos\gamma - \cos\alpha\sin\gamma & \sin\alpha\sin\beta\sin\gamma + \cos\alpha\cos\gamma & \sin\alpha\cos\beta \\ \cos\alpha\sin\beta\cos\gamma + \sin\alpha\sin\gamma & \cos\alpha\sin\beta\sin\gamma - \sin\alpha\cos\gamma & \cos\alpha\cos\beta \end{pmatrix}$$

$X = (x_1, x_2, x_3)^t$ and $X' = (x'_1, x'_2, x'_3)^t$ denote the coordinates of the transmitter and receiver respectively, $S$ is the position vector of the receiver with respect to Cartesian coordinate systems of the transmitter.

The receiver outputs the data of Eulerian angles, namely, $\alpha, \beta, \gamma$, the angles of rotation about $X_1, X_2$ and $X_3$ axes. Normally these data cannot be used directly as the features because inconsistent reference might exist since the position of the transmitter might be changed between the processing of training and that of testing. Therefore, it is necessary to define a reference point so that the features are invariant wherever the positions of transmitter and receivers are changed. The idea we propose to fix this problem is as follows. There is a receiver on each hand, and the third receiver is mounted at a fixed position on the body, such as the waist or the back. Suppose that $S_r, S_l$, and $S$ are the position vectors of the receivers at right hand, left hand and on the body. The invariant features are $RR_r^t, RR_l^t, R(S_r - S)$ and $R(S_l - S)$, where $R_l$, $R_r$, and $R$ are the rotation matrix of the receivers at right hand, left hand and on the body. $R_r^t$ is the transpose matrix of $R_r$ that is the rotation matrix of the receiver at the right hand respect to Cartesian coordinate systems of the transmitter. It is clear that the product $RR_r^t, RR_l^t, R(S_r - S)$ and $R(S_l - S)$ are invariant to the positions of the transmitter and the signer.

The raw gesture data, which in our system are obtained from 36 sensors on two datagloves, and three receivers mounted on the datagloves and the waist, are formed as 48-dimensional vector. A dynamic range concept is employed in our system for satisfying the requirement of using a tiny scale of data. The dynamic range of each element is different, and each element value is normalized to ensure its dynamic range 0-1.

# 5. Hidden Markov Models

The most popular framework for sign language recognition is the statistical formulation. One well-known and widely used statistical method is Hidden Markov Models (HMMs)[15], which have been used successfully in continuous speech recognition, handwriting recognition, etc. The underlying assumption of the HMM is that the signal can be well characterized as a parametric random process, and that the parameters of the stochastic process can be determined in a precise, well-defined manner. A HMM is a doubly stochastic state machine that has a Markov distribution associated with the transitions across various states, and a probability density function that models the output for every state. A key assumption in stochastic gesture processing is that the signal is stationary over a short time interval. We now give a summary of the basic theory behind HMMs, which is covered in detail in [15].

## 5.1. Definition of HMMs

An HMM is characterized by the following:

1.  N, the number of states in the model. Generally the states are interconnected in such a way that any state can be reached from other states. We label the individual states as $\{S_1, S_2, ..., S_N\}$, and denote the state at time $t$ as $q_t$.

2.  M, the number of distinct observation symbols per state.

3.  The initial state distribution $\pi = \{\pi_i\}$ in which

$$\pi_i = P[q_1 = i], \qquad 1 \le i \le N \qquad (3)$$

4.  The state-transition probability distribution $A = \{a_{ij}\}$

where $a_{ij} = P[q_{t+1} = j \mid q_t = i]$, $1 \le i, j \le N$, and $\sum_i a_{ij} = 1$. (4)

5.  The observation symbol probability distribution,

$$B = \{b_j(k)\}, \tag{5}$$

in which

$$b_j(k) = P[o_t = v_k \mid q_t = j], \, 1 \le k \le M, \tag{6}$$

defines the symbol distribution in state $j$, $j = 1,2,...,N$. When the observations were characterized as discrete symbols chosen from a finite alphabet, the HMM is called DHMMs (Discrete HMMs). But for speech recognition and sign language recognition, the observations are often continuous signals. Hence it would be advantageous to be able to used HMMs with continuous observation densities to model continuous signal representations directly, which is called CHMMs (Continuous HMMs). The probability distribution is a finte mixture of the form

$$b_j(o) = \sum_{k=1}^{M} c_{jk} N(o, \mu_{jk}, U_{jk}) , \, 1 \le j \le N \tag{7}$$

where $o$ is the observation vector being modeled, is the mixture coefficient for the $k$th mixture in state $j$ and $N$ is any log-concave or elliptically symmetric density (e.g., Gaussian). Without loss of generality, we assume that $N$ is Gaussian with mean vector $\mu_{jk}$ and covariance matrix $U_{jk}$ for the $k$th mixture component in state $j$. The mixture gains $c_{jk}$ satisfy the stochastic constraint

$$\sum_{k=1}^{M} c_{jk} = 1, \quad 1 \le j \le N$$

$$\tag{8}$$

$$c_{jk} \ge 0 , \, 1 \le j \le N , \, 1 \le k \le M$$

It can be seen from the above discussion that a complete specification of an HMM requires specification of two model parameters, N and M, specification of observation symbols, and the specification of the three sets of probability measures A, B, and $\pi$. For convenience, we use the compact notation

$$\lambda = (A, B, \pi) \tag{9}$$

to indicate the complete parameter set of the model. This parameter set, of course, defines a probability measure for O, i.e. $P(O \mid \lambda)$.

An example is given in Fig.4. The model given here is an example of a left-right model; that is, $a_{jk} > 0$ if and only if $j \geq k$. In other words, transitions only flow forward from lower states to the same state or higher states, but never backward. This topology is the most commonly used one for modeling processes over time.

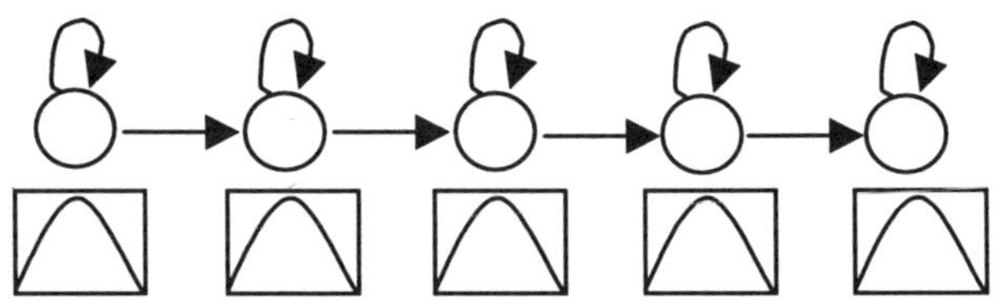

**Figure 4. Example left-right HMM with its transition and output probabilities.**

## 5.2. The Three Basic Problems For HMMs

Given the form of HMM of the previous section, three basic problems of interest must be solved for the model to be useful in real-world applications. These problems are the following:

1.  Given the observation sequence $O = (o_1 o_2 ... o_T)$, and a model $\lambda = (A, B, \pi)$, how do we efficiently compute $P(O \mid \lambda)$, the probability of the observation sequence, given the model?

2.  Given the observation sequence $O = (o_1 o_2 ... o_T)$, and the model $\lambda$, how do we choose a corresponding state sequence $q = (q_1 q_2 ... q_T)$ that is optimal in some sense (i.e., best "explains" the observations)?

3.  How do we adjust the model parameters $\lambda = (A, B, \pi)$ to maximize $P(O \mid \lambda)$?

The first problem is the evaluation problem; namely, given a model and a sequence of observations, how do we compute the probability that the observed sequence was produced by the model? We can also view the problem as one of scoring how well a given model matches a given observation sequence. The latter viewpoint is extremely useful. The solution to Problem 1 corresponds to maximum likelihood recognition of an unknown data sequence with a set of HMMs, each of which corresponds to a sign. For each HMM, the probability $P(O\,|\,\lambda)$ is computed that it generated the unknown sequence, and then the HMM with the highest probability is selected as the recognized sign.

In order to calculate the probability of the observation sequence, $O = (o_1 o_2 ... o_T)$, given the model $\lambda = (A, B, \pi)$, i.e., $P(O\,|\,\lambda)$. The most straightforward way of doing this is through enumerating every possible state sequence of length T (the number of observations). There are $N^T$ such state sequences. To calculate $P(O\,|\,\lambda)$, we need $(2T-1)N^T$ multiplications, and $N^T - 1$ additions. This calculation is computationally infeasible, even for small values of $N$ and $T$. Fortunately forward-backward procedure can be used to resolve this problem. The procedure is given in [15]. This method can compute $P(O\,|\,\lambda)$ in $O(N^2 T)$ time.

The second problem corresponds to finding the most likely path $Q$ through an HMM $\lambda$, given an observation sequence $O$, and is equivalent to maximizing $P(Q, O\,|\,\lambda)$. To implement this solution to Problem 2, a formal technique for finding this single best state sequence exists, based on dynamic programming methods, and is called the Viterbi algorithm.

The third problem is to determine a method to adjust the model parameters $(A, B, \pi)$ to satisfy a certain optimization criterion. There is no known way to analytically solve for the model set that maximizes the probability of the observation sequence in a closed form. We can choose $\lambda = (A, B, \pi)$ such that its likelihood, $P(O\,|\,\lambda)$, is locally maximized using an iterative procedure such as the Baum-Welch method.

## 6. Isolated Recognition

Isolated sign language recognition assumes that each sign can be extracted individually. This requires clearly marked boundaries between signs. Once there are clearly marked boundaries between signs, HMM recognition is comparatively straightforward. The recognition process extracts the signal corresponding to each sign individually. It then picks the HMM that yields the maximum likelihood for that signal as the recognized sign.

## 6.1. CHMMs with Different Numbers of States

Training the HMMs to maximize recognition performance is also comparatively straightforward. Initially, all signs in the training set are labeled. For each sign in the dictionary, the training procedure builds a HMM. But the numbers of basic gestures included in different words are variable. Some signs are simple, such as "chair". There is only one basic gesture in each one of these signs. It is enough to set 3 states in their HMMs. But some signs are complicated, such as Chinese idioms "hu-tou-she-wei". There are at least four basic gestures in these signs.

If the number of the states in HMMs is set to 3, each vector on the states in the complicated signs does not correspond to a gesture. The accuracy will be affected. On the other hand, if the number of the states in HMMs is set to the maximum number of the basic gestures included in one sign, the computational cost will be too much. The number of states in a HMM should be consistent with the number of basic gestures included in the sign. In our system, an approach based on dynamic programming is used to estimate the number of the states.

There is a problem of matching of long signs and short ones if the number of states is different. The minimum number of states is 3 and the maximum number is 5, and $a_{ij}$ is the probability of transferring from the state i to j. For the long signs, $a_{ij} < 1$ when $i, j \geq 3$. For the short signs, $a_{33} = 1$.

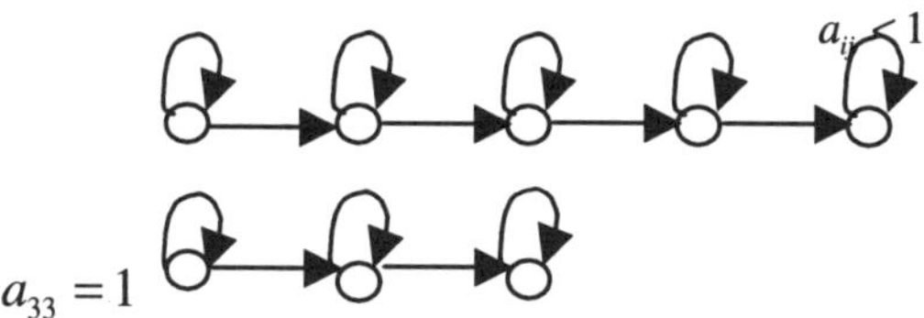


**Figure 5. The HMMs of long signs and short ones**

Given the observation sequence $O = (o_1 o_2 ... o_T)$, the best state sequence is $q = (q_1 q_2 ... q_T)$, where $q_1$ is the initial state. The probability of $O = (o_1 o_2 ... o_T)$ is obtained over the best state sequence $q$ can be written as

$$p(O \mid \lambda) = \pi_{q_1} b_{q_1}(o_1) a_{q_1 q_2} b_{q_2}(o_2) ... a_{q_{T-1} q_T} b_{q_T}(o_T) \tag{10}$$

The interpretation of the computation in the above equation is the following. Initially (at time $t = 1$) we are in state $q_1$ with probability $\pi_{q_1}$, and generate the symbol $o_1$ with probability $b_{q_1}(o_1)$. The clock changes generate the symbol $o_1$ with probability $b_{q_1}(o_1)$. The clock changes from time $t$ to $t+1$ and we make a transition to state $q_2$ from state $q_1$ with probability $a_{q_1 q_2}$, and generate the symbol $o_2$ with probability $b_{q_2}(o_2)$. This process continues in this manner until the last transition (at time T) from state $q_{T-1}$ to state $q_T$ with probability $a_{q_{T-1} q_T}$. Because $a_{ij} < 1$ (i,j>3) for long sign, the decrease of the probability of long signs is larger than that of short signs. A long sign is easily recognized as the short sign that is similar to the later half of the long one. To match the long signs and short ones, the transferring probabilities $a_{ij}(i,j \geq 3)$ in long signs are set to 1, namely the transfers between the later states are set to null.

## 6.2. State Tying

There are some gestures that appear in several signs, such as "Home", which is a part of "classroom", "school", "hospital" and "shop". Each state in HMMs are corresponding to a basic gesture, so there must be many parameters on the states are similar. The parameters can be tied. The aim of tying is to reduce computation load in decoding process. The tying can be carried out at different levels.

Sharing the same HMM among some different HMMs is named as "HMM tying in the whole sign space". This is the first level tying. Clustering different HMMs is very difficult because different HMMs may have different topologies, different transition probabilities and different state observation densities.

Clustering the Gaussians on the states of all of the models is named as "state tying in the whole sign space". This is the second level tying. Clustering the Gaussians means clustering the parameters.

From the temporal and spatial analysis, for each time instant, hand shape, hand position and hand orientation are three measurable factors forming a hand spatial unit in whole sign space. The basic spatial units include six data streams: the left hand shape, position, orientation, right hand shape, position and orientation. The number of possible combinations of these six parts can be approximately $10^8$, so tying at state level for sign language recognition is not as effective as that for speech recognition.

Therefore, tying in each data stream or in sign subspace is proposed, where the data streams include hand shape, hand position and hand orientation. This is the third level tying. It is named as "stream state tying". The tied streams are called "codeword". This level tying is more efficient for calculating state observation probabilities for sign language recognition. Unlike state tying in speech recognition, the stream state tying is taken in each data stream of a hand gesture. The basic idea is as follows: first of all, a whole spatial vector is form by using all streams vectors. For each sign, its HMM is trained with training samples. After all HMMs have been trained, the observation probability densities in each data stream of all signs are tied with a few probability densities. The advantage of this approach is that the computation time is greatly reduced, because the state observation probability density in a whole gesture space is the product of the state observation probability densities of the six streams. And because the state probability in log domain can be computed by summing all stream state probabilities in log domain as follows:

$$\log b_i(x) = \sum_{l=1}^{6} \log b_{il}(x_j) \tag{11}$$

$b_i(x)$ is the $i$'th state observation probability, $b_{il}(x_l)$ is the $l$'th data stream observation probability in the $i$'th state. For each data stream the stream state probabilities are clustered, the stream state probabilities belonging to the same class need to be computed only once. As the number of distinguishable patterns in each data stream is relatively small, for a given observation vector, after these six observation probabilities have been computed, the log likelihood of each signs can be easily gotten by a lookup table and by 5 times addition operations. In addition, the data stream of left hand and right hand can independently be used to select sign candidates during search, for example, the data stream of right hand position and shape can be used to select the sign candidates without need of computation of all streams.

## 6.3. *The algorithm for isolated sign recognition*

Each sign has its own start position, and the start positions of different signs may be different. For isolated sign recognition observation data of several frames near the start position can be used to select the sign candidates, computation load can be greatly reduced in this way.

For the isolated sign language recognition, the algorithm for isolated sign recognition is proposed as the following:

The sign vocabularies are clustered according to parameters in start state of each stream model and its corresponding codebook. Suppose that each stream codebook is $VQ_k$ ($k$=1-6), the sign vocabulary set is *WordSet*. A unique sign subset corresponding to each codeword $i$ in $VQ_k$ is denoted by $SubSet(k,i)$. For different codewords such as $i$ and $j$, their intersection set is empty, i.e.

$$SubSet(k,i) \cap SubSet(k,j) = \phi \qquad (12)$$

and

$$\bigcup_i SubSet(k,i) = WordSet \qquad (13)$$

Let the conditional probability of the observation vector $o_k$ with respect to the codeword $i$ and stream $k$ be $p(o_k|k,i)$. Its *posterior* probability can be calculated as the following,

$$p(i|o_k,k) = p(o_k|k,i) / \sum_{j \in VQ_k} p(o_k|k,j) \qquad (14)$$

If the *posterior* probability is greater than a threshold, then the sign subset $SubSet(k,i)$ is active, otherwise inactive. For each stream observation vector $o_k$ if a codeword is active, then its corresponding sign subset is active. Let all active sign subsets in all stream $k$ be WordCD($k$)($k$=1-6), the active sign subset in the all streams will be their intersection set as the following,

$$WordCD = \bigcap_k WordCD(k) \qquad (15)$$

Signs in active sign subset *WordCD* will be selected as candidates for further detailed match, and the final result is obtained.

Different stream combination coding schemes can be used to further reduce the computation time of the observation probabilities in whole sign space. The procedure can be formed as a hierarchical structure. For example, for left hand data stream when the intersection set of two different sign subsets in two streams is not empty, i.e. $SubSet(k_1,i_1) \cap SubSet(k_2,i_2) \neq \phi$, then the addition operation for signs in the intersection set only needs once to compute the whole observation densities. Based on the same principle, for the combinations over two streams, the similar approach can be obtained.


## 6.4. System Architecture

The architecture of this designed system is shown in Fig.6. The sign data collected by the gesture-input devices is fed into the feature extraction module, the output of feature vectors from the module is then input into the training module, in which a model is built for each sign. The number of the states of a model is set according to the transformation of the sign's signal. In order to decrease the computational cost, the Gaussians on the states are classified, then the index of the code word that is the nearest to the Gaussian on each state is recorded. When the sign is output from the decoder, the sign drives the speech synthesis module to produce the voice of speech.

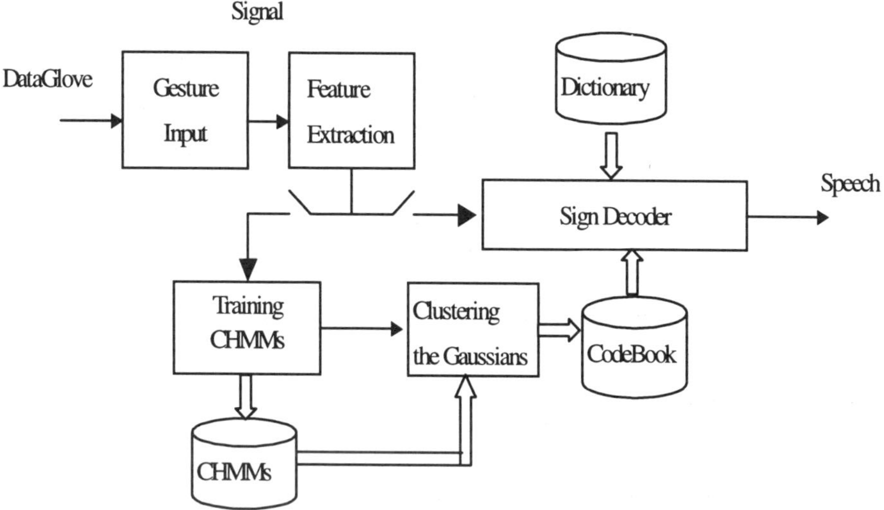


**Figure 6.  Sign Language Recognition.**

### 6.5. Experiments

The hardware environment is Pentium III 700MHz, with two CyberGloves and three receivers of 3D tracker; each Cyberglove is with 18 sensors. The baud rate for both CyberGlove and 3D tracker is set to 38400.

5100 signs in Chinese sign language are used as evaluation vocabularies. Each sign was performed five times, four times are used for training and one for testing. The minimum number of states in HMM of each sign is 3. The maximum number of states in HMM of each sign is 3~7. The recognition rates with different maximum number of states are shown in Table.1. According to Table.1, when the maximum number of states is 5  the best recognition accuracy is 95.0% and the average number of states is only 3.27. This result is very encouraging.

The results shown in Table 1 are with modifying the transferring probability. The comparison is given in Table 2. The recognition rate with modifying the transferring probability is 95% and the recognition rate without modifying the transferring probability is 93.8%. The results show that modifying the transferring probability has effect on the recognition rate.

| The maximum number of states | Average number of states | Rate |
|---|---|---|
| 3 | 3 | 93.9% |
| 4 | 3.162658 | 94.3% |
| 5 | 3.268776 | 95.0% |
| 6 | 3.349578 | 94.8% |
| 7 | 3.418354 | 94.78% |

Table 1. The recognition rates with different maximum number of states

| | |
|---|---|
| Without modifying the transferring probability | 93.8% |
| With modifying the transferring probability | 95.0% |

Table 2. The recognition rates of large vocabulary signs (5100 signs)

The recognition rates of isolated signs with different numbers of the codewords are shown in Table3. The test data are collected when the signs were recognized online.

| The number of codewords | | | | | | The |
| --- | --- | --- | --- | --- | --- | --- |
| Right position | Right orientation | Left position | Left orientation | Left hand shape | Right hand shape | recognition rates |
| 256 | 256 | 256 | 256 | 256 | 256 | 89.33% |
| 128 | 128 | 128 | 128 | 256 | 256 | 92.73% |
| 128 | 128 | 128 | 128 | 300 | 300 | 93.19% |
| 128 | 128 | 128 | 128 | 350 | 350 | 93.74% |
| 128 | 128 | 128 | 128 | 400 | 400 | 93.61% |
| 128 | 128 | 128 | 128 | 512 | 512 | 93.91% |

Table 3. The recognition rates of signs for different numbers of codewords

According to Table 3, considering both the accuracy and the speed, the numbers of codewords of right position, right orientation, left position, left orientation, left handshape and right handshape are set to 128, 128, 128, 128, 350, 350. It spends no more than 1 second to recognition a sign online and the recognition rate is more than 90%. Real-time recognition has been realized.

## 7. Continuous Sign Language Recognition

The standard approach to large vocabulary continuous sign language recognition is to assume a simple probabilistic model of sign language production whereby a specified word sequence, $W$, produces an observation sequence $F$, with probability $P(W,F)$. Let $W = \{w_1, w_2, ..., w_N\}$ be a sequence of words. Suppose $F$ is the feature extracted from input gestures. The recognizer must choose a word string $\hat{W}$ that maximizes the probability given that the feature evidence of $F$ was observed. This problem can be significantly simplified by applying the Bayesian method to find $\hat{W}$:

$$\hat{W} = \arg_W \max P(F \mid W)P(W) \tag{16}$$

The probability, $P(F \mid W)$, that the feature $F$ was observed if a word sequence $W$ was gestured, is typically provided by the data model of hand gestures. A language model determines the likelihood $P(W)$ that denotes a priori chances of the word sequence $W$ being gestured.


## 7.1. Language Modeling

The purpose of the language model is to provide a mechanism for estimating the probability of some word $w_k$ in an utterance given the preceding words $W_1^{k-1} = w_1...w_{k-1}$. A simple but effective way of doing this is to use N-grams in which it is assumed that the probability of appearance of $w_k$ depends only on the preceding n-1 words, that is

$$P(w_k \mid W_1^{k-1}) = P(w_k \mid W_{k-n+1}^{k-1}) \tag{17}$$

N-grams simultaneously encode syntax, semantics and pragmatics and they concentrate on local dependencies. This makes them very effective for languages where word order is important and the strongest contextual effects tend to come from the near neighbors. Thus to date, Bigram and Trigram language models dominate in the large vocabulary speech recognition. Bigram is used in our system.

In Bigram model, we make the assumption that the probability of appearance of any word only depends on the immediately preceding word. To make $P(w_i \mid w_0)$ meaningful, we assume that a sentence begins with a distinguished token<Bos>, that is, $w_0$ = <Bos>. For a word string $W$, the probability over $W$ is as

$$P(W) = P(w_1, w_2...w_n) = \prod_{i=1}^{n} P(w_i \mid w_{i-1}) \tag{18}$$

To estimate $P(w_i \mid w_{i-1})$, the frequency with which the word $w_i$ occurs given that the last word is $w_{i-1}$, we can simply count how often the couple occurs in some training corpus. If the training corpus is not large enough, many actually existing word successions will not be well enough observed which leads to many zero probabilities. So smoothing is critical to make the estimated probability robust for unseen data. In this chapter, we use the Katz smoothing [16].

The net result of the techniques is to limit the number of alternatives that must be searched for finding the most probable sequence of words. Hence the bigram language model reduces the search space. The corpus used in our case to estimate the bigram probabilities consists of about 30 million Chinese words in the Chinese newspapers from the year 1993 to 1995. But different from spoken language, the virtual words are always omitted in sign language, and sometimes the subject and the predicate are hyperbatic. Some adaptations to these linguistic characteristics are imposed to the Bigram.

## *7.2. Search Algorithms*

Viterbi[15] search and its variant forms belong to a class of breadth-first search techniques. All hypotheses are pursued in parallel and gradually pruned away as the correct hypothesis emerges with the maximum score. In this case, the recognition system can be treated as a recursive transition network composed of the states of HMMs in which any state can be reached from any other state. The signal sequence cannot be segmented in advance. The recognition result cannot be gotten until the end of the sequence is reached. Viterbi algorithm has the function of segmentation. In order to conserve the computing and memory resources, it is imperative to prune the low-scoring partial paths. In Viterbi-beam search only the hypothesis whose likelihood falls within a beam are considered for further growth. The beam threshold with respect to the best path scoring at that level is computed.

To speed up the decoding process and improve the recognition rate, the following techniques are proposed in time-synchronous search.

### 7.2.1. Word candidates

Each sign has its own trajectory in sign space, if an observation vector was close to the trajectory, the sign would be probably active at that time, otherwise the sign inactive.

For the observation vector of each frame how to judge whether a sign is active becomes very important to speeding up the recognition process. If only a small fraction of signs are active at a frame, the most probably active signs are what are active at the previous frame due to the continuity of gestures. Only these active signs need to be further searched at the next frame, thus a large mount of computation load is reduced.

The approach to selecting the active signs at a frame is as the following: let $U_i$ be a basic sign unit not including sign transition unit. If a state belongs to the state set of unit $U_i$, denote $j \in U_i$. For each frame the active score of stream $s$ of the unit is computed as the following,

$$P_{U_i}(t,s) = \max_{j \in U_i} \log b_j(s, O_t) \tag{19}$$

$b_j(s, O_t)$ is the state observation probability, and $P_{U_i}(t,s)$ denotes the active score. This score can be used as an active measure to order the recognition units. A threshold also can be used to select the active units. The active unit will be further searched at the next frame.

The following problems may exist in this approach:

Similar with other fast match approaches, this approach may cause the pruning errors, because if one unit is incorrectly pruned at some frame, the errors may not be recovered. The algorithm needs computing all state probabilities of all basic sign units. The computation load is relatively large for a fast match approach.

### 7.2.2. Still Frame Detecting

In the case of continuous sign language recognition, another difficult problem is the coarticulation, which means that both the sign in front and behind can affect a sign. If two signs are performed in succession, an extra movement from the end position of the first sign to the start position of the second sign appears sometimes. This phenomenon is called movement epenthesis. This problem is handled in speech recognition by adding extra context-dependent HMMs to describe the effect of coarticulation. But this idea is not efficient in large vocabulary sign language recognition. In speech recognition, phonemes are the basic units. There are about 50~60 phonemes. Plus context-dependent phonemes (TRIPHONE), there are about one thousand basic units. This number can be accepted. In CSL there are 2500~3000 "phonemes", so the number of possible "TRIPHONE" is too large to be accepted. In our system, the basic unit is the sign. In order to reduce the effect of the coarticulation, we use still frame detecting. The method is as follows. When a sign finishes, there maybe is a pause. So if a long standstill is detected, the probability of the current sign finishing is higher. In Viterbi search algorithm, when a step from one word to another one happens, a parameter is added to the current score. The parameter is set according to the number of the still frames. If there is no standstill or the standstill does not end, it is impossible that a sign ends, so the parameter is set to punish the transitions between signs. If the standstill finishes and the number of the still frames is big enough, it is probable that the current sign finishes, so the parameter is set to encourage the transitions. Besides, the next several frames maybe the movement epenthesis and their effect to the path should be reduced. If there is a pause keeping for about 1 second, the recognition rate can be improved greatly.

## 7.3. System Architecture

The system architecture is shown in Figure 7. The sign data collected by the gesture-input devices is fed into the feature extraction module, the output of feature vectors from the module is then input into the training module, in which one model is built for each sign. Because the system is signer dependent, there is only one mixture on each state. The parameters on the states are tied. The number of independent parameters in the models is reduced and the parameter estimation becomes simpler and more reliable. The language model that is used in our system is Bigram model. When the word sequence is output from the decoder, the sequence drives the speech synthesis module to produce the voice of speech.

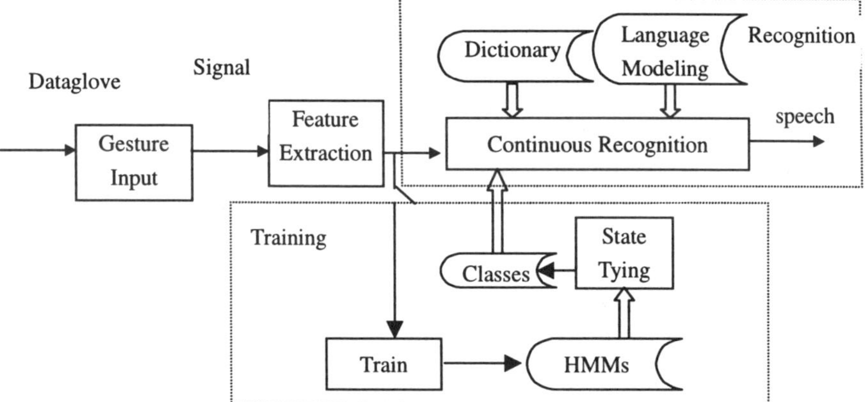


**Figure 7.   Continuous Sign language Recognition based on words**

## 7.4. Experiments

The vocabulary includes about 5100 words. For continuous sentence recognition, 1000 sentences are test. These sentences are made randomly. Each sentence consists of 2 to 10 words. The result is shown in Table 4. The accuracy is over 90%.

| Without still frame detecting | H=6156,D=116, S=2401,I=467,N=8673 |
|---|---|
| With still frame detecting | H=7819,D=42,S=812, I=243, N=8673 |

Table 4. The results of sentences recognition

Where H denotes the number of correct signs, D the number of delection errors, S the number of substitution errors, I the number of insertion errors, and N the total number of signs in the test set.

# 8. Sign Language Based On Phonemes

The greatest advantage of breaking down the signs into the individual phonemes is that it limits the number of HMMs that need to be trained. There are only a finite number of distinct phonemes, whereas the number of possibilities to combine them into signs is practically unlimited. It is a more practical way to make the large-scale applications possible. Especially when finger-spelling language is blended with gestures, this limited set of phonemes helps keeping CSL recognition tractable.

## *8.1. HMM-based Phone Model*

Each individual phone is represented by an HMM. An HMM has a number of states connected by arcs. HMM phone models typically have three emitting states and a simple left-right topology. These phone models can be joined together to form signs and signs can be joined together to cover complete sentences.

About 2400 phoneme continuous HMMs are built. A common technique for a "fast match" for efficient Gaussian calculation is to pre-cluster all the Gaussians into a relatively small number of clusters. During recognition, the likelihoods of the clusters are first evaluated and ranked, and these clusters whose scores are higher than the threshold are set active. Only those Gaussians corresponding to the active clusters are evaluated. The amount of computation that can be saved is good-sized. The method is similar to that of Sec.6.2

## *8.2. Decoding*

To find the sequence of signs with the maximum score is a search problem and its solution is the domain of the decoder. There are two main approaches: depth-first and breadth-first. In the depth-first designs, the most promising hypothesis is pursued until the end of the signal serial is reached. Examples of the depth-first decoders are the stack-decoders and the $A^*$-decoders. In the breadth-first designs, all the hypotheses are pursued in parallel. The breadth-first decoding exploits Bellman's optimality principle and is often referred to as Viterbi decoding. A most likely sequence of states can be found by Viterbi search. Replacing each state by the model that it belongs to, we can get the sequence of the models. Finally, these models are syncopated based on the code dictionary, and the sequence of signs is found. This method is simple, but the language model and the information of the sign language morphology cannot be used during the search.

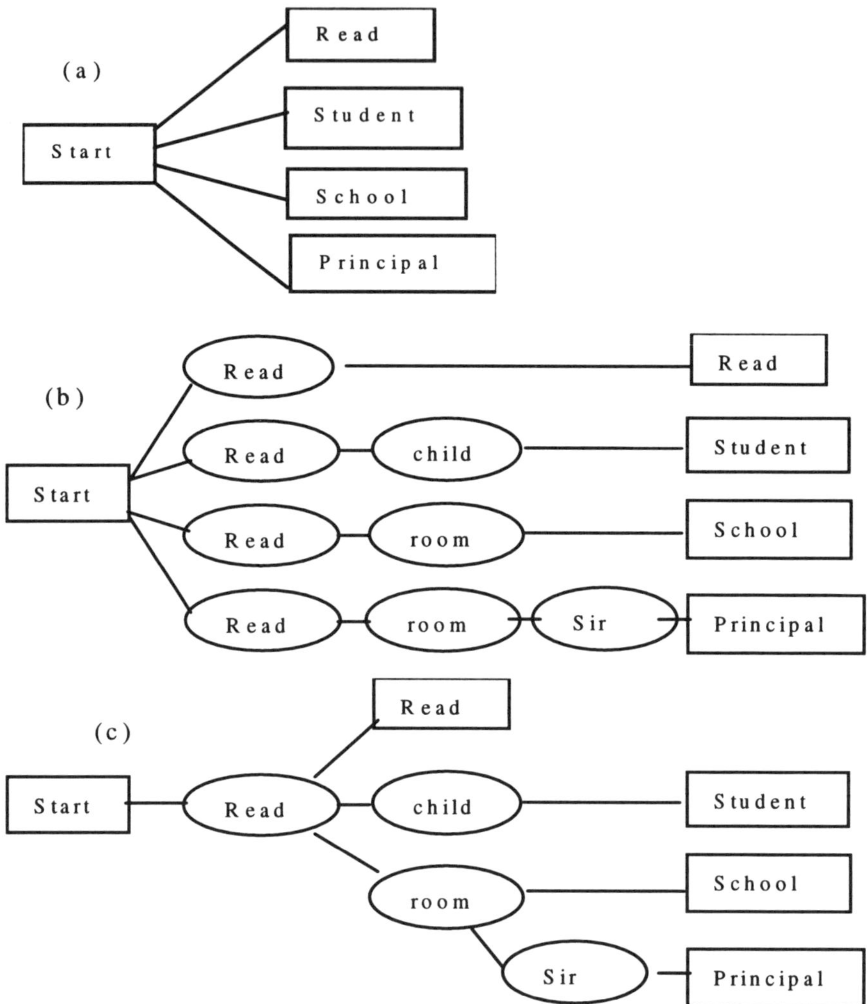



**Figure 8. Fragment of Decoder Network  (a) shows the network of signs (b) shows the same network decomposed into phonemes  (c) shows a tree beginning with the phoneme "Read". Clearly tree-structuring the network can reduce the size of the network.**

In order to use language model, the most likely models and the signs including the models are recorded at the same time. At the beginning, there is a branch to every possible start sign. All the first signs are then connected to all the possible subsequent signs and so on. This is shown in Fig. 8 (a). Then each sign in this network is replaced by the sequence of models according to the code dictionary. Fig. 8 (b) shows a fragment of the network expanding the signs into models. There are many signs include the common phonemes, which are duplicated, such as the phoneme "Read" in Fig. 8 (b). In order to merge all the identical phoneme models in identical contexts, the trees are built. The root of a tree is the phoneme that is the entry of some signs. The phonemes following the root in these signs are its sons. The leaves of the tree are the sets of the signs that consist of the phonemes appearing on the path from the root to them. One tree is illustrated in Fig. 8 (c). During one search, for each possible model, a tree node is recorded. If the node is a leaf, the possible signs can be found.

Even so, this search network is still too large for there are about 2400 models. So the pruning of the search space is necessary. A process called beam search is used. The low-scoring partial paths are pruned to conserve the computing and memory resources. In Viterbi-beam search only the hypothesis whose likelihood fall within a beam are considered for further growth. The beam threshold with respect to the best path scoring at that level is computed. Language model is important to select the actual sign when some models are similar.

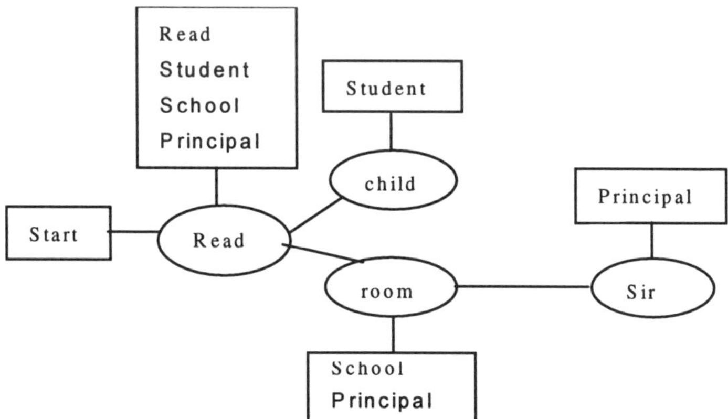


**Figure 9. The tree-structured network with a list of possible signs on each phoneme.**

However, in a tree-structured network, the language model cannot be applied until the end of the sign is reached. The delay severely limits the effectiveness of the language model for pruning. Besides, there are some signs that have the same "pronunciation", that is, they are comprised by the same sequence of phonemes. When their end is reached, there is more than one sign left. Language model is used to decide which one should be selected as the most likely sign. To solve this problem, at each frame, each active phone model carries a list of all the possible signs that it can belong to at that time (see Fig. 9). The list will shrink from the root to the leaves. The maximum probability is used as an estimate for the probability of the actual sign.

When there are two or more signs at the end, the subsequent sign is important to decide which is the most likely one. But the couple that has the maximum probability is probably not the correct selection. For example, sign1 and sign2 consist of the same sequence of phonemes. They have ended. Sign3 and Sign4 begin with the common phoneme (see Fig. 10). The matrix of the Bigram is as follows:

$$
\begin{array}{ccc}
 & \textit{Sign3} & \textit{Sign4} \\
\textit{Sign1} & 0.3 & 0.2 \\
\textit{Sign2} & 0.1 & 0.4
\end{array}
$$

According to the aforementioned method, the probability 0.4 is used as an estimate for this path. The preceding sign is recorded as sign2 here. But in fact the subsequent sign is sign3, the most likely preceding sign should be sign1. To solve this problem, a preceding sign is recorded for each possible latter sign. The current path does not plus the language model score until the end of the latter sign is reached. If sign1 and sign2 end with different phonemes, but with close scores, N-best-pass is an alternative.

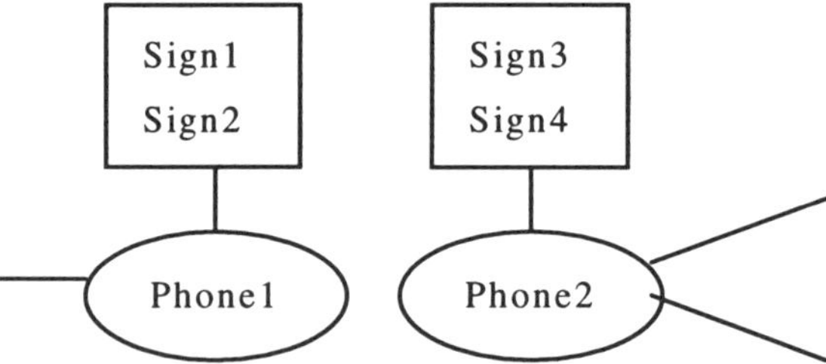


**Figure 10.  Sign1 and sign2 consist of the same sequence of phonemes. Sign3 and sign4 begin with the common phoneme.**

The search algorithm is as follows: For each frame, the active hand configurations, positions and orientations are found. If the six streams on a state are all active, the state is set to active, and the models including the state are active. Sometimes there are bad data gathered from the input devices. If this happens, the correct model may not be selected as the candidate at this frame. For the errors cannot be corrected in Viterbi, the recognition result must be erroneous. To avoid the effect of the "noise", the model candidates should also include those model candidates at the previous frame, whose scores are higher than a given threshold. The active models transit according to the tree-structured network. The current score and the history of each possible path are recorded. To reduce the impact of the movement between two signs, N-best-pass is used.

## 8.3. System Architecture

Current gesture recognition systems are firmly based on the principles of statistical pattern recognition. The basic methods of applying these principles to the problem of dynamic recognition were pioneered by Baker, Jelinek and their colleagues from IBM in the 1970's and have been used successfully in continuous speech recognition, handwriting recognition, etc. Our system uses statistical method, too. The structure of our system is shown in Fig. 11.

The sign data collected by the gesture-input devices is fed into the feature extraction module, and then the feature vectors are input into the training module, in which a model is built for each phoneme. The Gaussians on the states in the models are clustered, and then the indices of the Gaussians on the states are recorded. CHMMs become DHMMs. The signs are encoded based on the phonemes, and the phoneme-sequences of signs are stored in a codebook, based on which the tree-structured network is built. The language model that is used in our system is Bigram model. The decoder controls the search for the most likely priority of sign appearance in a sign sequence. Then the sign sequence is output from the decoder.

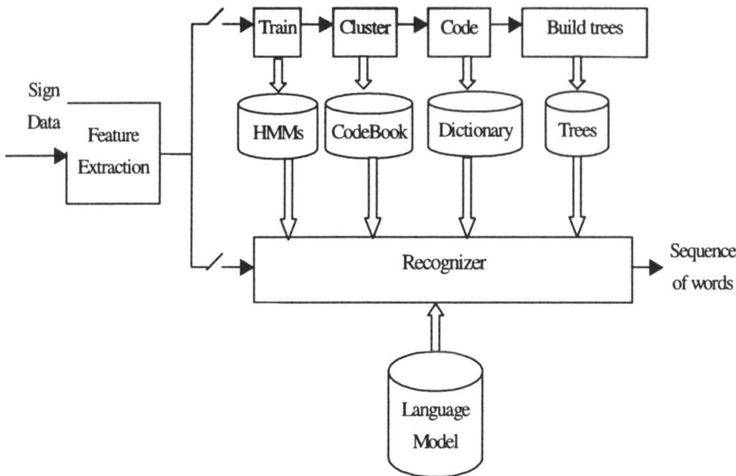

**Figure 11. Overview of Sign Language Recognition**

## 8.4. Experiments

This system is for signer dependent recognition task. 2439 phonemes defined for CSL are used as basic units. Each phoneme was performed five times by one signer, four times are used for training and one for testing. The number of states in HMMs is 3. The results of the isolated phonemes recognition are shown in Table5. The numbers of codewords of right position, right orientation, left position, left orientation, left hand configuration and right hand configuration are set to 128, 128, 128, 128, 350, 350 respectively.

We collected 5119 signs embodied in the dictionary. They are encoded. 200 sentences are test. These sentences are chosen randomly from the corpus used to train the language model. If the sentence does not appear in the corpus, the result of recognition is bad. By this token, the language model is useful. Each sentence consists of 2 to 10 signs. The results are shown in Table 5. The accuracy of these sentences is over 90%.

| 5119 signs | 92.8% |
|---|---|
| 200 sentences | H=781,D=5,S=81, I=34, N=867 |

Table 5. The results of recognition

Where H denotes the number of correct signs, D the number of delection errors, S the number of substitution errors, I the number of insertion errors, and N the total number of signs in the test set.

## 9. Conclusions

In this chapter, we have attempted to present the tools, techniques, and algorithms for attacking several fundamental problems in sign language recognition. A framework of large vocabulary, isolated and continuous sign language recognition is well established here. Techniques for training word or subword models have been developed and work well in practice. Recognition systems have been developed and , too, work well in practice. Recognition systems have been implemented with upward of 5000 word vocabulary. But, many unanswered questions remain. A key one is how to describe the effect of coarticulation. Other issues concern effectiveness of different spectral representations, including codebooks and tied-mixture densities, efficiency of implementation of search strategies, efficient implementations of task syntax, and signer-independent recognition. Large vocabulary recognition has come a long way, but a great deal remains to be done before such systems will be used for practical applications.

## References


C.Charayaphan, A. Marble, *Image processing system for interpreting motion in American Sign Language:* Journal of Biomedical Engineering, Vol.14, 419—425, 1992.

T.Starner, *Visual recognition of American Sign Language using hidden Markov models:* Master's thesis, MIT Media Laboratory, July. 1995.

S.S.Fels and G.Hinton, *GloveTalk:A neural network interface between a DataDlove and a speech synthesizer:* IEEE Transactions on Neural Networks, Vol.4, 2-8, 1993.

S.Sidney Fels, *Glove–TalkII: Mapping hand gestures to speech using neural networks-An approach to building adaptive interfaces:* PhD thesis, Computer Science Department, University of Torono, 1994.

Tomoichi Takahashi and Fumio Kishino, *Gesture coding based in experiments with a hand gesture interface device:* SIGCHI Bulletin, 23(2): 67-73, 1991.

Yanghee Nam and K. Y. Wohn, *Recognition of space-time hand-gestures using hidden Markov model:* ACM Symposium on Virtual Reality Software and Technology,1996.

R.-H.Liang and M.Ouhyoung, *A real-time continuous gesture recognition system for sign language:* In Proceeding of the Third International Conference on Automatic Face and Gesture Recognition, Nara, Japan, 558-565. 1998.

Kirsti Grobel and Marcell Assan, *Isolated sign language recognition using hidden Markov models*, In Proceedings of the International Conference of System,Man and Cybernetics, 162-167, 1996.

Christian Vogler and Dimitris Metaxas, *Adapting hidden Markov models for ASL recognition by using three-dimensional computer vision methods*, In Proceedings of the IEEE International Confference on Systems, Man and Cybernetics, Orlando, FL, 156-161, 1997.

ChristianVogler and Dimitris Metaxas, *ASL recognition based on a coupling between HMMs and 3D motion analysis, In Proceedings of the IEEE International Conference on Computer Vision,* Mumbai, India, 363-369,1998.

ChristianVogler and Dimitris Metaxas, *Toward scalability in ASL Recognition: Breaking Down Signs into Phonemes*, In Proceedings of Gesture Workshop, Gif-sur-Yvette, France, 400-404. 1999

Wen Gao, Jiyong Ma, Jiangqin Wu and Chunli Wang. *Large Vocabulary Sign Language Recognition Based on HMM/ANN/DP:* International Journal of Pattern Recognition and Artificial Intelligence, Vol. 14, No. 5, 587-602, 2000

Jiyong Ma,Wen Gao,Jiangqin Wu and Chunli Wang, *A Continuous Chinese Sign Language recognition system*, pp428-433, 28-31 March,FG'2000, Grenoble, France, 2000.

Vogler C. Metaxas D. *Parallel Hidden Markov Models for American Sign Language recognition:* Proceedings of the Seventh IEEE International Conference on Computer Vision. IEEE Comput. Soc. Part vol.1, pp.116-22, Los Alamitos, CA, USA, 1999.

L.Rabiner and B.Juang, *Fundamentals of Speech Recognition:* Publishing Company of TsingHua University, 1999.

S. X. Katz, *Estimation of probabilities from sparse data for the language model component of a speech recognizer:* IEEE Trans. Acous. Speech Sign. Proc. 35, 3, 400-401, 1987.

Jones, D., *Example of Reference Style in Stylesheets: Format Using Ctrl+Shift+F8.* Singapore: World Scientific, 1999

Smith, L., *The Next Sample Reference.* London: Imperial College Press, 1999.

# Helping Designers Create Recognition-Enabled Interfaces

A. Chris Long[1], James A. Landay[2], and Lawrence A. Rowe[2]

*Human Computer Interaction Institute, Carnegie Mellon University*

Recognition technology is becoming more prevalent in user interfaces. Interfaces using recognition of natural modalities, such as speech, handwriting, or pen-gesture can be easier to use than traditional WIMP (windows, icon, mouse, and pointer) interfaces. Unfortunately, using recognition in an interface introduces new challenges for users and designers of the interfaces. This chapter discusses a particular recognition-based interface technique, pen gestures. Gestures are marks made with a pen to invoke a command (see Figure 1).

**Figure 1.**    Example gesture.

## Benefits of Pens and Gestures

Interest in pen-based user interfaces is growing rapidly, and with good reason. Pen and paper has been an important, widely used technology for centuries. It is versatile and can easily express text, numbers, tables,

---

1 Based on work done at the Department of Electrical Engineering and Computer Sciences, University of California at Berkeley.

2 Department of Électrical Engineering and Computer Sciences, U.C. Berkeley.

diagrams, and equations [Meyer95]. Many authors list the benefits pen-based computer interfaces could enjoy on desktop and portable computing devices [Briggs93, Frankish95, Hanne92, Meyer95, Morrel-Samuels90, Walrath89]. In particular, commands issued with pens (i.e., *gestures*) are desirable because they are commonly used and iconic, which makes them easier to remember than textual commands [Morrel-Samuels90]. They are also faster, because command and operand are specified in one stroke.

Recently, more computer users have adopted pen-based computers. In 2000, 3.5 million handheld computers were sold, a substantial increase over 1999 sales of 1.3 million [Luening01]. The use of pen-based input for desktop systems is also growing as the cost of tablets and integrated display tablets fall. As pen-based devices proliferate, pen-based user interfaces become increasingly important.

Gestures have also become more prevalent recently. The Opera web browser supports a small set of gestures for navigation [Opera01]. Sensiva and KGesture provide gestures for common desktop applications and allows users to create their own gestures under Microsoft Windows and the Kommon Desktop Environment (KDE), respectively [Sensiva01, Pilone01].

In our work we have decided to concentrate on gestures in the spirit of copy editing [Lipscomb91, Rubine91] rather than marking menus [Tapia95], because we believe that traditional marks are more useful in some circumstances. For example, they can specify operands at the same time as the operation, and they can be iconic.


## Problems with Gestures

Although gestures have many benefits, they also have shortcomings. We discovered two drawbacks of gestures in a survey of Apple Newton and Palm Pilot users in 1997 [Long97, Long01].

The first problem we found is that sometimes the computer did not recognize gestures the users drew. Misrecognition is a problem with all recognition-based technologies, but it is especially troublesome for gestures because gestures are typically used to invoke commands. Misrecognition of entered information, such as handwriting, is easily detected by a user, whereas misrecognition of a command may not be noticed. If a gesture is misrecognized and an unintended operation is performed, users may be confused about what happened. Furthermore, an unintended operation is likely to be more difficult to correct than a misrecognized word. As a Palm user commented on our survey, "cut/copy gestures are risky."

The second problem our survey found was user dissatisfaction with gesture memorability. Traditional interaction techniques, such as buttons and menus, only require users to recognize commands, but gestures are not shown on the screen so users must recall them.

## A Prototype Gesture Design Tool

We believed that user interface designers needed help to create gestures that could be recognized more easily by the computer and remembered more easily by people. We created a prototype gesture design tool, *gdt*, based on gesture recognizer training tools (shown in Figure 2). Based on our use of other tools, we added new visualizations to *gdt* that we believed would help designers improve their gestures.

We used this prototype to study the gesture design process and determine how a tool could be helpful to designers [Long99]. We formulated several hypotheses:

- Participants could use *gdt* to improve their gesture sets.
- The visualizations *gdt* provided would aid designers.
- The performance of participants with art or design background would differ from that of participants with technical or computer science backgrounds.
- PDA users and non-PDA users would perform differently.

We recruited two types of participants: technical (mostly computer science undergraduates) and artistic (architects and artists). We ran ten pilot participants and ten in the experiment proper.

First, participants saw a demonstration of *gdt* and read a tutorial containing a practice task. To account for varying degrees of neatness across participants, the recognition rate in the practice task was recorded and used later as the target recognition rate in the experimental task. For the experimental task, participants used *gdt* to invent new gestures for specified commands and add them to a gesture set. We asked them to create gestures that the computer could recognize and that would be easy for people to learn and remember.

At the end of the experiment, participants filled out a questionnaire about the tool, the experiment, and demographic information.

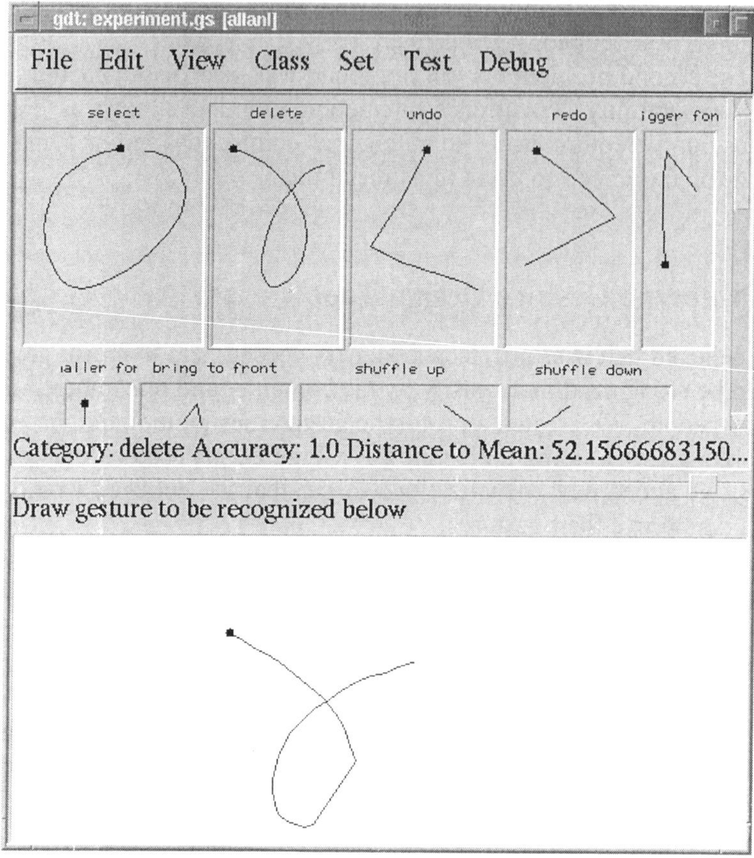


**Figure 2.**    *gdt* main window. A gesture was drawn and recognized as "delete."

## Results and Discussion

We found that people were able to improve their gesture sets with *gdt*, in terms of its recognizability. However, we were surprised to discover that none of the visualizations had any effect on the recognizability of the gestures. We found no difference between participants based on their artistic vs.

technical background, but we did find that people who had used PDAs created gesture sets that were less likely to be misrecognized.

Although participants were able to use gdt to improve their gesture sets, it was not an easy task. Following is a summary of problems participants encountered and strategies they employed:

- *Finding and fixing recognition problems.* Participants had difficulty finding and fixing recognition problems. On the post-experiment questionnaire, using a scale of 1 (difficult) to 9 (easy), finding recognition problems was ranked 5.8 and fixing them was ranked 4.6. Much of this was likely due to a lack of understanding of the recognizer, which many participants expressed verbally.

- *Adding new gesture types.* We also found that adding new gesture types caused a statistically significant drop of 2.4% in the recognition rate of the preexisting gestures ($p < 0.041$, 2-tailed t test). Most participants did not seem aware that this problem might occur. Many participants thought a low recognition rate was a problem with how they drew the gestures during the test.

- *New similar gesture type.* One way new gesture types were observed to cause a problem is by being too similar to one or more existing classes. Sometimes the participant noticed this problem by informally testing the recognition or with the visualizations. However, not all participants watched for this problem.

- *Outlier feature values.* Another way new gesture types were seen to cause recognition problems is by having feature values that were significantly different than the values of many old gestures.[3] The outlier values caused the values for old gestures, which were close together by comparison, to clump together. Unfortunately, these features were important for disambiguating the old gestures, and so by adding the new gestures the old ones became harder to correctly recognize.

- *Drawing gestures backwards.* Since several features used in the Rubine recognizer depend on the starting point, it is important for users to be consistent about the placement of the starting point and the initial direction. Unfortunately, some participants drew

---

3 Our work uses the Rubine recognizer, which uses geometric features such as length, initial angle, and size of bounding box.

test gestures backwards (i.e., starting at the end and going to the beginning), either because they had not learned the gesture well enough or because the start and end point of the gesture were too close together, and it was unclear which direction was the correct one.

- *Radical changes.* Participants also varied by what strategy they used to try to solve recognition problems. When they discovered that two gesture types were confused with one another, some participants made a small change in one of the two gesture types. Other participants made a dramatic change to one of the problem types. One of the metrics for success in the experimental task was how much the recognition rate improved from the beginning of the experimental task to the best recognition rate achieved during the experimental task. The improvement in recognition rate of participants who made radical changes was lower than the improvement of those who did not make radical changes (1.4% vs. 6.6%), and this difference was significant (p < 0.006, 2-tailed t test).

- *Over-testing.* When faced with a test score lower than the target, some participants elected to take the test again, because they thought they had been sloppy when entering the gesture. They thought if they were neater they would do better. Sometimes this strategy succeeded and other times it did not.

- *Limited test support.* Participants in the experiment relied heavily on the test procedure. *gdt* has only rudimentary support for testing how well a gesture set is recognized. The only test results available were the count of how many gestures of each gesture type were recognized and the overall recognition rate.

- *Multiple gestures for one operation.* Several participants wanted to experiment with different gestures for the same operation. For example, a participant wanted to experiment with several gestures for the "pen" operation and so made three types with three different gestures: *pen, pen 2,* and *pen 3.* Unfortunately, the alternative types affect the recognition of one another, which is undesirable since the final set will contain at most one of them.

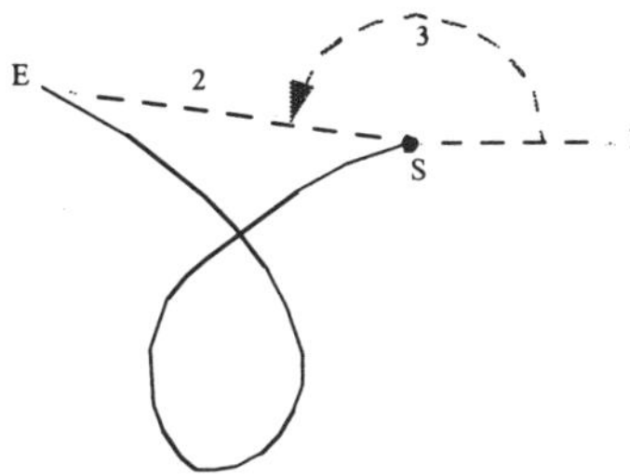



**Figure 3.**    Angle between first and last points visualization. *S* is the start point. *E* is the end point. 1 is a horizontal ray from *S*. 2 connects *S* and *E*. 3 represents the value of the feature, which is the angle between 1 and 2.

## *Lessons for gesture design tools*

Both the experiment and our own experiences with gesture design and *gdt* gave us ideas about what features a gesture design tool should have.

The single most important feature the experiment suggested is active feedback from the tool to the designer about problems. Specifically, a gesture design tool should provide warnings about: radical changes, gesture types that are too similar, gestures with outlying feature values, and drawing gestures backwards. The experiment also suggested that the tool should support testing better, because it was very popular in the experiment. Also, the ability to enable or disable an individual gesture type would be useful for conveniently trying out multiple gestures for the same operation.

We also learned from the experiment that the lack of understanding how the recognizer worked greatly hindered participants both in discovering and in fixing recognition problems. We want designers to be able to make gesture sets without being experts on gesture set design. Unfortunately, this knowledge is required to successfully use current tools.

One feature that would aid designers in understanding the recognition process is to graphically explain the features. For example, superimposing a graphic representation of each feature on top of a gesture would help designers understand what the features are and thus how to change one or more classes to make them less similar (see Figure 3).

Another capability we think would be useful is assistance in making a gesture type size- or rotation-independent. If the user indicated that a type should be size-independent, for example, the tool could generate training examples of different sizes by transforming existing examples. This feature could be extended to other types of independence besides size and rotation, such as drawing direction.

In summary, designing good gestures with existing tools was very difficult for designers. There are many pitfalls of which to be wary, and many of them are all but invisible to those unfamiliar with recognition technology. It was very difficult for the participants in our experiment to attain a good recognition rate for their gesture set, and we believe this was due in large part to difficulty in understanding the recognizer.

## Gesture Similarity

To make it easier for designers to create gestures that users would not perceive as too similar, we wanted our gesture design tool to predict similarity. Then, it could warn designers when their gestures would be seen as similar by people, and advise them how to make the gestures less similar. In two experiments and a web-based survey, we collected many judgments about gesture similarity from many participants. Using these data, we created computational, predictive models for human perception of gesture similarity. One model computes degree of similarity of a pair of gestures, and correlates 0.56 with reported similarity. Another model predicts whether two gestures will be perceived as similar by people or not, with an accuracy of 87.7%. These experiments and models are described in detail in [Long00, Long01].

## *quill*: an Intelligent Gesture Design Tool

We found that designers could create gestures with *gdt* and that, by trial and error, they could improve the recognition of their gestures. However, we believe users of pen-based user interfaces will demand better recognition than most participants in our study were able to achieve[4].

---

4Conventional wisdom is that even a 98% recognition rate is inadequate [BDBN93].

We created a new gesture design tool, called *quill*, that was inspired by *gdt* and the results of the *gdt* evaluation. It also incorporates the models derived from the similarity experiments to give feedback about human-perceived similarity of gestures.

## Goals

Based on our experience with *gdt*, three goals were developed for *quill*: 1) to provide active feedback, 2) to provide advice about human similarity and memorability and 3) to be easy for designers to use.

In the *gdt* evaluation, many participants had difficulty discovering that recognition problems existed in the gesture set they were designing. *gdt* included tables based on how the gestures would be recognized by the computer to help designers discover recognition problems. However, many participants did not consult these tables, and the tables were confusing to use.

The goal of active feedback was to help designers find problems, with both recognition and human perception, by informing the designer of possible problems without waiting for the designer to ask for the advice. Also, the active feedback should be in plain English and use diagrams so that designers with no recognition background can understand it.

Active feedback also addresses the problem designers had of not knowing how to fix recognition problems once they were discovered. When *quill* provides feedback to the designer about problems, it should also give advice about how the problem can be fixed.

It is frustrating to a user when gestures are misrecognized, but gestures are also not very useful if the user cannot remember them. If two gestures invoke different operations, the designer probably does not want them to appear similar since users may easily confuse one gesture for another, although our experiments have yet to show this correlation. To help the designer create gestures that will be easier for people to learn and remember, *quill* should give feedback to the designer about gestures that people may perceive to be similar.

Ease of use is a standard goal for user interfaces, and *quill* is no exception. This goal is challenging in *quill* because the application must explain to designers how to modify their gestures to better fit the requirements of the recognizer and human perception, both of which are complex systems. Few designers are trained in recognition or perception, so jargon and equations from those fields are inappropriate.

Instead, *quill* should avoid explaining how the recognizer works or how our perceptual model works as much as possible. Where we need to explain technical details, *quill* should use drawings and plain English that is intelligible to designers.

Before describing *quill* in more detail, we will describe how it organizes gestures.

### Gesture Hierarchy and Naming

Gestures are the actual objects that *quill* users want to manipulate, so it is important that the scheme used to organize them is easy for users to understand. This section describes how gestures are organized and how gesture structures are named.

In *quill*, we created the following 5-level hierarchy:

- Gesture: A single mark or glyph.
- Gesture category: A collection of gestures that define a type of gesture[5]. For example, a collection of left-to-right straight lines might define the "scroll right" gesture category.
- Gesture group: A collection of gesture categories, typically ones that perform related operations. For example, one might have an "Edit" group that contains the "cut," "copy," and "paste" gesture categories, and a "View" group that contains the "zoom in" and "zoom out" categories.
- Gesture set: A collection of gesture categories and gesture groups, typically all the categories and groups for a particular application (or a mode in an application for applications in which different sets of gestures are valid in different modes).
- Gesture package: A training set (i.e., a gesture set used to train the recognizer) and zero or more test sets (i.e., gesture sets used to test the recognition of the training set).

Gesture groups and gesture packages are not strictly necessary, but experience suggests they are useful for *quill* users. If an application has a large number of gesture categories, the designer may wish to organize them by type, which gesture groups support. Gesture packages were introduced to al-

---

5 In recognition literature, this is called a "class". We chose to use "category" instead because it sounds less technical and because "class" has another meaning in Java.

low tight coupling of test sets with a training set, which was suggested in the *gdt* evaluation.

Collectively, gesture packages, gesture sets, gesture groups, gesture categories, and gestures are called "gesture objects." Gesture objects that may have children (i.e., all except gestures) are "gesture containers."

## quill *example*

This section describes the *quill* interface and gives an example of using *quill*. An overview of the *quill* interface is given in Figure 4.

The first step in using *quill* is creating some gesture categories, and optionally some gesture groups to organize the categories. Then the designer enters training gestures by drawing them in the "drawing area." The designer can view the categories and training gestures simultaneously in *quill* sub-windows on the *quill* desktop, as shown in Figure 5.

Once training gestures have been entered, recognition can be tested. When the designer selects the training set and draws a gesture, *quill* recognizes it and displays the result, as shown in Figure 6.

More details about the *quill* interface are given in [Long01].

## *Active Feedback*

In our experiment with *gdt*, we found that people did not use the tables and graph that may have helped them find and fix recognition problems. We addressed this problem in *quill* by automatically detecting problems and alerting the user to them. This section describes the different types of problems *quill* detects and how these problems are detected.

### Recognizer similarity

If two gestures are similar to the recognizer, it is more likely that they will be misrecognized. To help designers find this potential problem, *quill* compares all pairs of gesture categories and reports when two of them are very similar, in terms of the metrics used by the gesture recognizer. It was challenging to determine the right threshold for declaring two categories to be similar. We had to experiment with different values to see which one gave useful results without too many false positives.

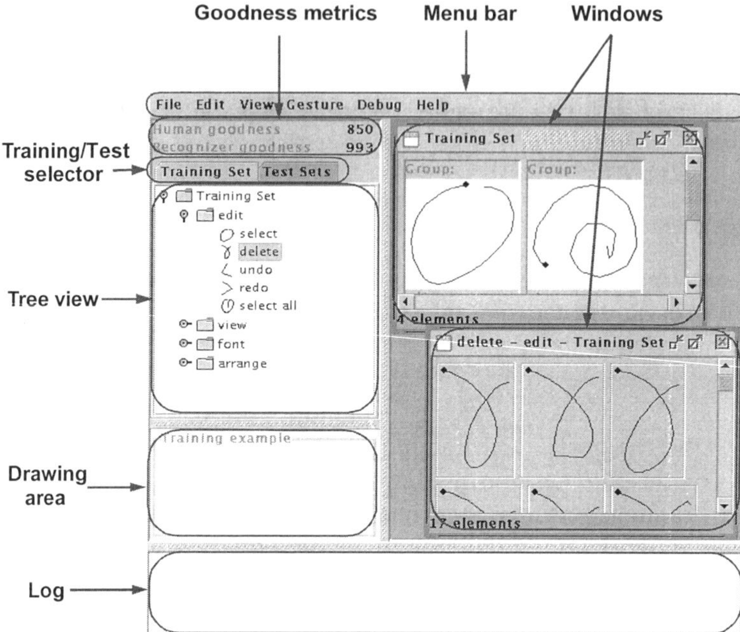



**Figure 4.**   *quill* main window

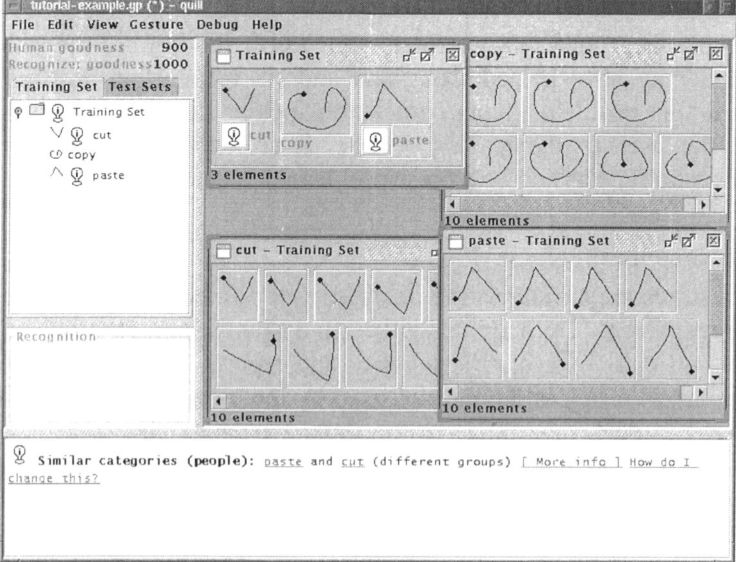



**Figure 5.**   *quill* desktop view of a gesture set, group, example (training gesture), and gesture category (clockwise from top left).

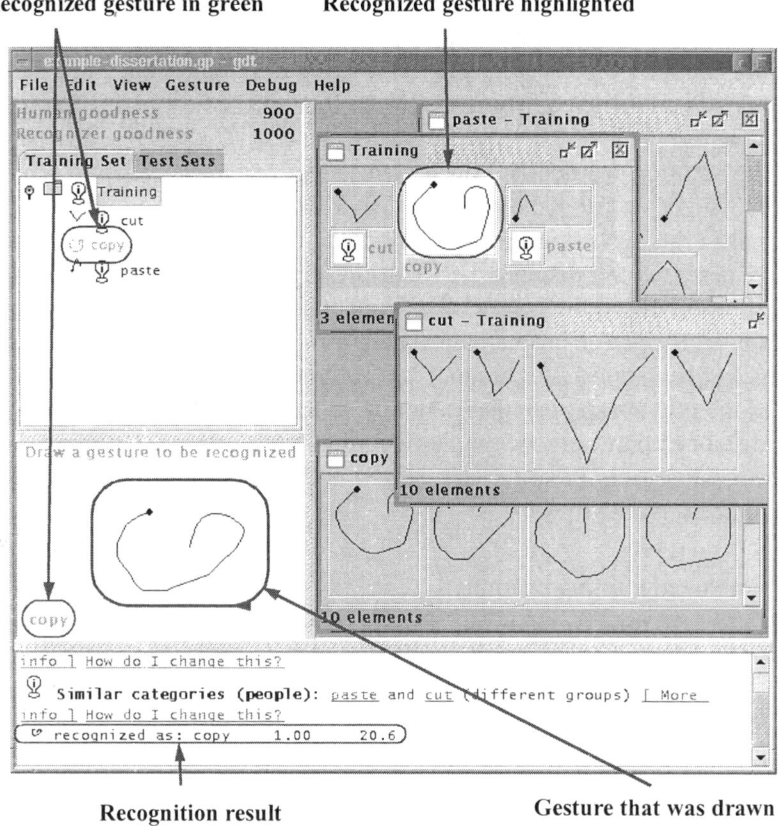


**Figure 6.**    *quill* recognizes a gesture and shows the result in several ways.

## Outlying category

The "outlying category" problem was observed during the gesture design study with *gdt*. It occurs when two categories are very similar because a third, outlying, gesture category is very different. When *quill* detects that this problem has occurred, it reports the problem as an outlying category problem, not a recognizer similarity problem, so the designer knows that the outlying category is causing the problem. The implication is that the outlier is causing the problem, not the two categories that are similar. Only very experienced gesture designers understand this problem, so *quill* can make a significant difference for less experienced designers.

To detect this problem, *quill* needs to compare the complete set of categories against the set without each category, in turn. Exactly what to compare was not obvious. We considered looking at the inter-category distances, distance of candidate bad category from other categories, and recognizer feature weights.

The solution we decided on is, when two categories are too similar for the recognizer, to try disabling all other categories, one at a time, and see if that makes the two categories farther apart. If disabling any category significantly increases the distance between the original two, suggest changing it This solution raised the issues of how must of a difference in distance is significant and, once a problematic category is identified, how it should be changed. *quill* reports a category as outlying if removing it from the set causes the two similar categories not to be too similar any more, and if their new distance apart is more than twice what it was with the potential outlier in the gesture set, in order to prevent a small change near the distance threshold from counting.

## Misrecognized training example

Normally, all training gestures should be recognized as the category of which they are a member. *quill* tests all training gestures and reports on ones that are not correctly recognized. Most misdrawn gestures are caught this way. This test also may indicate when two gesture categories are too similar for good recognition, since it's likely that if two categories are similar their training gestures will be easily confused.

Detection of misrecognized gestures is straightforward. To fix it, the designer needs to know which feature is causing the gesture to be different from its category. To determine which feature is most significant, *quill* takes the difference of feature values between the gesture and the average for its category and multiplies each difference by the weights that the recognizer uses for that feature and category. The product with the highest absolute value indicates the feature along which the gesture is most different from the category it is in.

## Outlying gesture

Usually if a training example is misdrawn it will be misrecognized and flagged as described in the previous section. However, sometimes a training example may be misdrawn yet still be correctly recognized. Misdrawn gestures give the recognizer false data about what the gesture category is supposed to be like, which may result in recognition problems. For this reason, *quill* looks for training examples that are very different from others in their category, and reports these outlying gestures to the user. The only issue for finding outlying gestures is deciding how far away it needs to be to be considered an outlier. Informal pilot testing revealed that it needs to be surprisingly far to avoid false positives (i.e., to avoid reporting a training example as an outlier when it is not). Five standard deviations was not enough, so *quill* uses ten.

## Human similarity

Previous warnings relate to how the recognizer sees the gestures. Another important factor in gesture usage is how easily gestures can be learned and remembered by people. To make their gestures easier to learn and remember, the designer may want gestures that invoke unrelated actions to appear dissimilar. To help the designer do this, *quill* checks all pairs of categories to determine if it's likely that people will perceive the two categories in the pair as very similar, based on the gesture similarity studies described above. If the gestures are in the different groups, *quill* reports this similarity to the user and suggests how to make the gestures less similar. If the gestures are in the same group, there is no warning because it is likely that gestures in the same group perform similar functions, and it may be helpful for gestures with similar functions to be perceptually similar. For example, the operations "scroll up" and "scroll down" should have similar gestures.

## Duplicate category or group name

Users of *quill* and end-users of the gesture sets designed in *quill* are likely to be confused if categories and groups are not named uniquely. For this reason, *quill* warns the designer if two (or more) categories or groups have the name.

## *Paper Prototype*

The *quill* interface was first prototyped on paper, using a combination of paper sketches and printed computer drawings, as shown in Figure 7 and Figure 8. We performed an informal user study with the paper prototype to test the usability of different components [Rettig94]. We received many suggestions from the participants and improved the interface design signifi-

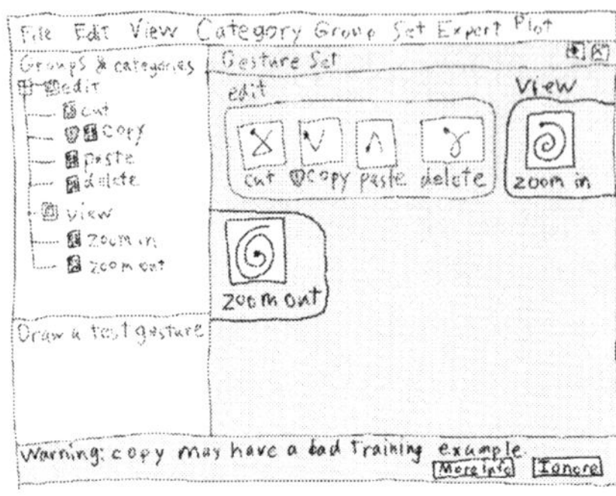

**Figure 7.**    Sketch of *quill* prototype.

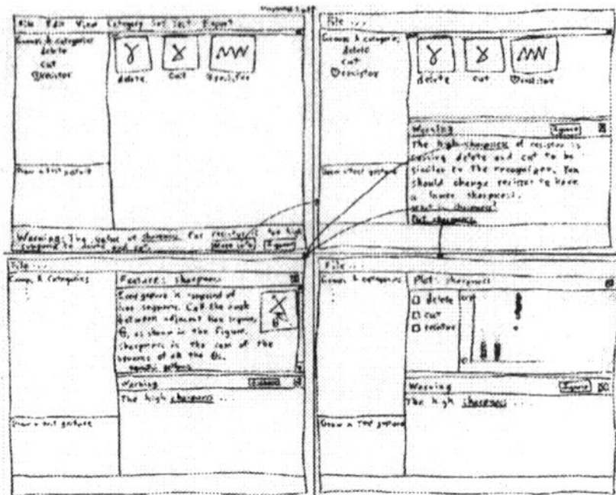

**Figure 8.**    Storyboard of *quill* prototype.

cantly. It was implemented in Java, and minor changes were later made, resulting in the version shown previously (Figures 4–6).

## *quill* evaluation

A human factors experiment was performed to evaluate the usability of *quill* and determine whether *quill* helps designers produce measurably better gestures. This experiment had two goals: 1) to observe designers using *quill* and qualitatively assess their usage and experiences and 2) to determine whether gesture sets designed with the aid of the active feedback in *quill* are measurably better than gesture sets designed without active feedback. We judged gesture set quality in terms of how confusable they would be for the recognizer and how similar people would perceive them to be, based on our human similarity metrics.

### *Participants and Equipment*

We wanted to find only professional designers. We chose to carry out the experiment at the Microsoft Usability Lab because they were able to recruit the type of participants we wanted. The Microsoft Usability Lab recruited 11[6] participants, 10 of whom were professional user interface designers and

---

6 Originally, 13 participants were recruited, but one canceled and another did not show up.

one of whom was a professional web designer. Participants were given gift certificates[7] for their participation.

Participants primarily interacted with the computer using a Wacom PL-300 display tablet, although they also used the keyboard.


## *Procedure*

The experimental procedure consisted of four parts: 1) a training exercise, 2) the first experimental task, 3) the second experimental task, and 4) a post-experiment questionnaire.

The two experimental tasks were a long gesture design task and a short gesture design task. For each participant, the active feedback in quill was enabled for one task, and for the other task it was disabled. The order of tasks and the feedback condition were randomized so that participants were evenly divided among the conditions (i.e., Latin Square design). Although each participant performed both tasks, it was not a true within-subjects design, because the tasks were not of equal difficulty or length, so performance across them could not be compared.

The training exercise was to read the *quill* and perform the tasks listed in it, which were short. Participants retained the tutorial for the remainder of the experiment.

The long experimental task was to design a gesture set for a presentation editing application (e.g., Microsoft PowerPoint). The gesture groups and categories are shown in Figure 9. Participants were given at most one and a half hours to complete this experimental task. After that time they were told to quit even if they had not finished creating and editing all the gestures.

The short experimental task was to create a gesture set for a web browser, with the groups and categories as shown in Figure 10. Participants were given one hour to complete this task.

After the second experimental task, participants filled out an online questionnaire using a different computer than the one used for the other tasks (to avoid negative effects suggested by [Reeves96]).

At the end, participants were given a post-experimental handout that gave more details about *quill* and the experiment. Also, the experimenter answered any remaining questions they had.

---

7 Participants chose whether they would receive a gift certificate from either Eddie Bauer or Tower Records and Video. This type of compensation is standard at the MS Usability Lab.

- Outline
  - New bullet
  - Select item
  - Indent
  - Unindent
- Format
  - Increase line spacing
  - Decrease line spacing
  - Left justify
  - Center justify
  - Right justify

- Font
  - Increase font size
  - Decrease font size
  - Change font
  - Bold
  - Italic
  - Underline
- Misc
  - Insert picture
  - New slide

**Figure 9.**    Operations for long task in *quill* evaluation.

## Quantitative Results and Analysis

The quantitative data from one participant, #4, had to be removed from consideration, because he did not follow instructions. He discovered a flaw in the human goodness metric that caused its value to be inflated when a very small number of training examples are entered (3–4 per gesture category). The experimenter instructed him to enter the same number of examples as the other participants for consistency, but he did not.

Three dependent variables were measured for each task for each participant:

1. The human goodness of the gesture set
2. The recognizer goodness of the set

- Navigate
  - Back
  - Forward
  - Home
  - Reload

- Bookmarks
  - Add bookmark
  - Edit bookmarks
- Misc
  - Add annotation
  - Email page

**Figure 10.**    Operations for short task in *quill* evaluation.

| | With feedback | Long task First | | | Short task First | | |
|---|---|---|---|---|---|---|---|
| | | No | Yes | Overall | No | Yes | Overall |
| Human goodness | No | 667 | 550 | 637 | 1000 | 800 | 900 |
| | Yes | 550 | 900 | 725 | 1000 | 1000 | 1000 |
| | Overall | 608 | 812 | 690 | 1000 | 900 | 940 |
| Recognizer goodness | No | 999 | 997 | 998 | 999 | 999 | 999 |
| | Yes | 996 | 992 | 994 | 1000 | 1000 | 1000 |
| | Overall | 998 | 993 | 996 | 999 | 999 | 999 |
| Time | No | 47.0 | 44.0 | 46.2 | 16.0 | 25.7 | 20.8 |
| | Yes | 43.7 | 65.0 | 54.3 | 13.0 | 29.7 | 25.5 |
| | Overall | 45.3 | 59.8 | 51.1 | 15.2 | 27.7 | 22.7 |

**Table 1.** Means for tasks in the *quill* evaluation. Goodness is on a scale of 0-1000, where 1000 is perfect. Time is in minutes.

3.   The time to finish the task.

The data for the tasks are summarized in Table 1.

A multivariate ANOVA was performed to find significant differences due to a) feedback, b) whether the task was first, and/or c) the task (long vs. short). Few statistically significant effects were found. The long task took participants significantly longer to perform than the short task (51.1 vs. 22.7 minutes, $p < 0.0092$), and had significantly lower human goodness (690 vs. 940, $p < 0.011$), with or without active feedback.

Also, when long and short tasks where considered together, there was a strong interaction between task order and whether it had feedback or not, as shown in Figure 11.

The effect of feedback alone was not statistically significant, and was positive in some cases and negative in others. In the long task, it had a positive effect on human goodness overall, but not for those who had feedback on their second task. In the short task it had a positive effect on human goodness for the first task, and no effect for the second (because it was at the maximum regardless of feedback). Recognizer goodness was slightly worse with feedback in the long task, but slightly better with feedback in the short task.

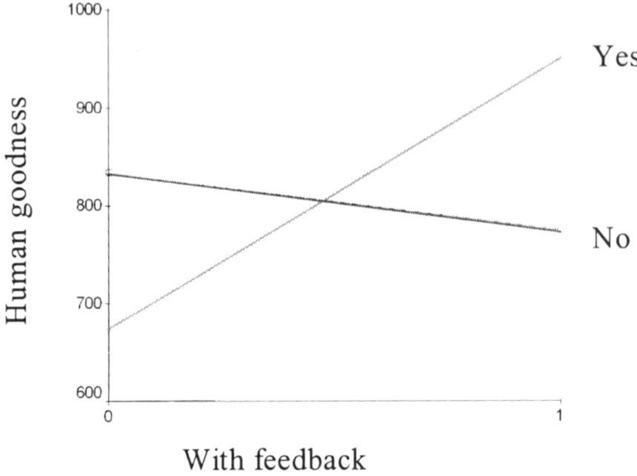


**Figure 11.**   Interaction between feedback and task order. Values are average human goodness (scale is 0-1000, higher is better).

## *Qualitative results*

This section describes common themes derived from comments participants made during the experiment and on the post-experiment questionnaire.

Participants had many comments about the suggestions *quill* gave about how to improve their gestures. Some participants read, understood, and used the feedback productively. However, some participants disagreed with some of the feedback, especially for gestures that were letters or contained letters, probably because the human similarity metric is derived from non-letter data. Other participants did not understand what *quill* was trying to tell them. In describing what was wrong with the gestures, *quill* used some mathematical terms, which prompted comments from some participants that the feedback was "too technical" and "That's not too good for humans; [it] might be good for mathematicians." It used diagrams to explain what the technical terms meant, but a few participants said that it would have been more useful if it had been more visual. One participant suggested explaining the geometric features (e.g., size of bounding box and sine of initial angle) using the actual gestures the user was working on, rather than stock images, "The error/suggestion text could potentially show my problem gesture with the error highlighted or overlaid."

A few participants wanted more information on or support for a larger context. For example, one participant wanted more information about the application in which the gestures would be used. Another wanted to be able to run the application for which the gestures were being designed and try out the gestures in context. She believed it would help her discover whether the gestures would be memorable and whether they made sense.

## Discussion

*gdt* provided a small amount of help to designers in figuring out how to make their gestures easier for the computer to recognize, but its tables of numbers were incomprehensible to most users. The suggestions in *quill* were designed to be more accessible by putting the information in English and supplementing it with pictures. In spite of this effort, many participants did not understand the suggestions, and the suggestions did not consistently help participants make better gesture sets. We believe the suggestions can be made more accessible by changing the language to be less technical, by using more diagrams, and by using dynamically generated diagrams based on the actual gestures entered by the designer.

We also believe that more training would be helpful in getting the most value from *quill*. The tutorial used for the experiment did not cover all the features in *quill*, and those that it did include were not covered in depth. We decided to keep the tutorial as short as possible to keep the length of the experiment as short as possible. (The long task took some participants nearly ninety minutes. A few participants took over 2.5 hours for the whole experiment.) In retrospect, participants may have been able to use *quill* more effectively if they had gone through longer training. In particular, some participants clearly could have benefited from more time spent on testing vs. training sets and on a step-by-step example of how to use *quill*'s suggestions. A professional technical writer helped edit an early version of the tutorial. Nevertheless, most participants did not read it carefully nor absorb it well, so it is unclear how much a longer tutorial would have helped.

Overall, the effect of feedback was mixed and in no case statistically significant. For the first task, feedback had a positive effect, but when feedback was provided in the second task, it had no effect or a negative effect. Unfortunately, it is impossible to determine the effect of feedback using a within-subjects analysis due to the difference in difficulty between the long and short tasks. There was great variance among participants in their understanding of *quill*'s feedback. Although it seemed more approachable than the tables and graph in *gdt*, it was still too technical for many participants.

Several subjective judgments about *quill* that were collected in the post-experiment questionnaire correlated with performance measures. For the long task, higher recognition goodness correlated with thinking the task was clear as opposed to confusing, entering new gesture categories was easy, and testing recognizability of gestures was easy. Also, people with a higher overall reaction to *quill* and people who thought *quill* had adequate power created gestures with higher human goodness. These correlations are not surprising, since we would expect that people who do better on the task would think it is easier. What is surprising is that people who took longer to perform the long task also tended to think that finding recognition problems was easy. We might expect that people who easily find recognition problems finish the task more quickly.

A problem with the human similarity suggestions is that they were not always right. The models used in *quill* to predict human similarity are not perfect, and participants rightly disagreed with it at times. *quill* seemed especially prone to overestimate similarity when a gesture was or contained a letter. This flaw is probably due to the similarity models being based entirely on non-letter gestures. It seems likely that people would perceive letter and non-letter shapes differently. A small difference in a non-letter shape might be perceived by people as a large difference in a letter. Ideally, *quill* would have separate similarity models for letter and non-letter gestures. Future experiments to measure similarity of letters are required to provide models for letter similarity.

A problem with this experiment is that the short task was too easy, as shown by the high goodness scores. In contrast, the scores in the long task did vary, so it is probably an appropriate length. Also, the tutorial needs to be improved, both in terms of including more information and in making it easier to read and absorb.

It is difficult to determine the ideal length for an evaluation of *quill*. On one hand, *quill* is not intended to be walk-up-and-use, but rather to be a tool like Photoshop, which designers use extensively and with which they become familiar. Therefore, an experiment such as the one we performed in which participants spend approximately twenty minutes learning the tool is unrealistic. On the other hand, it is difficult to perform an experiment with expert users of a research system. Ideally, the experiment would include a longer training session so that participants could learn the tool better. Unfortunately, the longer the experiment is, the more difficult it is to recruit participants, especially when the best participants are highly trained professionals.

## *Summary*

All participants were able to create gesture sets using *quill*, but the effect of feedback was mixed and not statistically significant. Some participants were helped by *quill*'s active feedback, but some were not. Also, feedback was helpful for the first task, but for the second task it was either neutral (for the long task) or slightly detrimental (for the short task).

The unclear effect of feedback is due in part to it being too technical for some participants. The feedback needs to be improved so that it is more accessible to non-technical designers.

## **Future Work and Conclusions**

There are several areas for future work on *quill*. *gdt* and *quill* were both developed as stand-alone tools, but a designer creating gestures with one of them would not be creating gestures for its own sake. As one of the participants in the *quill* study said, the tool would be much more useful if it were situated in a broader context. Interesting future work could be done to integrate *quill* into a pen-based user interface framework, possibly with a tool such as SILK [Landay95, Landay01].

Also, the interfaces for both tools were designed to be as modeless as possible, so that designers could take any action at any time. However, it may be useful to adopt a more workflow-oriented approach, such as Klemmer and colleagues used in SUEDE for helping speech interface designers prototype their interfaces [Klemmer00].

Although it is easy to add new features to Rubine's recognizer, *gdt* and *quill* use only the default features. In the similarity experiments, we discovered features such as curviness, aspect, and density that could be used in Rubine's recognizer. These features may improve accuracy and may make the recognizer behave more intuitively since these features are used by humans in their similarity judgments.

As well as extending Rubine's recognizer, it would be interesting to extend *quill* to use a different recognizer, such as one based on neural networks and/or a multistroke recognizer. Changing the recognition technology would change what gesture relationships constitute recognition problems, the way *quill* detects recognition problems, and the type of advice *quill* can offer about how to fix recognition problems. However, the general *quill* framework for editing, training, and offering advice could remain the same.

There are a number of features that would be helpful in *quill*. One would be the ability to specify a set of gesture categories for a command, rather than just one category. This could be helpful for recognition in a case where a gesture category is size independent and others in the set are not. If one gesture category is trained with gestures of greatly varying sizes, the recognizer may have difficulty differentiating other gestures based on size. If the designer could specify multiple size gestures for the same command, this problem could be avoided. Currently, this feature must be done in application code.

Another useful feature is the ability to show advice using gestures the designer has entered as examples rather than static images. Based on the *quill* evaluation, we believe this would help designers understand the advice in the context of their own design.

A challenging, but potentially useful feature for *quill* is automatic repair of recognition problems. For many recognition problems, *quill* can determine the gesture(s) causing the problem and can also determine which geometric feature(s) of the gesture(s) need to change and in what direction in order to fix the problem. Currently, the strategy is to tell the designer and let the designer change the gesture, because the designer can keep other properties about the gesture constant, such as its iconicness. However, it might be possible for *quill* to change the gesture(s) to fix the problem. Suppose gesture $g$ needs to be changed so that feature $f$ is smaller. A simple and general way to choose a new $g$ is to mutate $g$ in many different ways and choose the one that is most similar to the original $g$ except that its value for $f$ is smaller. One issue with this approach is what the best way to measure similarity is. Two possibilities are: 1) the human similarity metric from our similarity experiments and 2) recognizer similarity (i.e., distance in recognizer feature space).

It would also be helpful if there were a database of known gestures. New gestures could be automatically compared against this database to find potential conflicts. Also, this database could be searched by a designer by shape or keyword to find gestures that might be useful in a new application.

In conclusion, our work on *gdt* and *quill* produced several results. We discovered roadblocks in the gesture design process, such as the difficulty of finding and fixing recognition problems. We built the first intelligent tool for gesture design, *quill*, which helps designers improve the computer recognition of their gestures. Our evaluation of *quill* showed that advice can be helpful to designers in improving their gestures.

This work enables designers to create better gestures for pen-based user interfaces. It also allows a wider group of designers to create good gestures for pen-based UIs. Improving gestures and making gesture design more widely accessible is important because gestures are a powerful interaction technique, especially for pen-based user interfaces. People frequently use gestures on paper and other traditional media to communicate with other people. This work advances the state-of-the-art to allow people to more easily use gestures to communicate with computers.

# References

Briggs, R., Dennis, A., Beck, B., and Nunamaker, Jr., J. Whither the pen-based interface? *Journal of Management Information Systems*, 9(3):71–90, 1992-1993.

Frankish, C., Hull, R., and Morgan, P. Recognition accuracy and user acceptance of pen interfaces. In *Human Factors in Computing Systems (SIGCHI Proceedings)*, pages 503–510. ACM, Addison-Wesley, April 1995.

Hanne, K., and Bullinger, H. *Multimedia Interface Design*, chapter 8, pages 127–138. ACM Press, 1992.

Klemmer, S., Sinha, A., Chen, J., Landay, J. A., Aboobaker, N, and Wang, A. SUEDE: A Wizard of Oz prototyping tool for speech user interfaces. *CHI Letters: UIST*, 2(2):1–10, November 2000.

Landay, J. and Myers, B. Interactive sketching for the early stages of user interface design. In *Human Factors in Computing Systems (SIGCHI Proceedings)*, pages 43–50. ACM, Addison-Wesley, April 1995. http://www.acm.org/pubs/citations/proceedings/chi/223355/p63-landay/.

Landay, J. A. and Myers, B. A. Sketching interfaces: Toward more human interface design. *IEEE Computer*, 34(3):56–64, March 2001. http://www.cs.berkeley.edu/%7Elanday/research/publications/silk-ieee-publish%ed.pdf.

Lipscomb, J. A trainable gesture recognizer. *Pattern Recognition*, 24(9):895–907, September 1991.

Long, Jr., A. C., Landay, J. A., and Rowe, L. A. PDA and gesture use in practice: Insights for designers of pen-based user interfaces. Technical Report

UCB//CSD-97-976,    U.C.    Berkeley,    1997.    Available    at http://bmrc.berkeley.edu/papers/1997/142/142.html.

Long, Jr., A. C., Landay, J. A., and Rowe, L. A. Implications for a gesture design tool. *CHI 1999, ACM Conference on Human Factors in Computing Systems, CHI Letters,* 1(1), 40– 47.

Long, Jr., A. C., Landay, J. A., Rowe, L. A., and Michiels, J. Visual similarity of pen gestures. *CHI 2000, ACM Conference on Human Factors in Computing Systems, CHI Letters*, 2(1), 360–367.

Long, Jr., A. C. *Quill: a Gesture Design Tool for Pen-based User Interfaces.* PhD dissertation, University of California at Berkeley, Berkeley, CA, Dec. 2001. Available at http:// guir.berkeley.edu/pubs/quill/dissertation.pdf.

Luening, E. Study charts sharp rise in handheld sales. CNET WWW site, January 2001. http://news.cnet.com/news/0-1006-200-4601431.html.

Meyer, A. Pen computing. *SIGCHI Bulletin,* 27(3):46–90, July 1995.

Morrel-Samuels, P. Clarifying the distinction between lexical and gestural commands. *International Journal of Man-Machine Studies,* 32:581–590, 1990.

Opera Software. Mouse gestures in opera, 2001. Available at http:// www.opera.com/windows/mouse.html.

Pilone, M. KGesture, 2001. Available at http://www.slac.com/ %7Empilone/projects/.

Reeves, B. and Nass, C. *The media equation: how people treat computers, television, and new media like real people and places.* Center for the Study of Language and Information; Cambridge University Press, Stanford, Calif.: Cambridge [England]; New York, 1996.

Rettig, M. Prototyping for tiny fingers. *Communications of the ACM,* 37(4):21–27, April 1994.

Rubine, D. Specifying gestures by example. In *Computer Graphics (SIGGRAPH),* pages 329–337. ACM SIGGRAPH, Addison Wesley, July 1991.

Sensiva, Inc. Sensiva product brochure, 2001. Available at site http:// www.sensiva.com/.

Tapia, M. and Kurtenbach, G. Some design refinements and principles on the appearance and behavior of marking menus. In *Proceedings of the ACM Symposium on User Interface and Software Technology (UIST),* pages 189–195. ACM, November 1995.

Walrath, K. and Campione, M. *The JFC Swing Tutorial: A Guide to Constructing GUIs.* Addison-Wesley, July 1999.

# Part III  Information Retrieval

# Cross-Language Text Retrieval by Query Translation Using Term Re-weighting*

Insu Kang, Oh-Woog Kwon, Jong-Hyeok Lee, Geunbae Lee
Dept. of Computer Science & Engineering
POSTECH (Pohang University of Science & Technology)
KOREA
Email: {dbaisk, ohwoog, jhlee, gblee}@postech.ac.kr

## Abstract

In a dictionary-based query translation for cross-language text retrieval, transfer ambiguity is one of main causes of performance deterioration, but this problem has not received significant attention in this field. To resolve transfer ambiguity, this paper proposes a two-phase query translation based on term re-weighting, which uses a bilingual transfer dictionary, originally designed for machine translation. In general, source language query terms each show some word association with others, so that their correct translations should be more likely to co-occur in target documents. Based on this simple intuition, the first phase discriminates more relevant target documents from the others. Using statistical and ranking information from the highly relevant documents, the second phase then converts a translated query vector into re-weighted form to add an extra weight on probably correct target terms. In experiments, results were remarkable: the proposed method achieved almost the same performance as the monolingual IR system, actually contributing to an improvement of precision by about 9% over a baseline system.

*Extracted from International Journal of Pattern Recognition and Artificial Intelligence, Vol. 14, No. 5 Copyright World Scientific Publishing Company

# 1. Introduction

In Cross-Language Text Retrieval (CLTR), a user can query in one language but perform retrieval in another language [5]. Unlike Monolingual Text Retrieval (MLTR) in which the query and document languages are the same, CLTR thus requires a translation process to map both queries and documents into the same representation space (usually, into a single language) [6]. Such a translation process is normally conducted in two different directions: from a query language to a document language (query translation) and vice versa (document translation).

In document translation, a machine translation (MT) system may be used to translate documents into a query language and also to extract index terms. In general, MT system performs a deep linguistic analysis and takes advantage of rich surrounding contexts of sentences, so it can resolve word-sense ambiguities. But, document translation requires re-indexing of all translated documents, and moreover, due to the current unsatisfactory translation quality of most MT systems, the modular use of MT has not shown a promising result so far, which is why most researchers so far have been working on query translation rather than document translation.

In query translation, a query is translated into a document language using bilingual dictionaries, corpora, etc. The corpus-based approach is lacking in generality because corpora are domain-dependent and are not always readily available. The dictionary-based method usually employs a bilingual dictionary, originally intended for human readers. It features many paraphrased explanations and examples of usage and etymology. Such duplicated and spurious information is inappropriate for an automatic language translation, and often results in erroneous translation. So we use a bilingual transfer dictionary composed of only direct translations of each entry [2].

The ineffectiveness of a dictionary-based query translation is primarily caused by three factors: transfer ambiguity, phrasal concepts, and specialized vocabularies [8]. Out of them, the second and third ones are related with resources, which can be resolved by constructing phrasal dictionaries for phrasal concepts and by entering missing words into dictionaries. On the contrary, there is no direct solution to transfer ambiguity, which has not drawn attention in most previous research [2, 3, 8].

To resolve transfer ambiguity, this paper proposes a two-phase query translation based on term re-weighting scheme using a bilingual transfer dictionary, originally designed for machine translation. In general, source language query terms may have a word association with each other to some extent, so that their corresponding target terms, if translated correctly, would be likely to co-occur in documents as well. In the first phase, such word co-occurrence is used to discriminate more relevant documents from others. Such documents are expected to have more correct target terms. Second, based on statistical and ranking information from the highly relevant documents, the second phase produces a re-weighted query vector by adding an extra weight on probably correct target terms. So the re-weighted query makes it possible for documents more relevant to the user's query to rank higher during retrieval.

The rest of this paper is organized as follows: Section 2 describes the transfer ambiguity when translating source query terms into a target language. Section 3 proposes a two-phase query translation with a term re-weighting scheme to resolve transfer ambiguity. In Section 4, an experimental evaluation shows that our proposed method for CLTR can achieve almost the same performance as its underlined monolingual IR system. Finally, concluding remarks are given in Section 5. For representing Korean expressions, the Yale Romanization is used.

## 2. Transfer Ambiguity of Query

In query translation, transfer ambiguity arises when a single source language word (term) can potentially be translated into a number of different target words or expressions, not because the source language word itself is ambiguous but because it is ambiguous from the perspective of another language [10]. This ambiguity problem arises inevitably in a translation between different language pairs, which is one of the main causes of a performance drop in Cross-Language Text Retrieval (CLTR).

Given two Korean query terms *cikwu*($\Box\Box$) and *cikak*($\Box\Box$), Figure 1 shows all the possible combinations of their English translations. The first term *cikwu* has a translation set $T_1$ of two English words, *the earth* and *endurance*, the second term *cikak* a translation set $T_2$ of *crust* and *perception*. Thus, we can see a total of four possible translation combinations, which is a Cartesian product of the two translation sets. Now, our goal of query translation is to find a correct one from among all possible translation combinations.

The more ambiguous terms a source query possesses, the larger the number of all possible translation combinations would be. In such a case, finding one correct translation combination from the large search space results in a heavy burden of time and space complexities. Thus, most previous works on dictionary-based query translation have concentrated on a translated query obtained by expanding each query term in a source language into all of its possible translations in a target language. We call it an expanded query. An ideal disambiguation of ambiguous query terms, however, is to select only one correct combination of translated target terms. In an expanded query, this selection process is to discriminate the correctly translated terms from others, which can be conducted by a certain term weighting scheme of assigning more weights to correct target terms.

Usually, a document collection that we are trying to retrieve is written in the same language as that of translated query terms. So, a document collection can give us many linguistic clues on word usages of translated query terms from which we want to distinguish correct translations. In the following sections, we will describe the methods to utilize linguistic constraints of translated terms in documents.

## 3. Two-Phase Query Translation with Term Re-weighting

A query translation is a process of gradually converting a source language query into some other representations so that it may retrieve relevant documents to the user's original query. First, we start with an expanded query, in which all original query terms are expanded into all possible target terms using a bilingual transfer dictionary. Our retrieval system is based on a vector space model, so that the expanded query would be transformed into a query vector with weighting values. In a document discrimination phase, a retrieval model ranks the documents relevant to the query vector according to a query-document similarity measure based on a co-occurrence weighting scheme, which will be explained in Section 3.1. In the next term re-weighting phase, we collect distribution statistics of translated query terms from highly ranked documents of the first phase, and re-weight the importance of translated query terms. Finally, our model retrieves the documents relevant to the re-weighted query vector, which is expected to be much closer to a user's need. The whole model is depicted in Figure 2.

### 3.1 Phase 1: Document Discrimination

It is common practice in linguistics to classify words not only on the basis of their meanings but also on the basis of their co-occurrence with other words [9]. Co-occurring words in a text may restrict each other's meanings. For example, if two words *money* and *bank* co-occur in a text, then the meaning of *bank* is expected to be *an organization* or *a place that provides a financial service*. That is because the word *money* restricts the meanings of *bank*. This intuition is applicable to query translation. In Figure 1, a Korean word *cikwu(□□)* co-occurs with *cikak(□□)* in the original query statement. In this case, each of them restricts the other's meaning, so that the meaning of *cikwu* and *cikak* can be set to *the earth* and *crust*, respectively. In consequence, the first translation combination {*the earth, crust*} will be a plausible meaning of source language query terms *cikwu* and *cikak*. Observing these, we reach a conclusion that the meaning association of source query terms may also be captured from that of their target translations. In other words, if source language query terms share some meaning association with each other, then target translations which preserve associated meanings of source query terms are more likely to appear together in target language texts than other translation combinations.

In Figure 3, exemplifying weights of a translated term $tt_{ij}$ on documents $D_k$ at their crossing points, both of translated terms $tt_{11}$ and $tt_{22}$ co-occur in documents $D_2$ and $D_n$, but the other combinations of translated terms do not show the co-occurrence in those documents. This means that the pair of $tt_{11}$ and $tt_{22}$ is more likely to have some meaning association with each other, and they might be the correct translation of source language query terms $st_1$ and $st_2$. In this way, target language documents, which contain some co-occurrence usage of translated terms, can play an important role in resolving the ambiguity of source language query terms. To sum up, our approach relies on a simple intuition that if translated terms, each from a different source language query term, appear together in a document, they can be considered so much associated with each other that they might be the correct translation of the source query terms. This intuition leads to the fact that the more co-occurring target terms a document has, the more important role the document can play to resolve the transfer ambiguity. So, by assigning a larger query-document similarity to a document with more co-occurring translations, we may discriminate more relevant documents from the others. To embody this idea in the document discrimination phase, the query-document similarity is defined as Formula (1), where $C^{M-1}$ is called the co-occurrence weighting factor, which increases in proportion to the number of distinct original query terms of the target terms appearing in a document.

A document $D_1$ has six different target terms as shown in Figure 3, while the number of distinct source terms corresponding to them (denoted by M) is three. Thus, the co-occurrence weight between $D_1$ and the translated query is set to $C^{3-1}$. Similarly, a document $D_3$ has two target terms, all of which are only from a single source term, so the co-occurrence weight is set to $1(=C^{1-1})$ having no effect on the query-document similarity between $D_3$ and the translated query. In this way, Formula (1) can rank higher documents with target terms translated from more distinct source terms. Those documents are also supposed to have more correct translations than others.

In some cases, many different translations of a single source term may appear together in a document. For example, in Figure 3, three different translated terms $tt_{11}$, $tt_{12}$, and $tt_{13}$ from the same source term $st_1$ come out together in $D_1$ with their weights being 0.5, 0.8, and 0.6, respectively. In this case, a simple inner product of vectors produces 1.9, which is an overestimated weight of $st_1$. The goal of query translation is to differentiate correct target terms from the others. So, if an original query term can be translated into more than one different target terms appearing in a document, only one target term with the maximum weight will be selected, which is considered more representative than the others. In this sense, the weights of $st_1$ and $st_2$ on $D_1$ will be 0.8 and 0.9, respectively. Here, it is assumed that the weight of $st_1$ and $st_2$ on a source query Q is 1.

## 3.2 Phase 2: Term Re-weighting

In a standard information retrieval, relevance feedback is an effective method for raising both the average precision and recall rates at the same time by modifying the original query toward a user's intention [4]. In a similar way, relevance feedback in cross-language text retrieval is the process of adjusting the weights of target terms toward a source query's intention. In this phase, we modify the translated query vector of the first phase by adding extra weights on the target terms which are more likely to be correct translations. During the previous phase, we already obtained a ranked list of documents according to Formula (1), top N documents of which might be considered much more relevant to the user's need. As defined in Formula (2), using statistics of target terms obtained from the top N documents, the translated query can be modified much closer to the original user's need in view of relevance feedback.

It is obvious that not all the target terms appearing in the top N documents should be the correct translation. A document, in which some incorrect translation combinations happen to appear, for example, like {*the earth*, *perception}* in Figure 1, might be ranked high because of the co-occurrence weighting factor in Formula (1). However, as a whole, the highly ranked documents are much likely to have more correct translation combinations like *{the earth, crust}*. In Formula (2), the term $\Delta$ is intended to add an extra weight on the target term with high document frequency in the top N documents. In other words, incorrect target terms have such lower document frequencies that they would be given relatively small extra weights, thus having less effect on the re-weighting process.

Formula (2) has a weak point in that it ignores ranks of the top N documents. For example, both the first and the tenth ranked documents are handled with the same importance when collecting their document frequencies, which is unreasonable. Even though they are both the same highly ranked documents, the target terms in the first ranked document are more likely to be correct than those in the tenth ranked document. To reflect the ranking information during the re-weighting process, the term $\Delta$ is redefined in Formula (3), where the coefficient $\alpha$ plays the role of coordinating the relative importance of document frequency and ranking.

Consequently, the re-weighting process transforms a translated query vector into its re-weighted form. This process can have the same effect as the traditional query modification for relevance feedback, resulting in the improvement of both the average precision and recall rates.


## 4. Experiments and Evaluations

For an experimental evaluation of our proposed query translation method, we fixed a language pair of Cross-Language Text Retrieval for Korean and Japanese (CLTR-K/J), where Japanese documents would be retrieved from Korean queries. Experiments were conducted using a standard Japanese test collection called BMIR-J1 (Benchmark for Japanese IR Systems Ver. 1.0), which had been developed by a special working group of SIG-DBS, Information Processing Society of Japan. This test collection consists of 600 newspaper articles randomly taken from the CD-ROM version of the 1993 NIKKEI (Nihon Keizai) Shimbun on business and economics, and 60 short queries (average length is 4.1 Japanese words). In experiments, we used only 47 queries with more than 5 relevant documents, as the working group of SIG-DBS had recommended. To evaluate an effectiveness of query translation from Korean to Japanese, we need both Korean queries and Japanese documents with their relevance judgements. So Korean queries were created through manually translating the Japanese queries of BMIR-J1 into Korean by Japanese experts. In our experiments, we used a Korean-to-Japanese bilingual transfer dictionary, which was transformed from a Japanese-to-Korean bilingual dictionary of an existing high-quality machine translation system called COBALT-J/K(Collocation-Based Language Translator from Japanese to Korean) [1].

As for parameters in formulas, the co-occurrence weighting factor C and the number N of highly ranked documents in Formula (1),(2),(3) were set to 1.4 and 10, respectively, and the coefficient $\alpha$ in Formula (3) to 0.6, all of which were determined through experiments to achieve the best performance. A total of five retrieval systems below were built and evaluated to show the effectiveness of our proposed method.

**JJ** (Japanese monolingual retrieval system): JJ retrieves Japanese documents using Japanese queries of BMIR-J1. It ranks the documents according to the inner product similarity measure supplemented with the co-occurrence weighting factor in Formula (1) which showed better performance when used. JJ is a baseline system of our evaluation.

**KJ-1** (simple CLTR-K/J system): KJ-1 retrieves Japanese documents using Korean queries. It translates Korean queries into Japanese just by looking up a transfer dictionary. KJ-1 can show the pure effect of the transfer dictionary on CLTR because it only uses a simply expanded Japanese query and performs retrieval based on the basic inner-product similarity, and KJ-1 is a baseline system for an evaluation.

**KJ-2** (CLTR-K/J system using word association): KJ-2 performs up to the document discrimination phase based on Formula (1). It can show the effectiveness of the use of word association.

**KJ-3** (CLTR-K/J system 1 using term re-weighting): KJ-3 performs the full process of the proposed query translation, up to the term re-weighting phase based on Formula (2).

**KJ-4** (CLTR-K/J system 2 using term re-weighting): KJ-4 is the same as KJ-3 except that it uses Formula (3) for the term $\Delta$ of Formula (2).

In Table 1, which, for each retrieval system, summed up their precisions at 11 points of recall by interpolation, the simple KJ-1 system showed almost the same performance, up to 92% (= 0.3895/0.4235) of the corresponding monolingual system JJ. The results are remarkable, considering that most previous dictionary-based approaches have achieved only 50 ~ 75% performance against monolingual IR[7]. Such outstanding performance results from several reasons. The first is the high quality of bilingual transfer dictionary for query translation. In most previous works, a "general" bilingual dictionary (or its variations) have been used, which are basically designed not for machines but for human readers, so that they may have too much spurious information liable to cause translation errors. On the contrary, our CLTR-K/J system uses a bilingual transfer dictionary, which was transformed from a machine tractable dictionary used for an existing machine translation system. The second is related to the language similarity between Korean and Japanese, especially the fact that most nouns of the two languages have their same origin from Chinese, and a noun is regarded as a meaningful part of speech as an index term in Korean IR. This language similarity might also result in less transfer ambiguity. Third, the test collection was small in size and its domain was restricted only to business and economics.

In Table 1, KJ-2, as compared to KJ-1, improves the precision considerably at up to 10% recall points, on the average by 6.83% (= (0.4161-0.3895)/0.3895), indicating that the use of word association in the form of co-occurrence weighting could be very effective. KJ-3 and KJ-4 also achieved improvements over KJ-2 by 1.54% and 1.8%, respectively. It shows the positive effect of the term re-weighting through the use of document frequencies and ranks, respectively. To sum up, our two-phase method for resolving transfer ambiguity resulted in an improvement of precision by about 9% (= (0.4236-0.3895)/0.3895) over a baseline system KJ-1.

Table 2 shows the average precision at top 1, 5, ..., 25, and 30 retrieved documents for each retrieval system. It is noteworthy that, at up to 10 retrieved documents, KJ-3 and KJ-4 achieved better performance than the baseline system, the Japanese monolingual retrieval system JJ. That will be because the term re-weighting scheme could re-order target documents with more correct translations in higher ranks. The proposed query translation model can be also applied to a monolingual retrieval model, except for *max* operation in Formula (1), because a monolingual IR has no transfer ambiguity in retrieval. We already used Formula (1) except for *max* in JJ and obtained a better performance. Of course, if JJ performs up to the term re-weighting phase, it will be better than our CLTR systems.

## 5. Conclusions

For cross-language text retrieval, most previous dictionary-based approaches suffer from a significant performance drop, achieving 50 ~ 75% of their corresponding monolingual retrieval[7]. This is mostly because of transfer ambiguity. To cope with the problem, this paper proposes a two-phase query translation method based on term re-weighting. The simple intuition that source language query terms may be somewhat related in meaning leads to the inference that their correct translations should more likely co-occur in target documents. In the first phase, our proposed method uses this word co-occurrence data to distinguish more relevant documents, which contain more correct translations, from the others. Based on statistical and ranking information from highly relevant documents, the second phase then converts a translated query vector into a re-weighted form by adding extra weights on probably correct target terms. This may have similar effect on standard query modification for relevance feedback, but we did not conduct any query expansion techniques. In addition, unlike most of previous works, we used a bilingual transfer dictionary, originally designed for machine translation.

Experiments confirm that our proposed method remarkably achieved almost the same performance as the monolingual IR system, contributing to an improvement of precision by about 9%. Even though the test collection was small in size and restricted to a specific domain, and the language pair is very similar, our proposed method turned out to be very effective in resolving transfer ambiguity. Further research involves the test collection, which will be scaled up to include other language pairs for more objective evaluation. We are also working on the integration of our proposed method with query expansion, and anticipate further refinements to result.

# References


1. Chul-Jae Park, Jong-Hyeok Lee, Geunbae Lee, K. Kakechi, "Collocation-Based Transfer Method in Japanese-Korean Machine Translation," *Transaction of Information Processing Society of Japan*, 38(4), 1997, pp.707~718.

2. David A. Hull, Gregory Grefenstette, "Querying Across Languages: A Dictionary-Based Approach to Multilingual Information Retrieval," *in Proceedings of the 19<sup>th</sup> International ACM SIGIR Conference on Research and Development in Information Retrieval(SIGIR '96)*, 1996, pp.49-57.

3. David A. Hull, "Using Structured Queries for Disambiguation in Cross-Language Information Retrieval," *In AAAI Symposium on Cross-Language Text and Speech Retrieval*, 1997.

4. Donna Harman, "Relevance Feedback Revisited," *in Proceedings of the 15<sup>th</sup> International ACM SIGIR Conference on Research and Development in Information Retrieval(SIGIR '92)*, 1992, pp.1-10.

5. Douglas W. Oard, "Alternative Approaches for Cross-Language Text Retrieval," *In AAAI Symposium on Cross-Language Text and Speech Retrieval*, 1997.

6. Douglas W. Oard, and Bonnie J. Dorr, "A Survey of Multilingual Text Retrieval," *Technical Report UMIACS-TR-96-19, Institute for Advanced Computer Studies, University of Maryland*, 1996.

7. Douglas W. Oard, and Paul Hackett, "Document Translation for cross-language text retrieval at the university of maryland," *In Proceedings of the sixth Text Retrieval Conference(TREC6), Gaithersburg, MD:National Institute of Standards Technology(NIST)*, November 1998.

8. Lisa Ballesteros and W. Bruce Croft, "Phrasal Translation and Query Expansion Techniques for Cross-Language Information Retrieval," *in Proceedings of the 20<sup>th</sup> International ACM SIGIR Conference on Research and Development in Information Retrieval(SIGIR '97)*, 1997, pp.84-91.

9. Kenneth W. Church, "Word Association Norms, Mutual Information, AND Lexicography," *Computational Linguistics, 16(1)*, 1990, pp.22-29.

10. W. John Hutchins and Harold L. Somers, "An Introduction to Machine Translation," *ACADEMIC PRESS INC.*, 1992.

*a Korean source query :* $'cikwu'$ $(\Box\Box),$ $'cikak'$ $(\Box\Box)$

*a translation set* $T_1$ *of* $'cikwu'$ : *{ the earth, endurance }*

*a translation set* $T_2$ *of* $'cikak'$ : *{ crust, perception }*

*a translation combination* $K_j \in X_{i=1}^{2} T_i, j = 1,2,3,4$

$K_1 =$ *{ the earth, crust }*

$K_2 =$ *{ the earth, perception }*

$K_3 =$ *{ endurance, crust }*

$K_4 =$ *{ endurance, perception }*

**Figure 1. Possible translation combinations of source query terms**

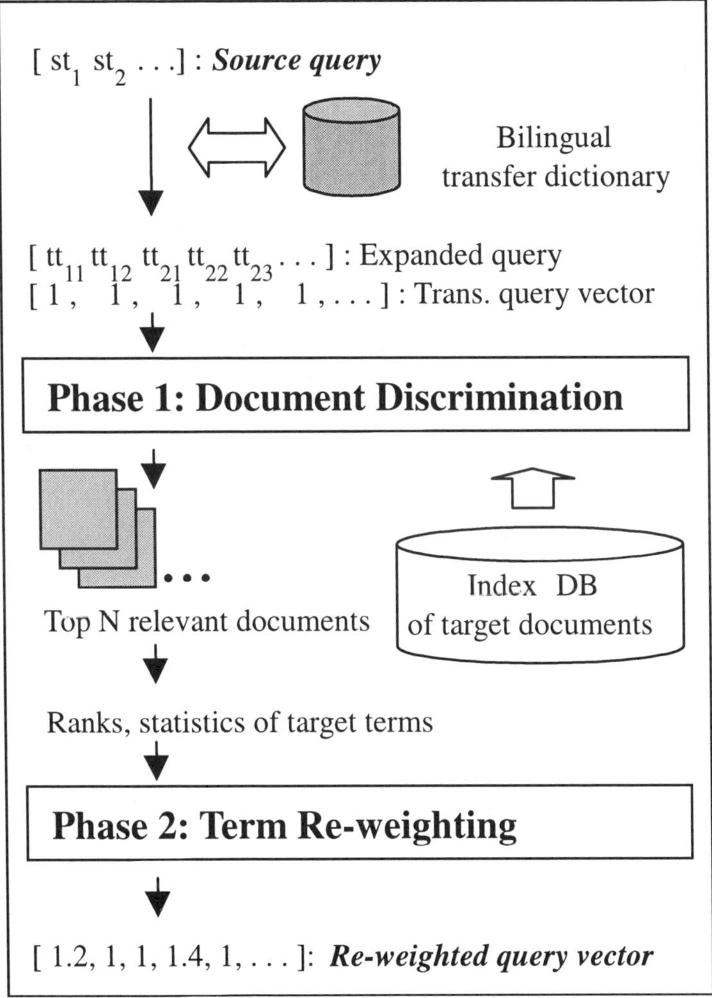



**Figure 2. Two-Phase Query Translation Model**

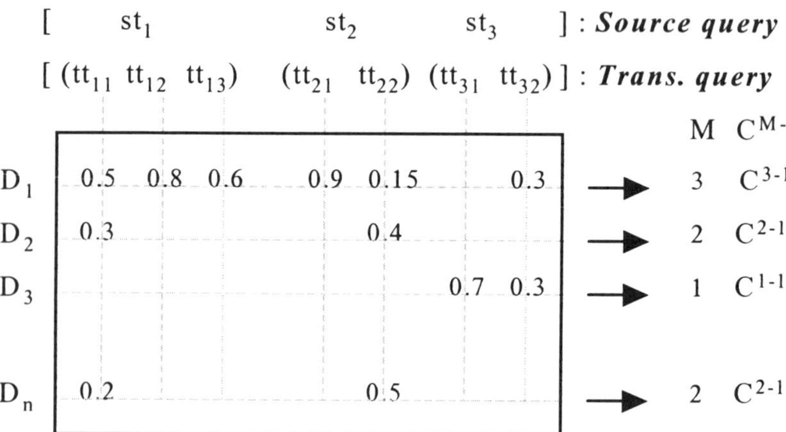



$st_i$ : $i$ - *th term of a source query*

$tt_{ij}$ : $j$ - *th translation of source query term* $st_i$

$M$ : *the number of original query terms* $st_i$

   *corresponding to the target terms* $tt_{ij}$ *that appear in a document D*

$C$ : *co - occurrence weighting factor*

**Figure 3. Weights of translated terms on documents**

$$sim(Q,D) = C^{M-1} \sum_{st_i} \max_{tt_{ij}} (W_{Q,tt_{ij}} \times W_{D,tt_{ij}}) \quad \text{-----------------} (1)$$

$Q$ : *an original source language query*

$D$ : *a document in a document collection*

$C$ : *co - occurrence weighting factor*

$M$ : *the number of original query terms* $st_i$ *corresponding to*

    *the target terms* $tt_{ij}$ *that appear in a document D*

$st_i$ : *i - th term of Q*

$tt_{ij}$ : *j - th translation of an original query term* $st_i$

$W_{Q,tt_{ij}}$ : *a weight of* $tt_{ij}$ *on Q*

$W_{D,tt_{ij}}$ : *a weight of* $tt_{ij}$ *on D*

**Formula 1. Query-document similarity function based on co-occurrence weighting**

$$W_{Q,tt_{ij}} = \Delta_{tt_{ij}} \times W_{Q,tt_{ij}} \quad \text{---------------------} (2)$$

$$\Delta_{tt_{ij}} = (1 + 0.5 \times \frac{df_{tt_{ij}}}{\max_{i,j}(df_{tt_{ij}})})$$

$W_{Q,tt_{ij}}$ : *a weight of* $tt_{ij}$ *on Q*

$tt_{ij}$ : *j - th translation of an original query term* $st_i$

$df_{tt_{ij}}$ : *document frequency of a target term* $tt_{ij}$

    *in the top N documents*

**Formula 2. Target term weighting function based on document frequency**

$$\Delta_{tt_{ij}} = \left(1 + \alpha \times \frac{df_{tt_{ij}}}{\max\limits_{i,j}(df_{tt_{ij}})} + (1 - \alpha) \times \frac{\sum\limits_{K \in R} N + 1 - K}{\sum\limits_{K=1}^{N} K}\right) \text{-----------------(3)}$$

$\alpha$ : a relative importance factor

between document frequency and ranking $(0 \leq \alpha \leq 1)$

$R$ : a rank set of highly ranked $N$ documents with a target term $tt_{ij}$

$N$ : the number of highly ranked documents retrieved in the first phase

**Formula 3. Target term weighting function based on relative importance between document frequency and ranking**

| Rec. | JJ | KJ-1 | KJ-2 | KJ-3 | KJ-4 |
|---|---|---|---|---|---|
| 0 | 0.7738 | 0.6833(-11.7) | 0.7988(+3.23) | 0.8071(+4.30) | 0.8106(+4.76) |
| 0.1 | 0.7117 | 0.6542(-8.08) | 0.7282(+2.32) | 0.7451(+4.69) | 0.7500(+5.38) |
| 0.2 | 0.6035 | 0.5601(-7.19) | 0.5807(-3.78) | 0.5938(-1.61) | 0.5946(-1.47) |
| 0.3 | 0.5057 | 0.4592(-9.20) | 0.4773(-5.62) | 0.4852(-4.05) | 0.4860(-3.90) |
| 0.4 | 0.4464 | 0.4160(-6.81) | 0.4286(-3.99) | 0.4305(-3.56) | 0.4298(-3.72) |
| 0.5 | 0.402 | 0.3767(-6.29) | 0.3941(-1.97) | 0.3998(-0.55) | 0.4005(-0.37) |
| 0.6 | 0.3613 | 0.3406(-5.73) | 0.3497(-3.21) | 0.3577(-1.00) | 0.3576(-1.02) |
| 0.7 | 0.2857 | 0.2774(-2.91) | 0.2788(-2.42) | 0.2831(-0.91) | 0.2836(-0.74) |
| 0.8 | 0.2408 | 0.2201(-8.60) | 0.2274(-5.56) | 0.2286(-5.07) | 0.2303(-4.36) |
| 0.9 | 0.1811 | 0.1659(-8.39) | 0.1747(-3.53) | 0.1766(-2.48) | 0.1768(-2.37) |
| 1 | 0.1462 | 0.1309(-10.5) | 0.1389(-4.99) | 0.1395(-4.58) | 0.1395(-4.58) |
| Avg. | 0.4235 | 0.3895(-8.03) | 0.4161(-1.75) | 0.4225(-0.24) | 0.4236(+0.02) |

**Table 1. Precision at 11 points of recall by interpolation, (): the improvement rate on the baseline JJ**

| Top N | JJ | | KJ-2 | | KJ-3 | | KJ-4 | |
|---|---|---|---|---|---|---|---|---|
| | Rec. | Pre. | Rec. | Pre. | Rec. | Pre. | Rec. | Pre. |
| 1 | 0.0668 | 0.617 | 0.0700(+4.79) | 0.6596(+6.90) | 0.0700(+4.79) | 0.6596(+6.90) | 0.0700(+4.79) | 0.6596(+6.90) |
| 5 | 0.2602 | 0.4979 | 0.2578(-0.92) | 0.4936(-0.86) | 0.2611(+0.35) | 0.5021(+0.84) | 0.2621(+0.73) | 0.5064(+1.71) |
| 10 | 0.2971 | 0.3277 | 0.2927(-1.48) | 0.3234(-1.31) | 0.3014(+1.45) | 0.3340(+1.92) | 0.3020(+1.65) | 0.3362(+2.59) |
| 15 | 0.3805 | 0.2879 | 0.3686(-3.13) | 0.2794(-2.95) | 0.3716(-2.34) | 0.2823(-1.95) | 0.3716(-2.34) | 0.2823(-1.95) |
| 20 | 0.3969 | 0.2255 | 0.3746(-5.62) | 0.2117(-6.12) | 0.3820(-3.75) | 0.2149(-4.70) | 0.3776(-4.86) | 0.2128(-5.63) |
| 25 | 0.4377 | 0.1974 | 0.4081(-6.76) | 0.1847(-6.43) | 0.4105(-6.21) | 0.1864(-5.57) | 0.4132(-5.60) | 0.1872(-5.17) |
| 30 | 0.4477 | 0.1709 | 0.4315(-3.62) | 0.1624(-4.97) | 0.4343(-2.99) | 0.1645(-3.74) | 0.4329(-3.31) | 0.1645(-3.74) |
| Avg | 0.3267 | 0.3320 | 0.3148(-3.66) | 0.3307(-0.41) | 0.3187(-2.45) | 0.3348(+0.84) | 0.3185(-2.51) | 0.3356(+1.06) |

**Table 2. Average Precision and Recall at top 1,5,...,25, and 30 retrieved documents**

# Direct Feature Extraction in DCT Domain and its Applications in Online Web Image Retrieval for JPEG Compressed Images


Guocan Feng [a b], A. Armstrong [a] and Jianmin Jiang [a]

[a] *(gfeng, ajarmstr, jjiang)@glam.ac.uk, School of Computing, University of Glamorgan, UK*

[b] *Faculty of Mathematics and Computing Science, Zhongshan University, Guangzhou, China*


## 1. Introduction

The current trends in computer and Internet use show a significant increase in the amount of media data being distributed and stored. This increase in data has already outstripped the ability of current systems as to its efficient archival and storage, and indexing. The classical means based on keyword indexing or simply browsing are quite far from the currently increasing requirements in the above areas. The content-based image retrieval (CBIR) systems, which can provide the ability to retrieve all similar images with a query image in content such as texture, shape, color and so on, aim to meet the requirements [2-3, 5, 7, 9, 13, 16-18]. At present, most of CBIR systems are based on pixel domain. However, almost all of images are stored in a compressed format. This means that images must be decoded before key construction or feature extraction [2-3, 9,16].

The majority of the compressed images, especially on the Internet, are currently stored in the JPEG compression format (jpg files). This format applies DCT-based data compression techniques to achieve large amount of compression and thus the file size has been significantly reduced. Although the area of image processing has gone through many years of research and development represented by tasks such as enhancement, segmentation, feature extraction, and pattern classification etc, they all are developed in *pixel-domain*. While DCT-based data compression greatly improves the transmission efficiency and the management of limited storage space, the compressed visual data will have to be processed in many cases before being displayed, further transmitted, and printed. Some of the frequently employed processing functions include scaling, filtering, rotation, translation, feature extraction and classification. To this end, conventional approaches would have to convert (decompress) the data from the DCT domain to the pixel domain before those existing algorithms can be applied [17]. These will lead to significant increase of the overhead computing cost and storage expense in the entire chain of image processing and compression. It is not only time consuming, but also a major factor of increasing the complexity of algorithm design and development. Therefore, to avoid the need of decompression, it is highly desirable to have algorithms capable of operating directly in compressed domain. As a result, a new wave of research efforts is now focusing on image processing in compressed domain or DCT domain [6,8, 17, 22, 25].

Shen *et al.* [22] presented an algorithm of the edge extraction directly from DCT domain. They used an ideal edge model to estimate the strength and orientation of an edge in terms of the relative values of different DCT coefficients of a block. The experimental result shows the coarse edge information from DCT-domain images can be extracted up to 20 times faster than conventional edge detectors. Similarly, Abdel-Malek *et al.* [1] have proposed the technique to detect oriented line features using DCT coefficients. Ng *et al.* [19] have proposed a segmentation technique by using local variance of DCT coefficients. In this technique, 3x3 DCT is computed at each pixel location using the surrounding points. The local variance of each DCT coefficient is then computed using 15x15 sliding window. Changes in the local variance are used to segment the image.

Smith *et al.*[25] proposed a method based on the 16 DCT coefficients of 4x4 block in the image/video indexing. The variance and the mean absolute values of each of these coefficients are computed over the whole image. The feature of the entire image is then represented by this 32 component vector. And then the feature vector can be further processed (such as dimension reduction) or can be directly used in the indexing. Reeves *et al.* [21] also proposed similar indexing technique based on the DCT domain. However, block size considered in their work is 8x8.

In the area of image watermarking, J. R. Hernandez *et al.* [12] have proposed to apply the generalized Gaussian distributions to model the DCT coefficients of the original image, and show how the resulting detector structures lead to considerable improvements in performance with respect to the correlation receiver. As a result, an analytical framework is provided that allows examining the performance of a given watermarking method in the DCT domain.

In developing a face recognition system of JPEG images, Eickeler [6] *et. al* even directly employs the first 15 coefficients of DCT block along the zigzag as face feature. The system does not only get a less recognition times (1.5 seconds) but also achieves better recognition for test on Olivetti Research Laboratory (ORL) face database. These enlighten the bright future of exploring the direct processing technique in the compressed domain.

Following the technique of direct feature extraction in compressed domain, this chapter firstly presents the spatial relationship between a DCT-block and its subblocks. The detailed derivation is given. The results can be used in converting the size of DCT blocks so as to easily extract the local feature from DCT domain. Secondly, we proposed an algorithm to take out pseudo color information from DCT domain. At last, Further to these results, we implement an on-line image indexing and retrieval technique based on a pseudo-pixel extraction algorithm. As it is suitable for WEB image browsing, we also describe our design of an automatic and WEB-based image retrieval system named as *ImageHunter*. The experiment results show the retrieval effectiveness of the system is comparable with that of full decompression, but it is more efficient than conventional algorithms because of without decompression involving.

The remainder of this chapter is organized as follows. Section 2 gives a brief overview of DCT and JPEG as a preliminary. In Section 3, we drive some theoretical deduction for spatial relationship of a block and its subblocks. While we describe an algorithm design for extracting pseudo-pixels directly from DCT domain without full decompression in section 4. And then exploiting the algorithm in the key construction, we describe the system design for *ImageHunter,* our WEB-based image browser in Section 5. Finally we give some discussion and conclusion in last section.

## 2. Overview of DCT and JPEG

As a preliminary, This section briefly gives the overview of DCT and JPEG standard.

Discrete cosine transform (DCT) is one of most commonly used in signal processing, which has good properties such as (a) close to the optimal Karhunen-Loève transform (KLT); (b) signal independent and capable of eliminating the shortcoming of KLT; and (c) orthogonal transform and real coefficients. Therefore it has been widely used in image/video compressed standard (JPEG/MPEG and H261/H263) and feature representation [6]. The basic computation in a 2-D DCT-based system is transformation of an N×N image block from the spatial domain to the DCT domain. For the image compression standards, N usually takes 8 because of hardware and software implementation viewpoint.

For 2-D signal x(i,j), the NxN forward DCT transform are expressed as

$$C(u,v) = \frac{2}{N}\alpha(u)\alpha(v)\sum_{i=0}^{N-1}\sum_{j=0}^{N-1}x(i,j)\cos\left(\frac{(2i+1)u\pi}{2N}\right)\cos\left(\frac{(2j+1)v\pi}{2N}\right) \quad (1)$$

where

$$\alpha(u) = \begin{cases} \sqrt{\dfrac{1}{2}} & for\ u = 0 \\ 1 & otherwise \end{cases} \quad (2)$$

The essence of DCT is to project the signal to a family of the orthogonal basis function. The 64 waveforms composing the DCT basis functions are depicted in Figure 2(a). The inverse DCT (IDCT) can be represented as

$$x(i,j) = \frac{2}{N}\sum_{u=0}^{N-1}\sum_{v=0}^{N-1}\alpha(u)\alpha(v)C(u,v)\cos\left(\frac{(2i+1)u\pi}{2N}\right)\cos\left(\frac{(2j+1)v\pi}{2N}\right) \quad (3)$$

An important property of the 2D DCT and IDCT transform is separability. This implies that the 2-D DCT or IDCT can be obtained by first performing 1-D DCTs of the rows of x(i,j) followed by 1-D DCTs of the columns. On the other hand, DCT is of a high ability of de-correlation, thus itself is one of tool of the feature extraction in image processing and pattern analysis.

The JPEG is a compression standard based on block-DCT, which is widely used in lossy image compression of photographic images. It reduces the visual information that is not significant for the human vision and it de-correlates the pixels and therefore eliminates redundancy. But it makes automatic processing difficult and the processing has to be adapted to the compression method [26].

The JPEG compression standard uses the block-based DCT. The image is sampled using non-overlapping blocks of the size 8x8 pixels, which are transformed utilizing the 2D. The coefficients of the transformed block are quantized and then coded by Huffman entropy encoder. Its decoder is just composed of the inverse process steps in reverse order. Figure 1 shows a typical block diagram of JPEG decoder for the special case of single-component (grayscale) image. Color image coding or decoding then can approximately be regarded as coding/decoding of multiple grayscale images[26].

Along with the diagram, the DCT is the last step of the proceedings. As mentioned as the above, DCT itself is a one of the best filters for the feature extraction, which has properties of good energy compact, and image independent. Thus, direct feature extraction from DCT domain in JPEG image will disregard the any necessity of decomposing the image and then exploring its features in pixel domain. It will greatly alleviate the computational cost caused. At present, the feature extraction algorithms and image index techniques directly based on the compressed domain are widely intended [17] especially in DCT domain.


## 3. The Spatial Relationship between a Block and its Subblocks in DCT Domain

While more and more image processing algorithms are proposed in compressed or DCT domain to take the advantage of reducing the computing cost and improving the processing speed, new problem could occur from the fact that various DCT block sizes have to be used in order to ensure optimized performances. These include $8 \times 8$ blocks used in JPEG, $4 \times 4$ blocks used in image indexing [25] and $16 \times 16$ macro-blocks in MPEGs etc [4]. To deal with inter-transfer of DCT coefficients from different blocks with various sizes, traditional approach would have to recover the pixel data in spatial domain first via IDCT, and re-divide the pixels into the required block size to apply DCT again and produce the DCT coefficients. It is obvious that the approach is inefficient. To this end, direct derivation of DCT coefficients from those of various block sizes can be made possible if the spatial relationship is fully revealed and analyzed. Along this line of research, Kou *et al.* [15] first proposed the so-called 'direct computation method', which gave the algorithm of composing the 2 N-point DCTs into 1

2N-point DCT directly. The algorithm reduced the computing cost in combining the two given adjacent blocks into 1 block in DCT domain. Recently, Skodras [24] also discussed the topic and gave the similar result for 1D signal as well. However, their work only focused on the case of the relationship between a block and its two adjacent sub-blocks. For 2-D signal, their work will be unable to produce a satisfactory solution. Since the DCT of a global range of blocks is more convenient to extract global information or features than the DCT of their sub-blocks, it remains an important research issue to reveal the full relationship between an image block with any size and all of its sub-blocks. To this end, we propose a concept of the spatial relationship of the DCT coefficients between a block and its sub-blocks and describe analytic expressions to characterize the interchange from a group of DCT coefficients to another directly in DCT domain.

## 3.1. Problem Description

Given a block of pixels, $B$, its number of rows and columns can be represented as a product of two integers such as $L \times N$ rows and $M \times N$ columns, in order to obtain a convenient representation of its sub-blocks. Correspondingly, this block $B$ can be divided into $L \times M$ sub-blocks represented as $SB_{ij}$ with the size of $N \times N$ ( $i$ =0,1, ..., L-1, j=0,1, ..., M-1)

pixels. As an example, a block of $6 \times 6$ pixels can be regarded as having $2 \times 3$ rows and $2 \times 3$ columns, and thus it can be divided into 4 ($L \times M$) sub-blocks, all of which would have $3 \times 3$ pixels. Assuming that the DCT coefficients of the block $B$ and its sub-blocks $SB_{ij}$ are represented as $C_B$ and $C_{ij}(u,v)$

respectively ($i=0,1,..., L-1; j=0,1,...,M-1; u,v=0,1,...N-1$), the problem to be formulated is to determine the spatial relationship between $C_B$ and $C_{ij}(u,v)$, i.e., the relationship between the DCT coefficients of the block $B$ and that of its sub-blocks $SB_{ij}$ .

## 3.2. Derivation

According to the definition of DCT in equation (1), a general 2-dimensional block $B$ with $LN$ rows and $MN$ columns would have its DCT being defined as follows:

$$C_{\mathrm{B}}(u,v) = \sqrt{\frac{4}{LN \times MN}}\alpha(u)\alpha(v)\sum_{i=0}^{LN-1}\sum_{j=0}^{MN-1} x(i,j)\cos\left(\frac{(2i+1)u\pi}{2LN}\right)\cos\left(\frac{(2j+1)v\pi}{2MN}\right) \quad (4)$$

where $\alpha(u)$ satisfies the equation (2). Here, for convenience, we normalize $\alpha(u) = 1$ for all $u$ only in this section. For the image block $SB_{lm}$, its corresponding DCT can be expressed as

$$C_{lm}(u,v) = DCT(SB_{lm}) = \frac{2}{N}\sum_{i=0}^{N-1}\sum_{j=0}^{N-1} x(lN+i, mN+j)\cos\left(\frac{(2i+1)u\pi}{2N}\right)\cos\left(\frac{(2j+1)v\pi}{2N}\right) \quad (5)$$

$(l=0,\ldots,L\text{-}1; m=0,1,\ldots,M\text{-}1; u,v=0,\ldots, N\text{-}1)$

As above described, the problem is to determine the relationship between $C_B$ and $C_{lm}$. Denote 2-D basis functions as $\Phi_{uv}(i,j)$. In fact, it is the product of 2 1-D basis functions $\Phi_u^1(i) = \cos\left(\frac{(2i+1)u\pi}{2LN}\right)$ and $\Phi_v^2(j) = \cos\left(\frac{(2j+1)v\pi}{2MN}\right)$.

On the same domain as the above, we reconstruct new basis functions as follows (refer to Figure 2)

$$\Psi_{uv}(i,j) = \begin{cases} \cos\left(\dfrac{2(i\bmod N)(u\bmod N)\pi}{2N}\right)\cos\left(\dfrac{2(j\bmod N)(v\bmod N)\pi}{2N}\right) & \begin{aligned} & when\ [i/N]=[u/N] \\ & and\ [j/N]=[v/N] \end{aligned} \\ 0 & othewise \end{cases} \quad (6)$$

Similarly, which can also expressed as the product of 2 1-D basis functions

$$\Psi_u^1(i) = \begin{cases} \cos\left(\dfrac{2(i\bmod N)(u\bmod N)\pi}{2N}\right) & when\ [i/N]=[u/N] \quad (i,u=0,1,\ldots,LN\text{-}1) \\ 0 & othewise \end{cases} \quad (7)$$

and

$$\Psi_v^2(i) = \begin{cases} \cos\left(\dfrac{2(j\bmod N)(v\bmod N)\pi}{2N}\right) & when\ [j/N]=[v/N] \quad (j,v=0,1,\ldots,LM\text{-}1) \\ 0 & othewise \end{cases} \quad (8)$$

In fact, in order to construct the new $LN \times MN$ DCT basis function, the operations of translating the basis function of $N \times N$ block with $M$ steps along row direction and with $L$ steps along column direction are applied respectively. Figure 2 illustrates how a new $16 \times 16$ DCT basis function can be constructed from that of $8 \times 8$ blocks, in which part (a) presents the $8 \times 8$ DCT basis functions with 64 coefficients, and part (b) the $16 \times 16$ DCT basis functions with 256 coefficients and (c) new $16 \times 16$ DCT basis functions.

According to the definition of the basis functions $\Psi_{uv}$, $\Psi_u^1$ and $\Psi_v^2$. We have

$$\sum_{i=0}^{LN-1}\sum_{j=0}^{MN-1} x(i,j)\Psi_{uv}(i,j) = \sum_{i=0}^{LN-1}\sum_{j=0}^{MN-1} x(i,j)\Psi_u^1(i)\Psi_v^2(j) = \frac{N}{2}C_{[u/N][v/N]}((u\bmod N),(v\bmod N)) \quad (9)$$

And furthermore, because $\Phi_u^1(i)$ and $\Psi_u^1(i)$ are 1-D basis functions on the same space, $\Phi_u^1(i)$ can be represented the linear combination of $\Psi_u^1(i)$ as follows.

$$\Phi_u^1(i) = \sum_{k=0}^{LN-1} \beta_k^u \Psi_k^1(i) \quad (u = 0,1, ..., LN\text{-}1) \tag{10}$$

where $\beta_k^u$ are the parameters with respect to $\Phi_u^1(i)$ and $\Psi_k^1(i)$, which can be uniquely determined by substituting the value of $i(i=0,1,...,LN\text{-}1)$. Similarly for $\Phi_v^1(j)$,

$$\Phi_v^2(i) = \sum_{l=0}^{MN-1} \beta_l^v \Psi_l^2(j) \quad (v = 0,1, ..., MN\text{-}1) \tag{11}$$

Denote matrices $\{\beta_k^u\}$ and $\{\gamma_l^v\}$ as $D_{LNxLN}$ and $F_{MNxMN}$. Consider equation (4). Substituting the results obtained in equation (10) and (11) into (4), equation (4) can be rearranged into:

$$C_B(u,v) = \sqrt{\frac{4}{LN * MN}} \begin{pmatrix} \beta_0^u & \beta_1^u & ... & \beta_{LN-1}^u \end{pmatrix} * \tag{12}$$

$$\sum_{i=0}^{LN-1} \sum_{j=0}^{MN-1} \left( x(i,j) \begin{pmatrix} \Psi_0^1(i)\Psi_0^2(j) & \Psi_0^1(i)\Psi_1^2(j) & ... & \Psi_0^1(i)\Psi_{MN-1}^2(j) \\ \Psi_1^1(i)\Psi_0^2(j) & \Psi_1^1(i)\Psi_1^2(j) & ... & \Psi_1^1(i)\Psi_{MN-1}^2(j) \\ \vdots & \vdots & ... & \vdots \\ \Psi_{LN-1}^1(i)\Psi_0^2(j) & \Psi_{LN-1}^1(i)\Psi_1^2(j) & ... & \Psi_{LN-1}^1(i)\Psi_{MN-1}^2(j) \end{pmatrix} \begin{pmatrix} \gamma_0^v \\ \gamma_1^v \\ \vdots \\ \gamma_{LN-1}^v \end{pmatrix} \right)$$

Exploiting the results in equation (9) into the above equation, we have

$$C_B(u,v) = \sqrt{\frac{1}{L * M}} \begin{pmatrix} \beta_0^u & \beta_1^u & ... & \beta_{LN-1}^u \end{pmatrix} * \tag{13}$$

$$\begin{pmatrix} C_{0,0}(0,0) & ... & C_{0,0}(0,N-1) & & C_{0,M-1}(0,0) & ... & C_{0,M-1}(0,N-1) \\ \vdots & ... & \vdots & ... & \vdots & ... & \vdots \\ C_{0,0}(0,0) & ... & C_{0,0}(N-1,N-1) & & C_{0,M-1}(0,0) & ... & C_{0,M-1}(N-1,N-1) \\ & \vdots & & ... & & \vdots & \\ C_{L-1,0}(0,0) & ... & C_{L-1,0}(0,N-1) & & C_{L-1,M-1}(0,0) & ... & C_{L-1,M-1}(0,N-1) \\ \vdots & ... & \vdots & ... & \vdots & ... & \vdots \\ C_{L-1,0}(0,0) & ... & C_{L-1,0}(N-1,N-1) & & C_{L-1,M-1}(0,0) & ... & C_{L-1,M-1}(N-1,N-1) \end{pmatrix} \begin{pmatrix} \gamma_0^v \\ \gamma_1^v \\ \vdots \\ \gamma_{LN-1}^v \end{pmatrix}$$

Applying the form of matrix and block matrix, the equation can be shown in concise form as follows.

$$C_B = \sqrt{\frac{1}{LM}} D \begin{pmatrix} C_{0,0} & C_{0,1} & ... & C_{0,M-1} \\ C_{1,0} & C_{1,1} & ... & C_{1,M-1} \\ \vdots & \vdots & ... & \vdots \\ C_{L-1,0} & C_{L-1,1} & ... & C_{L-1,M-1} \end{pmatrix} F^T \tag{14}$$

where **D** and **F** are square matrices of the parameters with dimensions $LN \times LN$ and $MN \times MN$ respectively, which can be uniquely determined by equation (10) or (11) in advance since they are only relevant to those basis functions. Note that each element $C_{ij}$ represents the set of DCT coefficients for sub-block $SB_{ij}$, and thus itself is a matrix with $N \times N$ elements. For the special case of $L=M$, we have: D=F, and hence equation (14) can be further simplified as:

$$C_{\mathbf{B}} = \frac{1}{M} \mathbf{D} \begin{pmatrix} C_{0,0} & C_{0,1} & \cdots & C_{0,M-1} \\ C_{1,0} & C_{1,1} & \cdots & C_{1,M-1} \\ \vdots & \vdots & \cdots & \vdots \\ C_{L-1,0} & C_{L-1,1} & \cdots & C_{L-1,M-1} \end{pmatrix} \mathbf{D}^T \qquad (15)$$

The analytic expression (14) and (15) generalizes the spatial relationship of DCT coefficients between a block and its sub-blocks, and the relationship is represented as a concise linear combination of its sub-blocks' DCT coefficients.

Finally, Since the matrices **D** or **F** are the transferring matrices between orthogonal basis function, they are invertible. The block matrix $\{C_{ij}\}$ also can be expressed into the linear combination of $C_B$, i.e.

$$\begin{pmatrix} C_{0,0} & C_{0,1} & \cdots & C_{0,M-1} \\ C_{1,0} & C_{1,1} & \cdots & C_{1,M-1} \\ \vdots & \vdots & \cdots & \vdots \\ C_{L-1,0} & C_{L-1,1} & \cdots & C_{L-1,M-1} \end{pmatrix} = \sqrt{LM}\,\mathbf{D}^{-1} C_{\mathbf{B}} \mathbf{F}^{T^{-1}} \qquad (16)$$

This means, for any block of DCT coefficients, the DCT of its sub-blocks can also be obtained directly in DCT domain. The result reveals that any DCT block can be decomposed into sub-blocks in an iterative manner similar to pyramid algorithms. At this case, $L$ and $M$ usually take 2.


### 3.3. Illustrative Example

In order to explore the potential applications of the above derivation, this section gives a detailed implementation for the exchanges between an image with size 4x4 and its 4 2x2 subblocks on the DCT domain.

Cropping a 4x4-window at the hat of the image Lena. The spatial relationship of the coefficients between the 4x4 window and its 4 2x2 subimage on the DCT domain will be discussed as following two phases.

From 4 2x2 blocks to 1 4x4 block: Calculate the transferring parameter matrix **D** between 2-dimension basis functions and 4-dimension basis function according to equation (10) in advance. Divide the 4x4 window into

4 2x2 subblocks, then carry out the DCT transform on each subblock so as to get the DCT coefficients of the subblocks. Employ the formula (12) to transform the DCT coefficients of 4 2x2 subblocks into that of 1 4x4 block. We can find the corresponding DCT coefficients are same as that gotten from the DCT.

From 1 4x4 block to 4 2x2 blocks: The process of calculating the DCT coefficients of 4 2x2 blocks from 1 4x4 block is inverse of the above. Figure 3 presents the detailed diagram of the example the exchange between 4x4 block and its four 2x2 subblocks on DCT domain.

## 3.4. Remarks

- Computation cost

Equation (14) conveys the linear relationship between a block and its subblocks on the DCT domain respectively for 2D signal. The corresponding result for 1-D is the special case of 2D signal. From the point of view on the mathematical form, the computation cost of DCT coefficients by composing and decomposing is almost same as that from the original signal. However, since the transferring matrix $\mathbf{D}$ or $\mathbf{F}$ is sparse matrix, the computation cost is greatly reduced by comparing with the traditional algorithm. The comparison of computation complexity between the traditional algorithm and the proposed algorithm of transferring a block and its ¼ size subblocks is tabulated as Table 1. The table shows that the addition operations and multiplication operations are respectively almost ¼ of the traditional algorithm of 2D signal for the block composition. For the decomposition, when $N$ is greater, the result is almost same as the composition.

- Comparison with the existed algorithms

The similar work originated Kou et al. [15]. They gave the 'so-called' direct computational algorithm for DCT coefficients of a signal block taken from two adjacent subblocks. Recently, Skodras *et al.* [24] also gave a novel algorithm. Their work mainly focused on composing the length-2N block from 2 adjacent length-N block on DCT domain for 1D signal. Their algorithms have shown the improvement on saving computation cost. Comparing with their works, the paper has the following contributions

i) Extend the available region from the composition of 2 length-N blocks to the general case M length–N blocks on DCT domain; and give the concise linear expression.

ii) Extend the result for 1D signal to 2D signal.

iii) Give out an answer to the inverse of the original problem. This is, the proposed algorithm in this paper includes that decomposing a block into subblocks on DCT.

## 4. Direct Information Extraction

In pixel domain, color information is regarded as one of the most important characters of image. Most of all features, such as histogram, texture, shape, can be extracted or transformed from this information. There are several various color spaces, for instance RGB, YCrCb, YUV and $C_4C_5C_6$ color space etc [4, 14], which can be exchange each other. The color space adopted in JPEG is luminance-chrominance color space YCrCb, where component Y presents the intensity.

Among currently image indexing techniques based on color, RGB and $C_4C_5C_6$ color space is commonly used in extracting image feature. Moreover, in order to improve the efficiency in image indexing, the coarse information is enough [2, 22], and trivial is often omitted. Following this idea, starting from those DCT coefficients, a series of rearrangement of their mathematical relationships and simplifications are described in this section, which enabled us to extract color information directly from DCT domain without incurring any significant computing cost. Since color information converts to pixel intensity values for gray level images, the work reported here could also serve a robust bridge between pixel domain and DCT domain. In other words, all image processing techniques developed in pixel domain could directly be applied in DCT domain with our proposed algorithm without going through full decompression and IDCT. As a result, significant savings on computing and storage spaces could be achieved.

### 4.1. Color Space Conversion between $YC_bC_r$ and RGB in DCT domain

Images and videos are usually displayed and indexed in RGB color space. However, the original data are typically compressed in a type of luminance-chrominance color space, such as $YC_bC_r$ [4] in JPEG standard. In this section, we briefly describe the relationship of both in their DCT domain as a starting point towards a full algorithm design for color extraction from DCT domain.

As we know, $YC_bC_r$ is the most commonly used color coordinate system for the compression of image and video signals such as JPEG/MPEG standards, among which $Y$ is the luminance component, $C_b$ and $C_r$ are the chrominance components. Further, there exists a linear relationship between the space of $YC_bC_r$ and that of RGB[8]. Given the primary RGB inputs($R$, $G$ and $B \in [0,1]$), we have:

$$\begin{bmatrix} Y \\ C_b \\ C_r \end{bmatrix} = \begin{bmatrix} 0.299 & 0.587 & 0.114 \\ -0.169 & -0.331 & 0.500 \\ 0.500 & -0.419 & -0.081 \end{bmatrix} \begin{bmatrix} R \\ G \\ B \end{bmatrix} = M_R \begin{bmatrix} R \\ G \\ B \end{bmatrix} \tag{17}$$

In turn, Given a $YC_bC_r$ input ($Y \in [0\ 1]$ and $C_b$, $C_r \in [-0.5, 0.5]$), the RGB values can also be derived from:

$$\begin{bmatrix} R \\ G \\ B \end{bmatrix} = \begin{bmatrix} 1 & 0 & 1.4021 \\ 1 & -0.3441 & -0.7142 \\ 1 & 1.7718 & 0 \end{bmatrix} \begin{bmatrix} Y \\ C_b \\ C_r \end{bmatrix} = M_Y \begin{bmatrix} Y \\ C_b \\ C_r \end{bmatrix} \tag{18}$$

where $[Y\ C_b\ C_r]^T$ and $[R\ G\ B]^T$ are the corresponding color components in the $YC_bC_r$ and RGB color space respectively, and $M_R$ and $M_y$ represent the corresponding transferring matrix as described in equation (17) and (18).

To extract color information from the compressed images, the conventional methods would conduct IDCT to convert $YC_bC_r$ from the DCT domain to the pixel domain, and then transform the $YC_bC_r$ signal into RGB color space. To save the computing cost in this process, the first step is to construct the conversion from the space of $YC_bC_r$ to that of RGB and vice versa in DCT domain. Let $Y(i, j)$, $C_b(i,j)$ and $C_r(i,j)$ be the value of $Y$, $C_b$ and $C_r$ at pixel $(i,j)$ in $YC_bC_r$ coordinate system ($i,j=0,1,...,N-1$). In the compression domain, $i$, $j$ may vary as $0,1,...$, $N/2$ for $C_b$, $C_r$. However, this can be extended to $N \times N$ without losing generality. Hence, given $R(i,j)$, $G(i,j)$ and $B(i,j)$, the color pixel components in RGB space, their DCT transform can be expressed as:

$$C_\Omega(u,v) = \frac{2}{N}\alpha(u)\alpha(v)\sum_{i=0}^{N-1}\sum_{j=0}^{N-1}\Omega(i,j)\cos\left(\frac{(2i+1)u\pi}{2N}\right)\cos\left(\frac{(2j+1)v\pi}{2N}\right) \tag{19}$$

where $\Omega \in$ color set$\{R, G, B\}$. Since the DCT is a linear transform [11], the DCT of a linear combination of signal set $\{x_p(i, j), p=1, 2, ..., M\}$ can be represented as the linear combination of its DCTs, i.e. if

$$x(i,j) = \sum_{p=1}^{M} a_p x_p(i,j), \quad \text{then} \quad C_x(u,v) = \sum_{p=1}^{M} a_p C_{x_p}(u,v), \quad \text{where} \quad a_p \ (p=1,2,$$

..., $M$) are constant parameters. Therefore, by considering equation (17) and (19), we have:

$$C_R(u,v) = C_Y(u,v) + 1.4021 C_{c_r}(u,v)$$

$$C_G(u,v) = C_Y(u,v) - 0.3441 C_{Cb}(u,v) - 0.7142 C_{Cr}(u,v) \qquad (20)$$

$$C_B(u,v) = C_Y(u,v) + 0.7718 C_{Cb}(u,v)$$

where $C_x(u,\,v)$ stands for the DCT coefficient of $x(i,j)(i,j,\,u,\,v = 0,1,\ldots,N\text{-}1)$. The above results can be rearranged in a matrix form:

$$\begin{bmatrix} C_R(u,v) \\ C_G(u,v) \\ C_B(u,v) \end{bmatrix} = M_Y \begin{bmatrix} C_Y(u,v) \\ C_{Cb}(u,v) \\ C_{Cr}(u,v) \end{bmatrix} \qquad (21)$$

and:

$$\begin{bmatrix} C_Y(u,v) \\ C_{Cb}(u,v) \\ C_{Cr}(u,v) \end{bmatrix} = M_R \begin{bmatrix} C_R(u,v) \\ C_G(u,v) \\ C_B(u,v) \end{bmatrix} \qquad (22)$$

where, $M_Y$ and $M_R$ are the coefficient matrices as described in equation (17) and (18) respectively.


## 4.2. Pseudo Pixel Extraction

We present a pseudo pixel extraction to extract color information directly from a limited number of DCT coefficients. The detailed mathematical derivation and experiments will be depicted in this section.

Without loss of generality, let us consider the DCT of $8 \times 8$ blocks that is commonly adopted in the compression of images and videos. In the pixel domain, the color values of the block do not change significantly due to the small block size. Therefore, we divide the block into four equivalent sub-blocks with the size $4 \times 4$ as shown in Figure 4(a). For each sub-block, we further assume that color values in the sub-block are homogenous and thus the averages of the 4 sub-blocks can be represented as $M_{11}$, $M_{12}$, $M_{21}$, $M_{22}$ respectively. The assumption is reasonable since the sub-block size is very small.

For 8x8 DCT defined in equation (1), as $i$ and $u$ varies, the angle $(2i+1)u\pi/16$ ranges within $[0,7\pi)$. To reduce the estimate error caused by Taylor extension, we initially transfer the angle into acute angle by a certain mathematical treatments. In fact, the expression $(2i+1)u$ ($i=0,1,2...,$ 7; $u=1,2,...,7$) in (1) can be rearranged into

$$(2i+1)u = 8(4k+l) + \beta_{i,u} \tag{23}$$

where $\beta_{i,u} = (2i+1)u \bmod 8$; $l = (((2i+1)u - \beta_{i,u}) \bmod 32)/8$; $k = [(2i+1)u/32]$ and the operators **mod** , [] are modulus and integer division respectively. This rearrangement can be confirmed point by point when both $i$ and $u$ varies within $[0, 7]$.

From equation (23), it can be seen that: $0 \le \beta_{i,u} < 8$ and $0 \le l < 4$. Therefore, we have:

$$\cos\left(\frac{8(4k+l)\pi + \beta_{i,u}\pi}{16}\right) = \begin{cases} \cos\dfrac{\beta_{i,u}\pi}{16} = \cos\dfrac{\gamma_{i,u}\pi}{16} & r_{i,u} = \beta_{i,u}, l = 0 \\ -\cos\dfrac{(8-\beta_{i,u})\pi}{16} = -\cos\dfrac{\gamma_{i,u}\pi}{16} & r_{i,u} = 8-\beta_{i,u}, l = 1 \\ -\cos\dfrac{\beta_{i,u}\pi}{16} = -\cos\dfrac{\gamma_{i,u}\pi}{16} & r_{i,u} = \beta_{i,u}, l = 2 \\ \cos\dfrac{(8-\beta_{i,u})\pi}{16} = \cos\dfrac{\gamma_{i,u}\pi}{16} & r_{i,u} = 8-\beta_{i,u}, l = 3 \end{cases}, = (-1)^{\left\lfloor\frac{l+1}{2}\right\rfloor}\cos(\frac{\gamma_{i,u}\pi}{16}) \tag{24}$$

This equation essentially transfers the angle $\dfrac{(2i+1)u\pi}{16}$ into the first

quadrant, and $\dfrac{\gamma_{i,u}\pi}{16}$ is a cute angle.

According to Taylor series, $\cos\dfrac{\gamma_{i,u}\pi}{16}$ at $\pi/4$ can be expanded into:

$$\cos(\gamma_{i,u}) = \cos(\frac{\pi}{4}) + \cos'(\frac{\pi}{4})(\frac{\gamma_{i,u}}{16} - \frac{\pi}{4}) + \cos''(\frac{\pi}{4})\frac{(\frac{\gamma_{i,u}}{16} - \frac{\pi}{4})^2}{2!} + ...$$

Since $|\gamma_{i,u} - \pi/4| < 1$ for all $\gamma_{i,u}$ and $u \neq 0$, the nonlinear terms in the above equation can be ignored. Hence, the equation can be approximately expressed as

$$\cos(\gamma_{i,u}) \approx \frac{\sqrt{2}}{2}(1 + \frac{4\pi - \gamma_{i,u}\pi}{16}) \tag{25}$$

Considering four top left DCT coefficients $C(0,0)$, $C(0,1)$, $C(1,0)$ and $C(1,1)$ within each block, their relationship with the four mean values in pixel domain (refer to Figure 4), $M_{11}$, $M_{12}$, $M_{21}$, $M_{22}$, can be obtained as follows from the earlier assumptions and the DCT definition:

180   G. Feng, A. Armstrong and J. Jiang

$$C(0,0) = \frac{1}{8}\sum_{i=0}^{7}\sum_{j=0}^{7} x(i,j) \Rightarrow M_{11} + M_{12} + M_{21} + M_{22} = C(0,0)/2 \quad (26)$$

and

$$C(1,0) = \frac{\sqrt{2}}{8}\sum_{i=0}^{7}\cos\left(\frac{(2i+1)\pi}{16}\right)\sum_{j=0}^{7} x(i,j) \approx$$

$$\frac{1}{8}\left\{\left[(1+\frac{3\pi}{16})\sum_{j=0}^{7} x(0,j) + (1+\frac{\pi}{16})\sum_{j=0}^{7} x(1,j) + (1-\frac{\pi}{16})\sum_{j=0}^{7} x(2,j) + (1-\frac{3\pi}{16})\sum_{j=0}^{7} x(3,j)\right]\right.$$
$$\left. -\left[(1-\frac{3\pi}{16})\sum_{j=0}^{7} x(4,j) + (1-\frac{\pi}{16})\sum_{j=0}^{7} x(5,j) + (1+\frac{\pi}{16})\sum_{j=0}^{7} x(2,j) + (1+\frac{3\pi}{16})\sum_{j=0}^{7} x(7,j)\right]\right\} \quad (27)$$

In the above equation, a weighted mean of
$$\left\{\sum_{j=0}^{7} x(0,j), \sum_{j=0}^{7} x(1,j), \sum_{j=0}^{7} x(2,j), \sum_{j=0}^{7} x(3,j)\right\}$$ can be regarded as being introduced,
which is represented as follows:

$$\frac{(1+\frac{3\pi}{16})\sum_{j=0}^{7} x(0,j) + (1+\frac{\pi}{16})\sum_{j=0}^{7} x(1,j) + (1-\frac{\pi}{16})\sum_{j=0}^{7} x(2,j) + (1-\frac{3\pi}{16})\sum_{j=0}^{7} x(3,j)}{(1+\frac{3\pi}{16}) + (1+\frac{\pi}{16}) + (1-\frac{\pi}{16}) + (1-\frac{3\pi}{16})} \quad (28)$$

By replacing the weighted mean given in expression (28) with the expression
$\left(\sum_{j=0}^{7} x(0,j) + \sum_{j=0}^{7} x(1,j) + \sum_{j=0}^{7} x(2,j) + \sum_{j=0}^{7} x(3,j)\right)\Big/4$, equation (27) can be approximated
by:

$$C(1,0) \approx \frac{1}{8}\left[16(M_{11} + M_{12}) - 16(M_{21} + M_{22})\right] \quad (29)$$

The error caused by the approximation can be estimated as

$$E = \left|3\pi\left(\sum_{j=0}^{7} x(0,j) - \sum_{j=0}^{7} x(3,j)\right) + \pi\left(\sum_{j=0}^{7} x(1,j) - \sum_{j=0}^{7} x(2,j)\right)\right|\Big/64 \quad (30)$$

Since the difference of the color or luminance values between the columns or the rows in the small block is minor, the above absolute error $E$ is very small in relation to $M_{11}$, $M_{12}$ and thus can be ignored. Therefore, we have:

$$M_{11} + M_{12} - M_{21} - M_{22} = C(1,0)/2 \quad (31)$$

The same conclusion can also be obtained for other DCT components via similar approximation procedures, which can be given below:

$$M_{11} - M_{12} + M_{21} - M_{22} = C(0,1)/2 \quad (32)$$

and

$$M_{11} - M_{12} - M_{21} + M_{22} = \sqrt{2}C(1,1)/4 \tag{33}$$

By solving equations of (26) and (31-33), we can obtain unique solution of the means of 4 sub-blocks $M_{11}$, $M_{12}$, $M_{21}$, $M_{22}$. This can be illustrated as follows.

$$M_{11} = \frac{2C(0,0) + 2C(1,0) + 2C(0,1) + \sqrt{2}C(1,1)}{16}$$

$$M_{12} = \frac{2C(0,0) + 2C(1,0) - 2C(0,1) - \sqrt{2}C(1,1)}{16} \tag{34}$$

$$M_{21} = \frac{2C(0,0) - 2C(1,0) + 2C(0,1) - \sqrt{2}C(1,1)}{16}$$

$$M_{22} = \frac{2C(0,0) - 2C(1,0) - 2C(0,1) + \sqrt{2}C(1,1)}{16}$$

The formula (34) concludes that the mean value of each sub-block can be computed approximately from only 4 DCT coefficients by a few very simple operations (three additions and one division). Since the mean values of four sub-blocks, $M_{11}$, $M_{12}$, $M_{21}$, $M_{22}$, are the average of all pixels inside each sub-block, they essentially represent the color information, and hence can be used to extract various features by existing image processing algorithms developed in pixel domain. As a result, a smaller version of the original image, which is one fourth of the original size, can be reconstructed by all the mean values obtained by equation (34). One such an example can be illustrated in part (c) of Figure 5. For the convenience of feature extraction by existing algorithms in pixel domain, the image can be enlarged by simply repeating each average value, $M_{ij}$, twice along both row and column directions. This enlargement is illustrated in part (d) of Figure 5. To obtain better results, various interpolation techniques such as bi-linear interpolation can be adopted, which is beyond the category of this paper. The significance of (34) lies in the fact that all image processing algorithms developed in pixel domain could be directly applied in DCT domain via a few simple computing operations given in (34).

Essentially, the proposed algorithm can be regarded as reconstructing an image only from its four top left DCT coefficients of each 8×8 block, instead of all DCT coefficients. The reconstruction, however, is not through IDCT of the four DCT coefficients, but through simple operations given in (34). Consequently, the computational cost and the memory consumption of the proposed method can be expected to be significantly lower than that of conventional approaches via IDCT. To distinguish the proposed technique from conventional decompression, we name the pixel extracted this way as *pseudo-pixel extraction*.

## 4.3. Performance Assessment

In order to evaluate the proposed algorithm, we select two conventional algorithms to act as the benchmark and make comparisons among their performances. The first one is full decompression via IDCT of all coefficients and the second one is partial decompression via IDCT of only four top left coefficients corresponding to those used in equation (34). Since DCT itself is a lossless process, we design our evaluation directly based on the original images and assume that the original image is reconstructed via IDCT of all coefficients.

The first phase of our experiments is to prove that our proposed algorithm achieves significant savings on computing cost when images are reconstructed. During the reconstruction process, those mean values derived from (34) inside each block of $4 \times 4$ pixels are simply repeated along the row and the column directions, in order to make the image the same size as that of its original one. The process is illustrated in Figure 5, where part (a) is the original image, which is equivalent to the reconstructed image by full IDCT of all coefficients; part (b) is the image reconstructed by IDCT of only 4 DCT coefficient, part (c) is the image reconstructed by the proposed, but the size of which is only 1/16 of the original image; and part (d) is its enlarged image.

Table 2 shows a full comparison of the computational costs among all the above three approaches, i.e., a full IDCT, partial IDCT of its four top left coefficients and the proposed method. From this Table, it is indicated that the number of multiplication, addition and storage for the proposed algorithm is only 1/64, 1/24 and 1/16 of the partial IDCT approach, which is the closest competitor to the proposed algorithm. Compared with the full DCT illustrated in the first row of Table-2, the savings on computing cost are even more significant.

The second phase intends to prove that the reconstructed image by our proposed algorithm is of high quality benchmarked by the two conventional approaches, i.e., the full IDCT and partial IDCT. In other words, the reconstructed image by our proposed algorithm retains all features inside the original image since the difference between the two is indeed trivial. Following this line, we constructed a group of test images and applied our proposed algorithm to reconstruct all of them and then calculate their PSNR values with respect to their original ones. Table 3 presents all the results obtained through such experiments, from which it can be seen that high PSNR values are maintained throughout the whole group of sample images by our proposed algorithm. Consequently, it can be established that, since there exists little difference between the reconstructed images and their original ones, any pixel-domain image processing techniques, when applied to the reconstructed image by our proposed algorithm, will achieve similar or competitive performances in comparison with that of original images (full IDCT). Yet the computing cost incurred will be substantially lower than that of full IDCT.

Table 3 also shows that the PSNR values obtained by partial IDCT are slightly higher than that of our proposed algorithm. To illustrate that the two reconstructed images are indeed very close, the third row of Table 3 offers the average distance between the image reconstructed by partial IDCT and the image reconstructed by the pseudo pixel method for all samples tested. The results show that the distance for all images are less than 0.02 (maximum intensity is 255), which is indeed insignificant, considering the enormous savings achieved on computing cost.

To further illustrate the quality comparison between the reconstructed image by the proposed algorithm and the original one, Figure 6 presents all samples for visual inspection, in which reconstructed image is enlarged by simple repetition of mean values of $M_{11}$, $M_{12}$, $M_{21}$, $M_{22}$.


### 4.4. Remarks and Discussions

This section developed a novel algorithm to extract color information directly from DCT domain. Due to the fact that the color information extracted by the proposed algorithm is essentially the average of pixels inside a small sub-block, all image processing algorithms developed in pixel domain can be directly operated for those DCT coefficients with only a small amount of overhead computing cost. Therefore, the work can be regarded as creating a bridge between the pixel domain and the DCT domain, which allows the image processing techniques designed in pixel domain directly operate in DCT domain without compromising their performances. This is supported by two phases of our experiments. The first phase certifies that significant savings on computing cost can be achieved by the proposed algorithm. The second phase confirms that the reconstructed image bears little difference from the original image.

## 5. Application in the Online Web Image Retrieval

The majority of images on the Internet are currently stored in the JPEG compression format (jpg files). This format applies DCT-based data compression techniques to achieve large amount of compression and thus the file size has been significantly reduced. Such compression is necessary to make it suitable for WEB-based applications in the sense that: (a)downloading speed is increased and (b) storage space is reduced. Yet on the other hand, most of content-based image retrieval techniques are developed in pixel domain where full images are always assumed to be available for feature extraction and analysis. For compressed images, this means that full decompression is the prerequisite for such image retrieval systems. To bridge the gap, research is now gathering paces to develop direct retrieval algorithms in compressed domain [13, 16-17, 20, 23]. In this direction, existing work can be classified as: (a) constructing indexing keys in the process of data compression [13, 16]; and (b) directly extract feature for indexing keys in compressed domain. The former category essentially builds up a signature containing a number of keys for each image before it is stored and compressed. When retrieval is performed, only the signature needs to be involved and the compressed images will not be touched until they are retrieved as the targets. This type of retrieval technique involving data compression is not suitable for WEB image retrieval simply because WEB images are already in compressed format at the source, and they are not indexed. The latter provides better tools in the sense that features of contents are directly extracted in compressed domain, in which majority of them extract features in transform domain, such as DCT [2, 23], wavelets [16], Fourier or principal components etc.[17], rather than compressed codes.

In this chapter, as an application of the pseudo pixel extraction in image indexing and retrieval in JPEG compressed domain, we develop an on-line image indexing and retrieval technique. As it is suitable for WEB image browsing, This section will describe our design of an automatic and WEB-based image retrieval system named as *ImageHunter*. Its framework is shown as Figure 7.


### 5.1. WEB-based On-line Image Retrieval System

As shown in Figure 1, the last step of DCT-based JPEG decoder is IDCT. According to the above description, for a given JPEG format image, the step is needed to display it, However, it is not obligatory to extract the features of the compressed image. Hence, our on-line image indexing system, *ImageHunter,* would require entropy decoding to get us into quantized DCT coefficients domain, and then perform feature extraction to build up indexing keys. Further browsing would also need distance calculation for those indexing keys and match with the query image to decide whether or not this image could be retrieved as one of our targets.

In the *ImageHunter* system, to extract content information from DCT domain, we exploit the equation (34) to extract approximated values of four average pixels inside each sub-block of $4 \times 4$ pixels. This is significant in the sense that we only need 8 additions , 4 multiplications and 4 units storage to extract the four average pixels without full decompression at all.

To build up a WEB-based image retrieval system, various image-indexing techniques are required. At this stage, however, our major concern is to see whether or not our proposed pseudo-pixel image can provide competitive performance for any existing indexing techniques, and prove the concept that direct searches on the WEB for similar image content is feasible. To this end, we adopted two existing image-indexing techniques based on color [10] and texture [3]. The color-based indexing technique maps the normal $\{R, G, B\}$ space into a so-called $\{C_4C_5C_6\}$ space by the following equation:

$$\{C_4C_5C_6\} = \begin{cases} C_4(RGB) = \dfrac{R-G}{R+G} \\ C_5(RGB) = \dfrac{R-B}{R+G} \\ C_6(RGB) = \dfrac{G-B}{R+G} \end{cases} \tag{35}$$

To extract invariant color features, a 3D histogram can be constructed by incrementing a counter each time a $\{C_4C_5C_6\}$ value is equal to a value of index $\{i,j,k\}$. The histogram is obtained as follows:

$$H(C_4C_5C_6) = \frac{\eta(\{C_4 = i\} \cap \{C_5 = j\} \cap \{C_6 = k\})}{X \times Y} \ \forall i, j, \ k \in \Omega = [0,255] \tag{36}$$

where $\eta(.)$ stands for the counting operation, $\cap$ the and operation, and $X \times Y$ the image size.

The texture key construction is carried out by a simple LBP (local binary partition) technique [3]. Each input image is processed as $3 \times 3$ blocks. Each centroid pixel $P$ is examined with its eight surrounding pixels to see if it is greater in intensity than its neighbors. If it is greater a bit value of 1 is stored, otherwise a bit value of 0 will be stored. In this way, the eight results can be stored in a single byte. A histogram can be constructed by counting the number of times that each state of $P$ is equal to an integer value varying from 1 to the total number of pixels inside the image. This is given as follows:

$$H(P) = \frac{\tau(state(P) = i)}{X \times Y} \qquad \forall i \in \Omega = [0, 255] \qquad (37)$$

It is worth noting that further gains can be made by processing the keys generated [2] so that they can represent the image more efficiently. In addition, more indexing key techniques can also be added to improve the retrieving performance, which would be left for further work since our concern here is to prove the concept.

The proposed system, *ImageHunter,* uses the framework described in Figure 7. The system has two modes of operation, real-time and offline. Real-time deals with queries and results, while the offline mode focuses on gathering addresses and indexing keys.

Online mode accepts two types of query, an example image in the JPEG format (upload) or the address of a query image as a URL (Uniform resource locator). The latter function can also be used to increase browser functionality, via a plug-in, to allow searches from images on any web site with the simple click of a button. Once the system is given an image it is transported to a temporary area of the system for processing. It is worth noting that the interface provided for image upload is via a standard Internet browser, allowing access from anywhere in the world.

Key generation normally requires the decoding of the image (full or otherwise). Using a generic decoding module, various methods can be used to obtain the pixel information needed. For the convenience of comparisons and options, we designed full IDCT, partial IDCT and the proposed pseudo pixel method to reconstruct pixel information within the same framework. The feature extraction code works on this data to produce color ($\{C_4 C_5 C_6\}$) or texture (LBP) keys. Once all the necessary key information is generated, the key data is then passed to the searching stage.

The distance measurement used in the database search is based on the simple 1D distance illustrated in equation (38), which is chosen on account of its simplicity and low computing cost.

$$Dist(Query, Test) = \sum_{i=1} \left| (Qh_i - Th_i) \right| \qquad (38)$$

where *Dist* is the distance calculated, *Qh* the query histogram, *Qh* the histogram being worked on and $i$ varies from 1 to the total number of elements inside the histogram.

Once all the distances between the query and the database images are calculated, the results parser removes any duplicate images and organizes the data to determine the top twelve matches. These results are then sent to the Output Generator whose function is to format the results for display. One example of our output is shown in Figure 9.

The output generator accesses the address information for the images and generates a page-using standard html (Hypertext Mark-up Language). Using the full URL (Uniform Resource Locator) the image thumbnails are displayed directly from the site they are stored. If a user wishes to download one of the images, they are redirected to the page where it was found. Any copyright issues are then placed at the discretion of the user. Figure 8 shows a sample screenshot for an output generated using texture-based keys.

One key feature of our system is the ability to allow the user to submit one of the returned images as a new query image. This 'More like these' function allows the user to refine searches based on those hits thought to be most suitable. This method produces results quickly as the necessary indexing keys are already generated.

The offline system runs independently of the real-time online mode. Concerned only with obtaining and indexing images, it is designed to run automatically and continuously. The offline system is capable of spawning a number of duplicate processes, allowing as many indexing and update processes as processor bandwidth allows.

Primarily the spiders deal with obtaining data from web sites; however they have options to work locally, i.e. server image databases. These spiders scan web pages looking for image files. When found, a process is initiated to generate the key for the image; this is stored in the database along with the full URL of the image. It is worth noting that once the keys are generated the image file downloaded is removed from the system; eliminating the need to actually store the original images, saving space and preventing copyright infringements. When all of the images on a page are exhausted, the spiders look for links to other sites and the process is repeated. In the case of the Internet these process run continuously, stopping only when either storage space is exhausted or when pre-defined criteria is met. The spiders can also be set to update the database, removing dead links and re-scanning pages that have been modified.

### 5.2. Experiments and analysis

To assess our system, we implemented 3 algorithms for both texture and color keys giving a total of 6, these are as follows:

Full decompression – the image is fully decompressed and the keys are generated using all pixel information available.

Partial IDCT – Keys are generated from the image reconstructed from using the IDCT only with the first four coefficients (following the zigzag), i.e., DC, $AC_1 - AC_3$.

Our pseudo pixel technique – The Keys are generated from the 1/16 sized reconstructed image from the pseudo-pixel information extracted.

In the experiment design, the two algorithms, full decompression and partial decompression, are mainly used as the benchmark to assess the proposed pseudo pixel method. The test images were each processed in the same way without any optimizations or pre-processing. The system analyzed the images and generated the keys off-line so that un-necessary, real-time, key generation was avoided. A database of over 10,000 images was processed in this way, resulting in 6 sets of keys.

Ten query images were selected at random, simulating the demands placed on a general-purpose image retrieval system. 50 volunteers were asked to rank the results of each query image for each algorithm. The scoring system involved the volunteer to rank the first five hits generated from the query image, with a score between 1 and 5 (5 being a very good match). These perceived relevancy results were then calculated as overall percentages for each of the decoding algorithms, which are summarized in Table 4. The following equations summarize the process:

$$E_p(i) = \frac{1}{k}\sum_1^k S_p(i) \tag{39}$$

$$\Gamma_p(i) = (\frac{E_p(i)}{n}) * 100 \tag{40}$$

$$Tr(i) = \frac{1}{x}\sum_{p=1}^x \Gamma_p(i) \tag{41}$$

where $k$ is the number of images in the set, $S_p$ is the score (between 1 and 5), $E_p(i)$ is the average score for rank $i$ for all images in the set. $\Gamma_p$ is the average rank score expressed as a percentage (n is the maximum score allocated, i.e. 5 for [1-5] range), Tr is the average rank score for all participants. $p$ is the index of each individual participant and $x$ the total number of participants.

Table 5 shows how much the alternative methods differ from the original. Percentages preceded by a minus symbol indicate that the difference was in favor of the alternative method. Little emphasis should be placed on those values, which suggest that the proposed methods perform better than the original, as the test is entirely perceptual. However, these results can be interpreted as indicating that the performance of all the systems is very similar in terms of retrieval accuracy.

As the database contained a large amount of random images, further experiments were carried out to perform searches on known images. Some 192 images were captured of people, objects and scenery with a digital camera. These contained several pictures of the same object, taken from several angles, filling various parts of the frame. There were some sixteen objects in the image set, each with twelve variants. Each method was tested and rated on how many of the 16 images were returned in the top twelve hits. The results varied between the color and texture keys but insignificantly between their variants. For images of a particular scene, texture keys returned good results, often returning the complete set of 12 images. Texture only faltered in scenes where the camera was rotated between shots this was a result caused by the lack of rotational invariance present in the LBP technique. Color keys successfully returned scenes of a similar color but not necessarily the siblings of the query image. Such results seemed to be caused by the limited amount of content data the color keys describe (unlike texture). It is suggested that a combination of both will return indeed better images.

The success of the methods can only be truly rated in relation to the application they are intended to be used for. For exact image matches, such as a face recognition system, both are unlikely to perform adequately. But is used in an image search system where not identical, but similar matches are required the systems will perform well, and at low cost.


### 5.3. Remarks and discussions

The results show that the keys generated from the proposed pseudo-pixel method produce results that were identical or very comparable to the keys generated from the fully reconstructed image and the partial decoded image (IDCT of four coefficients). The performance savings are significant - a very important factor when considering the vast amounts of image data that are stored on systems, especially via the Internet.

The performance of the retrieval system as a whole was good. Many suitable matches were found within the twelve results returned, primarily in the first three. Inclusions of feedback technology will no doubt increase the performance and tailor the results to the individual's requirements.

The results showed that what some people considered excellent results, others thought was only a reasonable match. The key problem areas lie in the user expectation. For example, if a car was sent as a query image, is the user looking for cars in general, that particular car, that particular color, similar scenes with the same background etc? It seems unlikely that a simple technology will be able to suffice all the various needs, however if in the ten or so highest matches returned the user can find what they are looking for, then the system will be very useful. In this paper, we mainly dealt with the efficiency problem by proposing a pseudo-pixel method to design a WEB-based image retrieval system, which features in extracting content information from JPEG compressed images without full decompression, yet the retrieval performance remains very competitive as evidenced by our experiments on texture and color keys. To improve the system, more robust indexing techniques such as object-based, shape based, spatial relationship, and relevance feedback etc. can be added to provide more choices for users to decide which key would best represent their intention for content search in an image database or the whole WEB. This can be regarded as further work for our WEB-based image retrieval system.

## 6. Conclusions

To directly extract the feature of image from DCT domain, we develop on the spatial relationship of DCT block and its subblocks, the pseudo pixel extraction from limited DCT coefficient. The first algorithm can be applied in transferring different size DCT blocks and JPEG image progressive decoding and pyramid algorithm. The latter and its application in web image retrieval for the JPEG compressed image. The fact that the reconstructed images by the pseudo pixel algorithm have competitive quality as that of images reconstructed by full decompression. Yet the computing cost and the storage expense of the proposed algorithm are significantly lower than that of full decompression. The significance of our contribution can be highlighted as enabling all image processing techniques developed in pixel domain being directly applied to DCT domain without going through full decompression or IDCT. This serves as a highly efficient bridge between the compressed images in JPEG compressed domain and all image processing techniques in pixel domain. As an application in image indexing and retrieval in JPEG compressed domain, we develop an on-line image indexing and retrieval technique based on a pseudo-pixel extraction algorithm. The results show that the keys generated from the proposed pseudo-pixel method produce results that were identical or very comparable to the keys generated from the fully reconstructed image and the partial decoded image. The performance savings are significant - a very important factor when considering the vast amounts of image data that are stored on systems, especially via the Internet.

## Acknowledgements

The authors would like to thank Dr. Mike Reddy, Dr. C. Grecos and Mr. G. Voulgaris for their useful discussions and suggestions related to the work presented in this chapter.

## References


1. Abdel-Malek, A. A. and Hershey, J. E., Feature cueing in the discrete cosine domain, *Journal of Electronic Imaging*, Vol.3, pp.71-80, 1994.
2. Armstrong A. and Jiang, J.  An efficient image indexing algorithm in JPEG compressed domain, Accepted by *Int. Conf. of IEEE Consumer Electronics(ICCE'2001)*, USA, June, 2001.
3. Berman A.P. and Shapiro L.G., A flexible image database system for content-based retrieval, *Computer Vision and Image Understanding*, Vol.75, No1-2, pp175-195, 1999 .
4. Bhaskaran. V. and Konstanti, K., *Image and Video Compression Standards: Algorithms and Architectures,* Boston: Kluwer Academic Publications, 1997.
5. Cox, I. J. *et al*, The Bayesian image retrieval system, PicHunter: theory, implementation, and psychophysical experiments, *IEEE Trans. on Image Processing*, Vol. 9, No.1, pp 20-37, 2000.
6. Eickeler, S.,  Muller, S. and Rigoll,G.,  Recognition of JPEG compressed face images based on statistical methods, *Image and Vision Computing,* Vol.18, pp.279-287, 2000.

7. Faloutsos C., Barber R. and Flickner, M. *et al*, Efficient and effective querying by image content, *Journal of Intelligent Information System,* Vol.3, No.3, pp.231-262, 1994.

8. Feng, G. C. and Jiang, J., Image spatial transformation in DCT domain, Accepted by *Int. Conf. of Image Procesing( (ICIP'2001)*, Greece, Oct, 2001.

9. Flickner, M. *et. al.*, Query by image and video content: The QBIC system, *IEEE Computer*, No.9, pp 23-32, 1995.

10. Gevers T. and Smeulders A., PicToSeek: Combining color and shape invariant features for image retrieval, *IEEE Trans. On Image Processing,* Vol. 9, No. 1, pp.102-119, 2000.

11. Gonzalez, R. C. and Woods, R., *Digital Image Processing*, Reading: Addison-Wesley Publications, 1993.

12. Hernandez, J. R., Amado, M. and Gonzalez, F. P., DCT-domain watermarking techniques for still images: Detector Performance Analysis and a New Structure , *IEEE Trans. On Image Processing*, Vol. 9, No.1, pp.55-68, 2000.

13. Jiang J., Image compression and indexing with neural networks *Journal of Visual Communication and Image Representation*. Vol.8, No.2, pp135-145, 1997.

14. Jiang, J., Liu, M. G. and Hou, C. H., Content-based image indexing in the process of lossless data compression , submitted to *IEEE Trans. on Image Processing*, Nov. 2000.

15. Kou, E. and Fjaellbrant, T., A direct computation of DCT coefficients for a signal block taken from two adjacent blocks , *IEEE Trans. Signal Processing*, Vol. 39, No. 7, pp.1692-1695, 1991.

16. Liang, K. C. and Kuo, C. C., Waveguide: a joint wavelet-based image representation and description system IEEE Trans. Image Processing, Vol.8, No.11, pp.1619-1629, 1999.

17. Mandal M. K., Idris, F. and Panchanathan S., A critical evaluation of image and video indexing techniques in the compressed domain, *Image and Vision Computing Journal*, Vol.17, pp. 513-529, 1999.

18. Methtre, B. M., Kankanhalli, M. S. and Lee, W. F., Shape measures for content based image retrieval: A comparison, *Information Processing & Management*, Vol.33, No.3, pp319-337,1997.

19. Ng, I.,Tan, T. and Kitter J., On local linear transform and Gabor filter representation of texture, *Proc. Of the 11<sup>th</sup> Intl. Conf. On Pattern Recognition*, pp.627-631, 1992.

20. Pajarola, R. and Widmayer, P., An image compression method for spatial search, *IEEE Trans. Image Processing*, Vol.9, No.3, pp357-365, 2000.

21. Reeves, R., Kubik, K. and Osberger, W., Texture characterization of compressed aerial images using DCT coefficients, *Proc. of SPIE: Storge and Retrival for Image and Video Databases V*, Vol.3022, pp.398-407, Feb, 1997.

22. Shen, B. and Sethi, I. K., Direct feature extraction from compressed images , *SPIE: Vol.2670 Storage & Retrieval for Image and Video Databases* IV, 1996.

23. Shneier, M. and Abdel-Mottaleb, M., Exploiting the JPEG compression scheme for image retrieval, *IEEE Trans on Pattern Analysis and Machine Intelligence*, No.8, 1996.
24. Skodras, A. N.,  Direct transform to computation , *IEEE Signal Processing Letters*, Vol. No.8, pp.202-204, 1999.
25. Smith, J. R. and Chang, S. F., Transform feature for texture classification and discrimination in large image database, *Proc. of IEEE Intl. Conf. on Image Processing*, Vol. 3, pp. 407-411,1994.
26. Wallace, G. K, The JPEG still picture compression standard, *Communication of the ACM*, Vol.34, No.4, pp31-45,1991.

| Traditional algorithm | | The proposed algorithm | |
|---|---|---|---|
| Addition | Multiplication | Addition | Multiplication |
| Composition from $N{\times}N$ to $2N{\times}2N$ | | | |
| 8N(N-1) | $8N^2$ | 4N(N-1) | $2N^2$ |
| Decomposition from $N{\times}N$ to $(N/2){\times}(N/2)$ | | | |
| 2(N-2)N | $2N^2$ | $2N+N^2$ | $(2N+N^2)/2$ |

Table 1. Comparison of computation cost

| Algorithms | Computation cost | | Storage expense |
|---|---|---|---|
| | Multiplication | Addition | |
| The full IDCT | 4096 | 4032 | 64 units |
| IDCT of only 4 coefficients | 256 | 192 | 64 units |
| The proposed method | 4 | 8 | 4 units |

Table 2. Comparison of computational complexity between conventional IDCT and the pseudo pixel

| Image Samples | | Lena | Baboon | Boat | Truck | Zelda | Jet | Barb | Clown |
|---|---|---|---|---|---|---|---|---|---|
| PSNR | Partial IDCT | 28.55 | 21.06 | 25.57 | 29.17 | 32.19 | 25.72 | 23.77 | 23.55 |
| | Pseudo pixel | 27.25 | 20.76 | 24.75 | 28.38 | 30.65 | 24.59 | 23.28 | 22.48 |
| Distance of two constructed images | | 0.0105 | 0.0124 | 0.0128 | 0.0082 | 0.0079 | 0.0143 | 0.0109 | 0.0361 |

Table 3. PSNR and distance of the reconstructed images by two algorithms

| Algorithms | Rank 1% | Rank 2% | Rank 3% | Rank 4% | Rank 5% |
|---|---|---|---|---|---|
| IDCT Colour | 52 | 43 | 64.5 | 52.5 | 60 |
| IDCT 4 Colour | 51 | 50 | 52 | 53 | 49.5 |
| PP Colour | 60 | 52.5 | 47 | 50 | 54 |

| IDCT Texture | 53.5 | 54.5 | 72 | 72 | 52.5 |
|---|---|---|---|---|---|
| IDCT 4 Texture | 54 | 73 | 66 | 53.5 | 48 |
| PP Texture | 62 | 80 | 80 | 72 | 76 |

Table 4. Test results showing perceived % relevancy

| Algorithms | Rank 1% | Rank 2% | Rank 3% | Rank 4% | Rank 5% |
|---|---|---|---|---|---|
| IDCT Colour | 52 | 43 | 64.5 | 52.5 | 60 |
| IDCT 4 Colour | 1 | -7 | 12.5 | -0.5 | 10.5 |
| PP Colour | -8 | -9.5 | 17.5 | 2.5 | 6 |
| IDCT Texture | 53.5 | 54.5 | 72 | 72 | 52.5 |
| IDCT 4 Texture | -0.5 | -18.5 | 6 | 18.5 | 4.5 |
| PP Texture | -8.5 | -25.5 | -8 | 0 | -23.5 |

Table 5. Test results indicating difference between % relevancy
Note: IDCT – full decompression; IDCT4 – partial decompression via IDCT of four
coefficients (DC, $AC_1$ to $AC_3$); and PP – pseudo-pixel method.

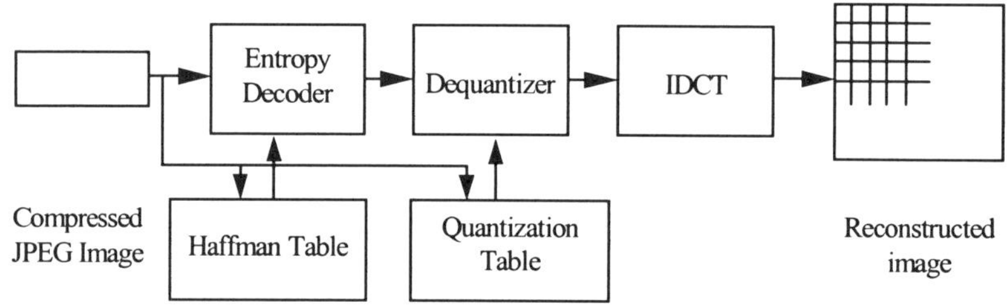


Figure 1. Block diagram of a DCT-based JPEG decoder

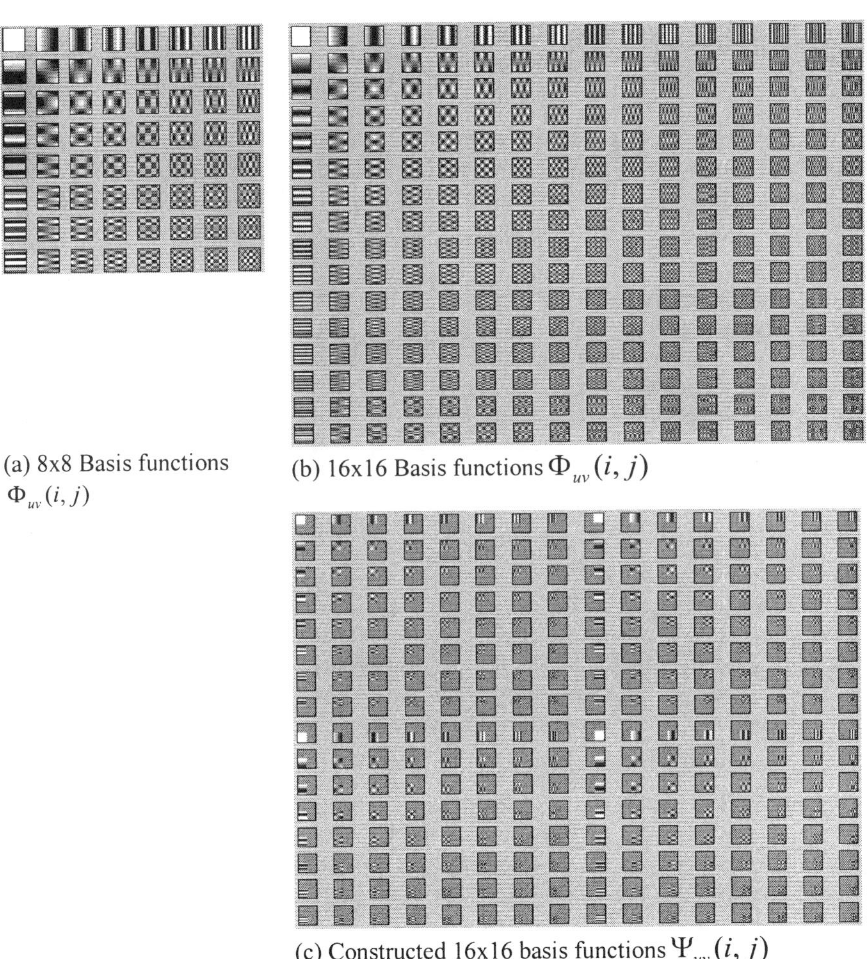

(a) 8x8 Basis functions $\Phi_{uv}(i,j)$

(b) 16x16 Basis functions $\Phi_{uv}(i,j)$

(c) Constructed 16x16 basis functions $\Psi_{uv}(i,j)$

Figure 2. Basis functions for 2-D DCT

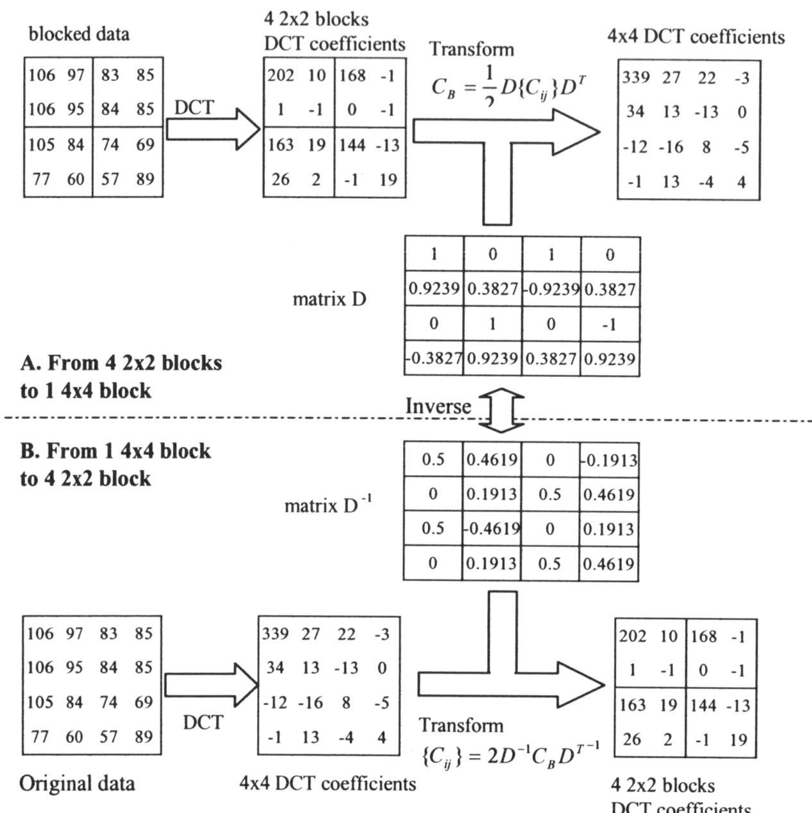


$$C_B = \frac{1}{2} D\{C_{ij}\}D^T$$

$$\{C_{ij}\} = 2D^{-1}C_B D^{T^{-1}}$$

Figure 3. The example for DCT coefficients exchange between 4 2x2 blocks and 1 4x4 block

| $x_{0,0}$ $x_{0,1}$ $x_{0,2}$ $x_{0,3}$ | $x_{0,4}$ $x_{0,5}$ $x_{0,6}$ $x_{0,7}$ |
|---|---|
| $x_{1,0}$ $\quad\quad x_{1,3}$ | $x_{1,4}$ $\quad\quad x_{1,7}$ |
| $x_{2,0}\quad M_{11}\quad x_{2,3}$ | $x_{2,4}\quad M_{12}\quad x_{2,7}$ |
| $x_{3,0}$ $x_{3,1}$ $x_{3,2}$ $x_{3,3}$ | $x_{3,4}$ $x_{3,5}$ $x_{3,6}$ $x_{3,7}$ |
| $x_{4,0}$ $x_{4,1}$ $x_{4,2}$ $x_{4,3}$ | $x_{4,4}$ $x_{4,5}$ $x_{4,6}$ $x_{4,7}$ |
| $x_{5,0}$ $\quad\quad x_{5,3}$ | $x_{5,4}$ $\quad\quad x_{5,7}$ |
| $x_{6,0}\quad M_{21}\quad x_{6,3}$ | $x_{6,4}\quad M_{22}\quad x_{6,7}$ |
| $x_{7,0}$ $x_{7,1}$ $x_{7,2}$ $x_{7,3}$ | $x_{7,4}$ $x_{7,5}$ $x_{7,6}$ $x_{7,7}$ |

(a)  Pixel domain

| $C_{0,0}$ | $C_{0,1}$ | $C_{0,2}$ | $C_{0,3}$ | $C_{0,4}$ | $C_{0,5}$ | $C_{0,6}$ | $C_{0,7}$ |
|---|---|---|---|---|---|---|---|
| $C_{1,0}$ | $C_{1,1}$ | $C_{1,2}$ | $C_{1,3}$ | $C_{1,4}$ | $C_{1,5}$ | $C_{1,6}$ | $C_{1,7}$ |
| $C_{2,0}$ | $C_{2,1}$ | $C_{2,2}$ | $C_{2,3}$ | $C_{2,4}$ | $C_{2,5}$ | $C_{2,6}$ | $C_{2,7}$ |
| $C_{3,0}$ | $C_{3,1}$ | $C_{3,2}$ | $C_{3,3}$ | $C_{3,4}$ | $C_{3,5}$ | $C_{3,6}$ | $C_{3,7}$ |
| $C_{4,0}$ | $C_{4,1}$ | $C_{4,2}$ | $C_{4,3}$ | $C_{4,4}$ | $C_{4,5}$ | $C_{4,6}$ | $C_{4,7}$ |
| $C_{5,0}$ | $C_{5,1}$ | $C_{5,2}$ | $C_{5,3}$ | $C_{5,4}$ | $C_{5,5}$ | $C_{5,6}$ | $C_{5,7}$ |
| $C_{6,0}$ | $C_{6,1}$ | $C_{6,2}$ | $C_{6,3}$ | $C_{6,4}$ | $C_{6,5}$ | $C_{6,6}$ | $C_{6,7}$ |
| $C_{7,0}$ | $C_{7,1}$ | $C_{7,2}$ | $C_{7,3}$ | $C_{7,4}$ | $C_{7,5}$ | $C_{7,6}$ | $C_{7,7}$ |

(b) DCT domain

Figure 4. (a) Division of 8x8 block into sub-blocks; and (b) 4 selected upper-left
DCT coefficients

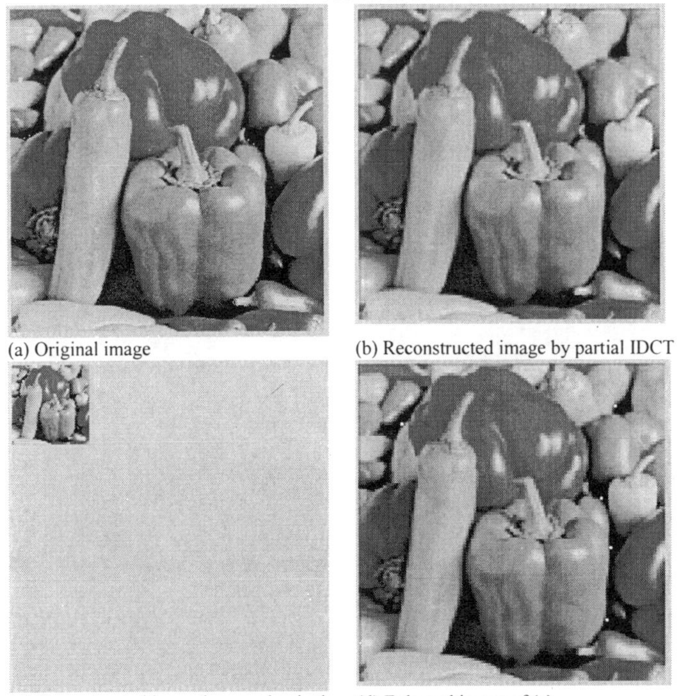

(a) Original image

(b) Reconstructed image by partial IDCT

(c) Reconstructed image by pseudo pixel

(d) Enlarged image of (c)

Figure 5. Comparison of images between the proposed method and the benchmarks

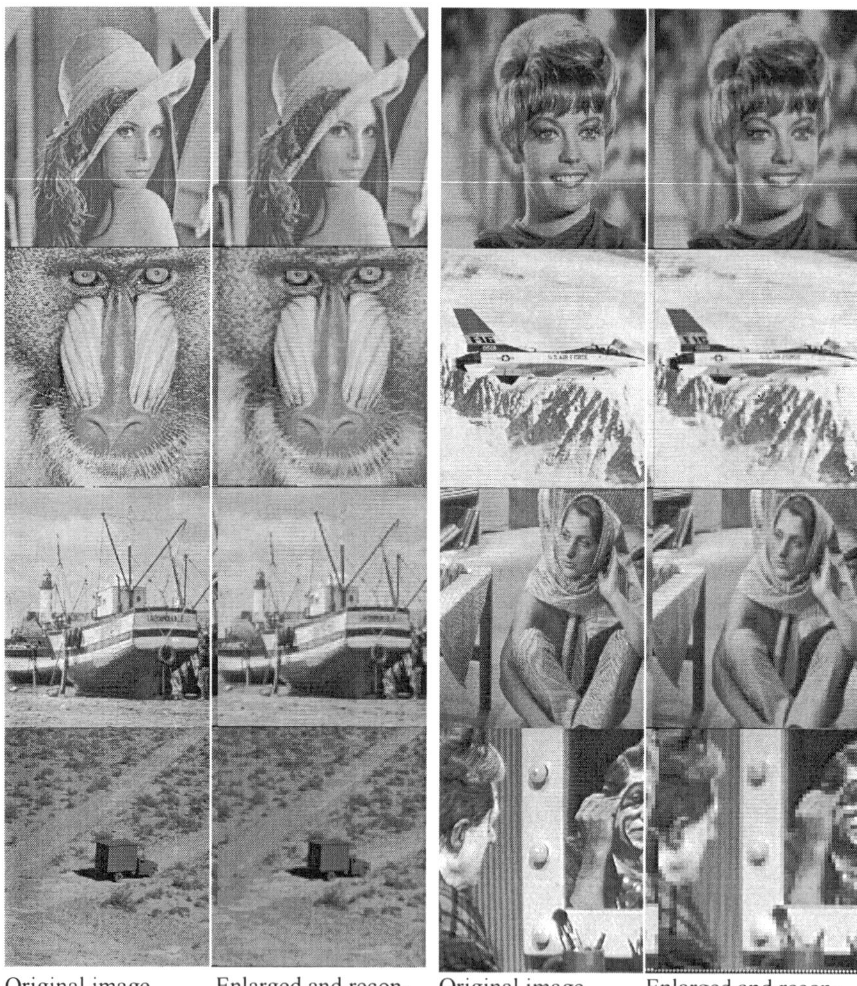

<table>
<tr><td>Original image</td><td>Enlarged and recon-<br>structed image</td><td>Original image</td><td>Enlarged and recon-<br>structed image</td></tr>
</table>

Figure 6. Visual comparison between the original images and the reconstructed ones by pseudo pixel extraction

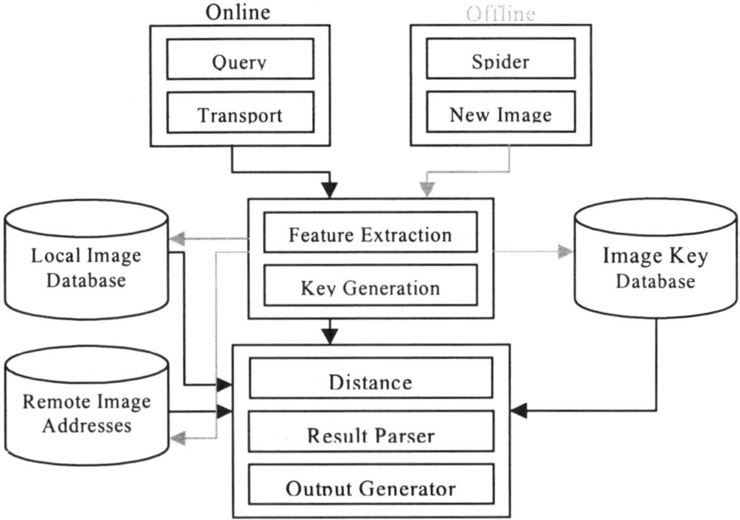


Figure 7. Image retrieval framework

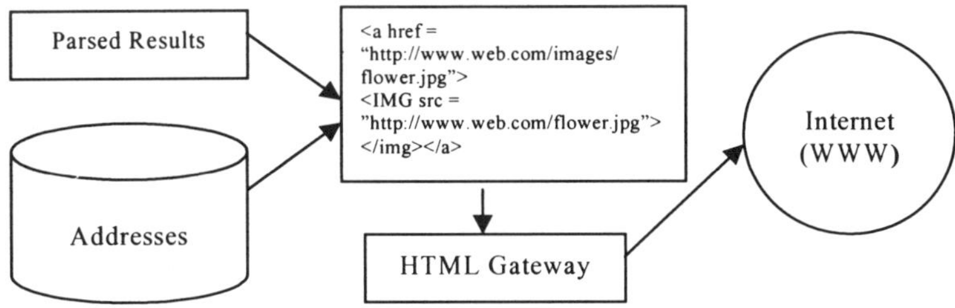


Figure 8. The output module, converts local and remote references to standard HTML for web browsers

Figure 9. Sample database output (PP Texture)

# Part IV  Multimodality Systems

# Advances in the Robust Processing of Multimodal Speech and Pen Systems[‡]

Sharon Oviatt

*Center for Human-Computer Communication*

*Department of Computer Science & Engineering*

*Oregon Graduate Institute of Science & Technology*

*20000 N.W. Walker Road, Beaverton, Oregon USA 97006*

*Email: oviatt@cse.ogi.edu*

Multimodal systems have developed rapidly during the past decade, with progress toward building more general and robust systems, as well as more transparent and usable human interfaces. These next-generation multimodal systems aim to improve the expressive power and efficiency of human interfaces, to expand the accessibility of computing for diverse and disabled users, to enhance the performance stability and robustness of recognition-

[‡] This research was supported by **Grant No.** IRI-9530666 from the National Science Foundation, Special Extension for Creativity (SEC) Grant No. IIS-9530666 from the National Science Foundation, Contracts DABT63-95-C-007 and N66001-99-D-8503 from DARPA's Information Technology and Information Systems offices, and Grant No. N00014-99-1-0377 from ONR. Figures 1 & 2 are reprinted here with permission of LEA, Inc.

based systems, and to support new forms of computing. In this chapter, we describe the QuickSet multimodal pen/voice system, including its functionality, interface design, natural language processing and fusion techniques, overall architecture, applications and performance. We also summarize results from two recent empirical studies with QuickSet in which its multimodal architecture is shown to decrease failures in spoken language processing by 19-41%. This performance improvement mainly is due to the mutual disambiguation of input signals that is possible within a multimodal architecture, which occurs at higher levels for challenging user groups (accented versus native speakers) and usage environments (mobile versus stationary use). This research demonstrates that new multimodal architectures can stabilize error-prone recognition technologies, and yield major improvements in system robustness.


## Introduction

Multimodal systems have developed rapidly during the past decade, with progress toward building more general and robust systems, as well as more transparent and usable human interfaces (Oviatt et al., 2000). Major developments have occurred in the hardware and software needed to support component technologies incorporated within multimodal systems, as well as in techniques for integrating parallel input streams. Multimodal systems also have diversified to include new mode combinations, including speech and pen input, speech and lip movements, speech and manual gesturing, and gaze tracking and manual input (Benoit & Le Goff, 1998; Cohen et al., 1997; Stork & Hennecke, 1995; Turk & Robertson, 2000; Zhai, Morimoto & Ihde, 1999). In addition, the array of multimodal applications has expanded rapidly, and presently ranges from map-based and virtual reality systems for simulation and training, to person identification/verification systems for security purposes, to medical and web-based transaction systems that will transform our daily lives (Neti, Iyengar, Potamianos, & Senior, 2000: Oviatt et al., 2000; Pankanti, Bolle, & Jain, 2000). These next-generation multimodal systems aim to improve the expressive power and efficiency of human interfaces, to expand the accessibility of computing for diverse and disabled users, to enhance the performance stability and robustness of recognition-based systems, and to support new forms of computing.

Cumulative evidence now clarifies that a well-designed multimodal system that fuses two or more information sources can be an effective means of reducing recognition uncertainty (Adjoudani & Benoit, 1995; Neti et al., 2000; Oviatt, 1999 & 2000; Tomlinson, Russell, & Brooke, 1996). Furthermore, the error suppression achievable with a multimodal system, compared with a unimodal spoken language system, can be relatively large (Oviatt, 1999 & 2000). In the present chapter, the QuickSet multimodal system and its capabilities are introduced. In addition, the results of two recent empirical studies conducted with QuickSet are summarized. This research reveals that a multimodal architecture can support mutual disambiguation of input signals, which can substantially improve the robustness and performance stability of the system.

## The QuickSet Multimodal System

### *Interface and Application*

QuickSet is an agent-based collaborative multimodal system that runs on a handheld PC. QuickSet enables a user to create and position entities on a map with speech, pen-based gestures, and direct manipulation (Cohen et al., 1997). These entities then can be used to initialize a simulation. The user can create entities by speaking their names or descriptions, while simultaneously indicating their location or shape with an electronic pen. For example, a jeep could be created at a specific location and orientation by saying "Jeep facing this way <draws arrow>." Users also can control entities in a simulation, for example by saying "Jeep, follow this evacuation route <draws line>" while gesturing the exact route with the pen. The QuickSet interface is illustrated in Figure 1 running on a hand-held PC. In addition to processing combined multimodal input, user commands can be given just using speech or gesture as individual input modalities.

### *Gesture and Speech Signal Recognition*

QuickSet recognizes symbols and gestures such as points, lines, arrows, and deletion, as well as military symbology such as units and control measures (e.g., barbed wire, fortification). In Quickset, all pen-based and spoken input is time-stamped to mark its beginning and end. For pen-based input, time-stamping occurs for the beginning and end of each stroke, which is an internal data structure that represents tracking of the pen's x,y coordinates. This data structure then is sent to the gesture recognizer for signal-level processing. Gestures can be quite ambiguous, with the same stroke interpreted differently in different contexts. During processing, the gesture recognizer produces an n-best list of possible meaningful interpretations, each of which is associated with a probability estimate.

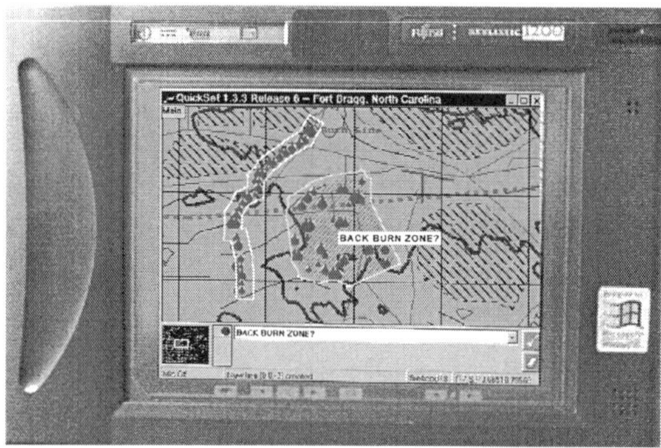


Figure 1. QuickSet system with a map-based interface
running on a handheld PC.

Gesture recognition is based on a hierarchical recognition technique called Member-Team-Committee (MTC) (Wu, Oviatt, & Cohen, 1999). The MTC weights the contributions of individual recognizers based on their empirically-derived relative reliabilities, and thereby optimizes pattern recognition robustness. It uses a divide-and-conquer strategy, wherein the members produce local posterior estimates that are reported to one or more "team" leaders. These team leaders then weight the scores, and pass results to a "committee" that weights the distribution of the team results. Using the MTC, the gesture recognizer can identify about 190 different gestures and symbols while achieving a recognition rate above 90%. Once recognized, gesture interpretations are passed on for processing by the natural language agent to create a gesture parse n-best list before being integrated with the parallel speech interpretation.

For spoken input, time-stamping begins and the speech recognition engine is engaged when an acoustic signal exceeding a minimum energy threshold is picked up. Time-stamping ends when the signal's energy falls below this threshold for a given duration, after which speech processing is completed. Since the interface is a tap-to-speak one, a pen-down event indicating that the user's input was intentional also is a prerequisite for time-stamping and processing. Like gesture processing, the speech recognizer generates an n-best list of lexical interpretations, each associated with a probability estimate that represents the likelihood that the incoming speech signal matches a particular string of phonemes in the speech recognizer's model.

QuickSet speech recognition is based on Dragon Systems' Naturally Speaking or can use other Microsoft SAPI-compliant engines, which are continuous speaker-independent recognizers. The speech recognizer produces an n-best list for each phrase. QuickSet's speech vocabulary is approximately 660 words, although the grammar specifies a larger number of valid phrases. Once the speech recognizer generates its n-best list of hypotheses, this is forwarded along with time stamp information to the speech natural language agent.

## Gesture and Speech Natural Language Processing & Fusion

To interpret a whole multimodal command, the time-stamps for speech and gestural input are compared by the integrator agent. Based on results of empirical analysis of the synchronization patterns typical of speech and pen input in a similar domain (Oviatt, DeAngeli, & Kuhn, 1997), an integration rule is applied to these time-stamped signals. The integrator will combine speech and pen signals and attempt to process their multimodal meaning in all cases for which there is temporal overlap between signals, and in cases involving sequential signals if the speech signal begins within four seconds of the end of gesture. When the architecture's synchronization rules permit joint processing, and one or more successful unifications (see details below) yield candidates for inclusion on the final multimodal n-best list, then these lexical items are listed and ranked according to their probability estimates.

In addition to temporal rules, the multimodal architecture imposes constraints based on authentication and semantic unification before joint processing of signals is completed for a multimodal command. During unification, each candidate string in the n-best list for both speech and gesture recognition is parsed by a unification-based parser, and then is assigned a feature-structure representation for its semantic interpretation. During this process, a definite-clause grammar produces typed-feature structures, or directed acyclic graphs of attribute-value pairs, as meaning representations for the speech signal. The gesture parser also produces typed-feature structures and there typically are multiple gesture interpretations for each recognition hypothesis. For example, a circle gesture can represent an area or selection of an object.

Both of these speech and gesture representations are partial until the modes are integrated during unification by the multimodal integration agent, at which point full interpretations are generated. Unification then compares the speech and gesture meaning fragments, and combines them into a single complete semantic interpretation, if they are compatible. This type of unification is a generalization of term unification in logic programming languages, such as Prolog. Typed feature-structure unification requires pairs of feature structures to be compatible in type (i.e., one must be in the transitive closure of the subtype relation with respect to the other) (Carpenter, 1992). The result of a typed unification is the more specific feature structure in the type hierarchy. Successful unification and constraint satisfaction results in a new set of merged feature structures. Typed feature-structure unification is ideal for multimodal integration, because it can combine complementary or redundant input from different modes, yet it rules out contradictory input (Cohen et al., 1997; Johnston, 1998).

So the multimodal integration agent effectively filters out combined interpretations that do not unify due to temporal or semantic constraints. The remaining "legal" unifications then comprise the final multimodal n-best list, which is rank-ordered by probability estimates. During this process, individual modes can disambiguate one another, which effectively suppresses errors (Oviatt, 1999). Finally, the top-ranked multimodal integration is sent to the architecture's application bridge agent, at which point this system interpretation is confirmed as the user's intended command.

## *QuickSet's Multi-agent Framework*

QuickSet has been developed as a set of autonomous and distributed software components that communicate using an agent communication language in the Adaptive Agent Architecture (AAA) (Kumar, Cohen, & Levesque, 2000), which is backwards compatible with the Open Agent Architecture (OAA) (Cohen, Cheyer, Wang, & Baeg, 1994). The AAA is a robust, facilitated multi-agent system architecture specifically adapted for use with multimodal systems. A multi-platform Java agent shell provides services that allow each agent to interact with others in the agent architecture. The agents can dynamically join and leave the system. They register their capabilities with an AAA facilitator, which provides brokering and matchmaking services to them. QuickSet's recognition, language understanding, and mode integration is coordinated by multiple agents working in parallel, which feed their results via the AAA facilitator to the user interface, application, and multimedia output agents.

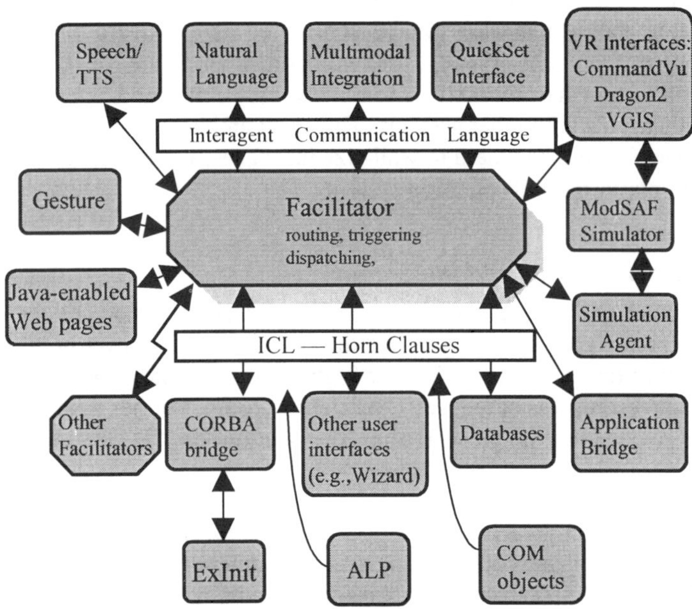


Figure 2. QuickSet's facilitated multi-agent architecture.

Among the agents that comprise QuickSet's main components (illustrated in Figure 2) are: (1) continuous speaker-independent speech recognition, (2) Members-Teams-Committee gesture recognizer, (3) multimodal natural language parser, (4) unification-based multimodal integration component, and (5) map-based user interface supporting different styles of confirmation. Other agents, shown in Figure 2, also can support text-to-speech output, bridges to other software integration frameworks (e.g., Corba and KQML), and so forth. Most agents can run stand-alone on a handheld PC, or they can be distributed over a network. The agents can be written in Java, C, C++, Prolog, Visual Basic, Common Lisp, and other languages.

Since QuickSet is based on a centralized facilitator architecture, when a second user interface is connected into the system, QuickSet becomes a collaborative application with the different user interfaces reflecting each other's contents. When a simple modification is made to this architecture in which the "wizard" (i.e., programmer assistant) becomes an unseen collaborator, the system also can be configured as a "wizard-of-Oz" data collection environment. Finally, the componential nature of QuickSet's agent architecture has resulted in relatively easy reuse and integration of QuickSet's agents with other systems. The agent architecture has enabled the system to scale from handheld to wall-size interfaces, and to operate across a number of platforms and operating systems.

## QuickSet's Evaluation and Integration

The QuickSet multimodal interface concept and early prototypes received extensive proactive user testing before the system itself was ever built. For a description of this work, as well as the high-fidelity simulation infrastructure upon which testing was based, see Oviatt et al. (2000). Further description of QuickSet evaluation is presented in the section on "Recent Empirical Studies."

The basic QuickSet system has been used to develop a variety of map-based and VR applications, including military simulations, training systems, 3-D virtual-terrain visualization systems, a community disaster management system, a medical informatics system, and others (Cohen et al., 1997; Cohen et al., 1999; Oviatt, 1999). QuickSet also has been transferred to the research laboratories of each of the US armed services, and to many government, commercial, and university sites, where it is being integrated with other software. For example, the QuickSet interface has been applied to the Naval Research Laboratory's 3D Dragon 2 virtual-reality system (Cohen et al.,

1999), to a mobile augmented reality application (Feiner, MacIntyre, Höllerer, & Webster, 1997), and it has provided the basis for the RASA tangible multimodal interface (McGee & Cohen, 2001).

## Recent Empirical Studies

Among the most noteworthy advantages of multimodal interface design is enhancement of system robustness. Such interfaces also can improve the stability of recognition-based systems, supporting larger performance advantages for challenging user groups (e.g., accented speakers) and usage contexts (e.g., mobile). In this section, two recent studies are reviewed that document these performance enhancements.

*Experiment 1:*

In the first study, performance evaluations were conducted with the QuickSet system to investigate whether a multimodal architecture could be designed to support higher recognition rates than unimodal spoken language processing, as well as larger performance improvements for accented users who normally would experience higher error rates with a spoken language system. In particular, the study investigated whether a multimodal architecture can support *mutual disambiguation* of ambiguous input signals, which functions to suppress errors.

Mutual disambiguation involves disambiguation of signal or semantic-level information in one error-prone input mode from partial information supplied by another. It can occur in a multimodal architecture with two or more semantically rich recognition-based input modes. As an example, if a user says "ditches" but the speech recognizer confirms the singular "ditch" as its best guess, then parallel recognition of several graphic marks could result in recovery of the correct plural interpretation. This recovery can occur in a multimodal architecture even though the speech recognizer initially ranked the plural interpretation "ditches" as a less preferred choice on its n-best list. When mutual disambiguation occurs, it leads to recovery from unimodal recognition errors within a multimodal architecture, with the net effect of suppressing errors experienced by the user and improving system robustness.

The participants in this first study were eight native speakers of English, and eight accented speakers with native languages representing diverse continents (e.g., Mandarin, Yoruba, Spanish). Everyone communicated 100 commands multimodally to the QuickSet system while they set up simulation exercises involving community flood and fire management. A record of all user speech and pen input, along with the system's performance, was recorded for 2,000 multimodal commands.

The results confirmed that the QuickSet multimodal architecture supported significant levels of mutual disambiguation, with one in eight user commands recognized correctly due to mutual disambiguation. Overall, a 41% reduction occurred in the total error rate for spoken language processed within a multimodal architecture, compared with spoken language processing as a stand-alone (Oviatt, 1999). Table 1 reveals that the speech recognition rate was poorer for accented speakers (–9.5%), as would be expected. However, their gesture recognition rate averaged slightly but significantly better (+3.4%). Table 2 summarizes that the rate of mutual disambiguation was significantly higher for accented speakers (+15%), compared with native speakers of English (+8.5%)— by a substantial 76%. As a result, the final multimodal recognition rate (shown in Table 1) for accented speakers no longer differed significantly from the performance of native speakers. The main factor responsible for closing this performance gap between groups was the higher rate of mutual disambiguation for accented speakers. Two-thirds of all signal pull-ups for accented speakers involved retrieving poorly ranked speech input.

| Type of Language Processing | % Performance Difference for Accented Speakers |
|---|---|
| Speech | −9.5% * |
| Gesture | +3.4% * |
| Multimodal | — |

* Significant difference present.

Table 1. Difference in recognition rate performance of accented speakers, compared with native ones, during speech, gesture and multimodal processing.

| | Native Speakers | Accented Speakers |
|---|---|---|
| Signal MD Rate | 8.5% | 15.0% * |
| Ratio of Speech Pull-ups | .35 | .65 * |

* Significant difference present.

Table 2. Mutual disambiguation (MD) rate and ratio of MD involving speech signal pull-ups for native and accented speakers

## *Experiment 2:*

In the second study, the investigation of whether a multimodal architecture could support mutual disambiguation and higher recognition rates was extended to testing in a noisy field environment while users were mobile. More specifically, a comparison was made of whether the mutual disambiguation rate would be higher in a noisy mobile environment than during quiet stationary use. If so, then a further goal of this study was to determine whether this difference would selectively target the mobile recognition rates for improvement, reducing the processing disadvantage associated with mobile use. Such findings would generalize the disproportionate robustness improvement observed in experiment 1 in favor of accented speakers.

The participants in the second study were twenty-two native English speakers, who interacted multimodally using the QuickSet system on a hand-held PC. They completed 50 commands while working alone in a quiet room averaging 42 decibels (e.g., "stationary" condition), and another 50 while walking through a moderately noisy public cafeteria that ranged 40-60 decibels (e.g., "mobile" condition). Testing included two opposite types of microphone. The first was a high-end close-talking noise-canceling Andrea microphone. The second was a built-in microphone on the handheld PC that lacked noise-cancellation. In total, data were analyzed on over 2,600 multimodal commands.

The results revealed 19-35% reductions in the total error rate, for noise-canceling versus built-in microphones, when speech was processed within the multimodal architecture (Oviatt, 2000). Once again, this substantial improvement in robustness was a direct result of the disambiguation between signals that occurred in the multimodal system. Table 3 confirms that the speech recognition rate was significantly degraded while the same users were mobile in a naturalistic noisy setting (−10%). However, their gesture recognition rates did not decline during mobility, perhaps in part because input primarily was 1-to-3-stroke gestures. Table 4 reveals that the mutual disambiguation rate also averaged substantially higher in the mobile condition (+16%), compared with the same subjects' stationary use (+9.5%). Depending on which microphone was engaged, the mutual disambiguation rate ranged from 50-100% higher during mobile system use. Since mutual disambiguation occurred at higher rates while mobile, Table 3 also confirms a significant narrowing of the gap between mobile and stationary recognition rates (to −8.0%) during multimodal processing, compared with spoken language processing alone.

| TYPE OF LANGUAGE PROCESSING | % PERFORMANCE DIFFERENCE WHEN MOBILE |
|---|---|
| Speech | −10.0% * |
| Gesture | — |
| Multimodal | −8.0% * |

* Significant difference present.

Table 3. Difference in recognition rate performance in noisy mobile environment, compared with quiet stationary use, for speech, gesture and multimodal processing

| | STATIONARY | MOBILE |
|---|---|---|
| Signal MD Rate | 9.5% | 16.0% * |
| Ratio of Speech Pull-ups | .26 | .34 * |

* Significant difference present.

Table 4. Mutual disambiguation (MD) rate and ratio of MD involving speech signal pull-ups in stationary and mobile environments.

In summary, although speech recognition as a stand-alone performed poorly for accented speakers and in mobile environments, results from these experiments reveal that a multimodal architecture decreased failures in spoken language processing by 19-41%. This performance improvement occurred mainly due to the mutual disambiguation of input signals that is possible within a unification-based multimodal architecture like QuickSet, which occurs at higher levels for challenging user groups and usage environments. These large robustness improvements in turn can reduce or eliminate the performance gap for precisely those users and environments in which speech technology is most prone to failure.

## Conclusion

This chapter summarized the current status of the QuickSet multimodal system, including its functionality, interface design, natural language processing and fusion techniques, overall architecture, applications and performance. It also reviewed results from two recent studies in which QuickSet's multimodal architecture decreased recognition errors in spoken language processing by 19-41%. This research demonstrates that future multimodal systems can be designed to function more reliably during real-world conditions. This new class of systems also can be designed to expand the accessibility of computing for diverse users and challenging mobile environments, both of which are key issues for future successful commercialization.

## References


Adjoudani, A., & Benoit, C. (1995). Audio-visual speech recognition compared across two architectures. *Proceedings of the Eurospeech Conference Vol.2* (pp. 1563-1566) Madrid, Spain.

Benoit, C., & Le Goff, B. (1998). Audio-visual speech synthesis from French text: Eight years of models, designs and evaluation at the ICP. *Speech Communication, 26*, 117-129.

Carpenter, R. (1992). *The logic of typed feature structures.* Cambridge, U.K.: Cambridge University Press.

Cohen, P. R., Cheyer, A., Wang, M., & Baeg, S. C. (1994). An open agent architecture. *AAAI '94 Spring Symposium Series on Software Agents*, 1-8. AAAI Press. (Reprinted in Huhns and Singh (Eds.). (1997). *Readings in Agents* (pp. 197-204). San Francisco: Morgan Kaufmann.)

Cohen, P. R., Johnston, M., McGee, D., Oviatt, S., Pittman, J., Smith, I., Chen, L., & Clow, J. (1997). Quickset: Multimodal interaction for distributed applications. *Proceedings of the Fifth ACM International Multimedia Conference*, 31-40. New York: ACM Press.

Cohen, P. R., McGee, D., Oviatt, S., Wu, L., Clow, J., King, R., Julier, S., & Rosenblum, L. (1999). Multimodal interaction for 2D and 3D environments. *IEEE Computer Graphics and Applications, 19(4),*10-13, IEEE Press.

Feiner, S., MacIntyre, B., Höllerer, T., and Webster, T. A (1997). Touring machine: Prototyping 3D mobile augmented reality systems for exploring the urban environment. *Proc. Int. Symp. on Wearable Computers*, 74-81, Cambridge, MA.

Johnston, M. (1998). Unification-based multimodal parsing. *Proceedings of the International Joint Conference of the Association for Computational Linguistics and the International Committee on Computational Linguistics*, 624-630, ACL Press.

Kumar, S., Cohen, P.R., and Levesque, H.J. (2000). The adaptive agent architecture: achieving fault-tolerance using persistent broker teams. *Proceedings of the International Conference on Multi-Agent Systems*, 159-166, IEEE Press.

McGee, D. R., Cohen, P. R. (2001). Creating tangible interfaces by augmenting physical objects with multimodal language. *Proceedings of the International Conference on Intelligent User Interfaces (IUI 2001)*, 113-119, ACM Press.

Neti, C., Iyengar, G., Potamianos, G. & Senior, A. (2000). Perceptual interfaces for information interaction: Joint processing of audio and visual information for human-computer interaction. In B. Yuan, T. Huang & X. Tang (Eds.), *Proceedings of the International Conference on Spoken Language Processing (ICSLP'2000), Vol. 3*, (pp. 11-14). Beijing, China: Chinese Friendship Publishers.

Oviatt, S. L. (1999). Mutual disambiguation of recognition errors in a multimodal architecture. *Proceedings of the Conference on Human Factors in Computing Systems (CHI'99)*, 576-583. New York: ACM Press.

Oviatt, S.L. (2000). Multimodal system processing in mobile environments. *Proceedings of the Thirteenth Annual ACM Symposium on User Interface Software Technology (UIST'2000)*, 21-30. New York: ACM Press.

Oviatt, S.L., Cohen, P.R., Wu, L.,Vergo, J., Duncan, L., Suhm, B., Bers, J., Holzman, T., Winograd, T., Landay, J., Larson, J. & Ferro, D. (2000). Designing the user interface for multimodal speech and gesture applications: State-of-the-art systems and research directions. *Human Computer Interaction, 15(4)*, 263-322. (to be reprinted in J. Carroll (Ed.) *Human-Computer Interaction in the New Millennium*, Addison-Wesley Press: Boston, to appear 2001).

Oviatt, S. L., DeAngeli, A., & Kuhn, K. (1997). Integration and synchronization of input modes during multimodal human-computer interaction. *Proceedings of Conference on Human Factors in Computing Systems (CHI'97)*, 415-422. New York: ACM Press.

Pankanti, S., Bolle, R.M., & Jain, A. (Eds.), (2000). Biometrics: The future of identification. *Computer, 33(2),* 46-80.

Stork, D. G., & Hennecke, M. E. (Eds.). (1995). *Speechreading by Humans and Machines.* New York: Springer Verlag.

Tomlinson, M. J., Russell, M. J. & Brooke, N. M., (1996). Integrating audio and visual information to provide highly robust speech recognition. *Proceedings of the International Conference on Acoustics, Speech and Signal Processing (IEEE-ICASSP) Vol. 2,* 821- 824. IEEE Press.

Turk, M. & Robertson, G. (Eds.). (2000). Perceptual user interfaces [Special issue]. *Communications of the ACM, 43(3),* 32-70.

Wu, L., Oviatt, S., &. Cohen, P. (1999). Multimodal integration—A statistical view. *IEEE Transactions on Multimedia, 1(4),* 334-341.

Zhai, S., Morimoto, C., & Ihde, S. (1999). Manual and gaze input cascaded (MAGIC) pointing. *Proceedings of the Conference on Human Factors in Computing Systems (CHI'99),* 246-253. New York: ACM Press.

# Information-Theoretic Fusion for Multimodal Interfaces

John W. Fisher III and Trevor Darrell

*MIT AI Laboratory
200 Technology Square
Cambridge, MA 02139
USA*

## Introduction

Multi-modal fusion is an important, yet challenging task for perceptual user interfaces. Humans routinely perform complex and simple tasks in which ambiguous auditory and visual data are combined in order to support accurate perception. In contrast, automated approaches for processing multi-modal data sources lag far behind. This is primarily due to the fact that few methods adequately model the complexity of the audio/visual relationship. Classical approaches to multi-modal fusion either assume a statistical relationship which is too simple (e.g. jointly Gaussian) or defer fusion to the decision level when many of the joint (and useful) properties have been lost. While such pragmatic choices may lead to simple statistical measures, they do so at the cost of modeling capacity.

A critical question is whether, in the absence of an adequate parametric model for joint audio and video, one can integrate measurements in a principled way without discounting statistical uncertainty. We discuss a nonparametric statistical approach to fusion which addresses these issues. Using principles from information theory we present an approach for learning maximally informative joint subspaces for multi-modal fusion. Specifically, we simultaneously learn projections of images in the video

"

sequence *and* projections of sequences of periodograms taken from the audio sequence. The projections are computed adaptively such that the video and audio projections have maximum mutual information (MI). The approach uses the methodology presented in [2,6,4] which formulates a learning approach by which the entropy, and by extension the MI, of a differentiable map may be optimized. In addition to the intuitive appeal of information theory as a motivation for the approach, we also discuss a statistical model for which the approach can be shown to be optimal.

Combining audio and video signals for dialog interface applications is an important goal for perceptual user interfaces. There has been substantial progress on feature-level integration of speech and vision. Several authors have shown how the integration of ``viseme" features into a standard Hidden Markov Model recognition system can dramatically improve recognition performance, since the visual feature can easily disambiguate articulation cues that are difficult to resolve in the audio domain. However, these systems generally assumed that no significant motion distractors are present and that the camera was ``looking" at the user who was uttering the audio signal.

Indeed, speech systems (both those that integrate viseme features and those that do not) are easily confused if there are nearby speakers also making utterances, either directed at the speech recognition system or not. If a second person says ``shut down" near a voice-enabled workstation, the primary user may not be pleased with the result! In general, it is clear that multimodal cues can aid the segmentation of multiple speakers into separate channels.

While the fusion approach we describe operates at the signal level, we demonstrate higher level functionality using the learned subspace. In this paper we present empirical results which demonstrate two different utilities. First we show that combining audio/visual data in the manner described successfully locates the speaker in the video in the presence of additional motion distractors (including other faces). Second we present experiments in which we use the method to decide whether the audio video signals come from the same source, that is, the detection of audio/video synchrony.


## Related Work

As mentioned above, there has been much work on feature level audio-visual speech recognition. For example, Meier [9] and Stork [12] (and others) have built visual speech reading systems that can improve speech recognition results dramatically. It is not clear whether these systems could be used to localize the speaker as they implicitly rely on localization having already been performed. In theory, these systems could be modified to verify if the sequence of observed visemes was consistent with the detected phonemes. We are not aware of a system which has been reported to do this to date, though it may be a successful approach. Our method works at a pre-feature level and does not presume detection of phonemes or visemes, so it may be advantageous in cases where a person-independent viseme model is hard to obtain. Also, since our method is not dependent on speech content, it would have the advantage of working on non-verbal utterances.

Other work which is more closely related to ours is that of Hershey and Movellan [7] which examined the per-pixel correlation relative to an audio track, detecting which pixels have related variation. An inherent assumption of this method was that the joint statistics were gaussian. Slaney and Covell [11] looked at optimizing temporal alignment between audio and video tracks, but did not address the problem of detecting whether two signals came from the same person or not. Their technique was more general than [7] in that pixels changes were considered jointly, although there is also an implicit Gaussian assumption. Furthermore, this technique makes use of training data.

The idea of simply gating audio input with a face detector is related to ours, but would not solve our target scenerio above where the primary user is facing the screen and a nearby person makes an utterance that can be mistakenly interpreted as a system command. We are not aware of any prior work in perceptual user interfaces which addresses signal-processing level estimators to do both video localization and classify audio-visual synchrony among individuals.

## Informative Subspaces

We now give a brief description of our information theoretic fusion approach. While the algorithm has been described in previous work [3], that discussion focused primarily on the information theoretic intuition which motivated the method. In this section we also present a statistical model from which the method can be derived and the conditions under which our fusion approach is optimal.

## *Information Theoretic Fusion*

Figure 1.1 illustrates our audio/visual fusion approach. Each image in the measured video sequence is treated as a single sample of a high-dimensional random variable (i.e. the dimension equals the number of pixels) . We denote $i$th image as $V_i$. The audio signal is converted to a sequence of periodograms (i.e. magnitude of windowed FFTs). Peridograms are computed at the video frame rate using a window equal to twice the frame period. Similarly to the video sequence, each periodogram ``frame" is also treated as a sample of a high dimensional random variable (whose dimension is equal to the number of frequency bins) and whose $i$th frame is denoted $U_i$.

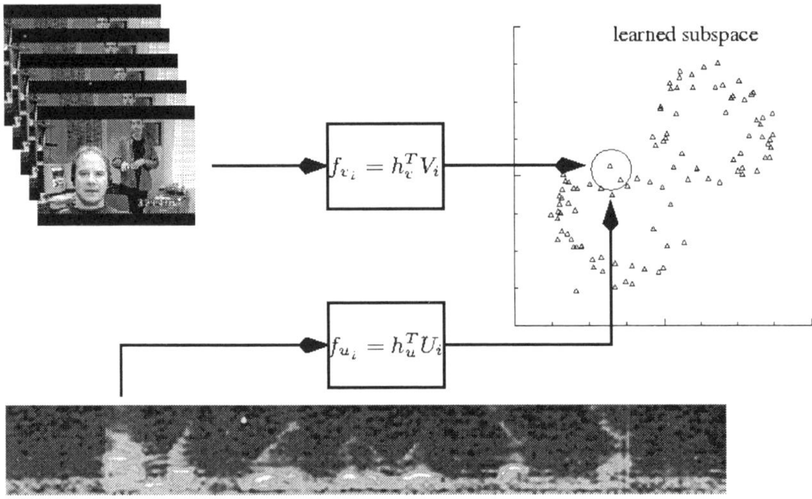



**Figure 1.1:** Maximally Informative Joint Subspace

Using the approach described in [3] we learn projections of the audio/video frames, denoted,

$$f_{V_i} = h_v^T V_i$$

$$f_{U_i} = h_u^T U_i$$

resulting in samples of low-dimensional features $f_{Vi}$ and $f_{Ui}$ (whose dimensionality is determined by the matrices $h_V$ and $h_U$, respectively). The criterion for learning the projection vectors, $h_V$ and $h_U$, is to maximize the MI between the resulting audio and video features $f_{Vi}$ and $f_{Ui}$.

Mutual information (in the case of continuous features) is defined as [1]

$$I(f_V, f_U) = h(f_U) + h(f_V) - h(f_V, f_U)$$

$$= \int_{R_U} p_{f_u}(x)\log p_{f_u}(x)\,dx + \int_{R_V} p_{f_v}(x)\log p_{f_v}(x)\,dx$$

$$- \int_{R_U \times R_V} p_{f_u,f_v}(x,y)\log p_{f_u,f_v}(x,y)\,dxdy$$

The difficulty with using MI as a criterion for adaptation is that it is an integral function of probability densities. Furthermore, in general we are not given the densities themselves, but samples from which they must be inferred. Consequently, we replace equation 1.3 with the approximation of [6]

$$\hat{I}(f_V, f_U) = \hat{h}(f_U) + \hat{h}(f_V) - \hat{h}(f_V, f_U)$$

$$= \int_{R_U} \left(p_{f_u}(x) - p_u(x)\right)^2 dx + \int_{R_V} \left(p_{f_v}(x) - p_u(x)\right)^2 dx$$

$$- \int_{R_U \times R_V} \left(p_{f_u,f_v}(x,y) - p_u(x,y)\right)^2 dxdy$$

where $R_U$ is the support of one feature output, $R_V$ is the support of the other, $p_u$ is the uniform density over that support, and $\hat{p}(x)$ is the Parzen density [10] estimate computed from the projected samples:

$$\hat{p}(x) = \frac{1}{N}\sum_i \kappa(x - x_i, \sigma)$$

where $\kappa(\ )$ is a (separable) gaussian kernel in our case and $\sigma$ is the standard deviation.

Note that this is essentially an integrated squared error comparison between the density of the projections to the uniform density (which has maximum entropy over a finite region). The consequence of using this approximation is that its gradient with respect to the projection coefficients can be computed *exactly* by evaluating a finite number of functions at a finite number of sample locations in the output space as shown in [5,6]. The update term for the individual entropy terms in 1.4 of the $i$th feature vector at iteration $k$ as a function of the value of the feature vector at iteration $k$ - 1 is (where $f_i$ denotes a sample of either $f_U$ or $f_V$ or their concatenation depending on which term of 1.4 is being computed)

$$\Delta f_i^{(k)} = b_r\left(f_i^{(k-1)}\right) - \frac{1}{N}\sum_{j \neq i} \kappa_a\left(f_i^{(k-1)} - f_j^{(k-1)};\sigma\right)$$

$$b_r(f_i)_l = \frac{1}{d^M}\prod_{j \neq i}\left(\kappa_1\left(f_{ij}^{(k-1)} + \frac{d}{2};\sigma\right) - \kappa_1\left(f_{ij}^{(k-1)} - \frac{d}{2};\sigma\right)\right)$$

$$\kappa_a(f_i;\sigma) = \kappa\left(f_i + \frac{d}{2};\sigma\right) * \kappa'\left(f_i + \frac{d}{2};\sigma\right)$$

$$= \frac{\exp\left(-\dfrac{f_i^T f_i}{4\sigma^2}\right)}{\left(2^{M+1}\pi^{\frac{M}{2}}\sigma^{M+2}\right)}f_i$$

where $M$ is the dimensionality of the feature vector $f_i$. Both $b_r(f_i)$ and $\kappa_a(f_i,\sigma)$ are $M$-dimensional vector-valued functions and $d$ is the support of the output of the mapping (i.e. a hyper-cube with sides of length $d$ centered at the origin). The notation $b_r(y_i)_l$ indicates the $l$th element of $b_r(f_i)$ while $\kappa_1(\ )$ indicates the one-dimensional kernel [6].

The process is repeated iteratively until a local maximum is reached using the update rule above. In the experiments that follow the dimensionality of $f_U$ and $f_V$ are set to unity while the number iterations is typically 150 to 300 iterations. Given that the mapping from data, $U_i$ and $V_i$, to features, $f_{Ui}$ and $f_{Vi}$, is linear we solve for mapping coefficients, $h_U$ and $h_V$, using a least squares method.

## Capacity Control

The method of [6] requires that the projection be differentiable, which it is in this case. Additionally some form of capacity control is necessary as the method results in a system of underdetermined equations. In practice we impose an $L_2$ penalty on the projection coefficients of $h_U$ and $h_V$ (sometimes referred to as ``ridge regression"). Furthermore, we impose the criterion that if we consider the projection $h_V$ as a filter, it has low output energy when convolved with images in the sequence (on average). This constraint is the same as that proposed by Mahalanobis [8] for designing optimized correlators the difference being that in their case the projection output was designed explicitly while in our case it is derived from the MI optimization in the output space.

The adaptation criterion, which we maximize in practice, is then a combination of the approximation to MI (equation 1.4) and the regularization terms:

$$J = \hat{I}(f_u, f_v) - \alpha_v h_v^T h_v - \alpha_u h_u^T h_u - \beta h_v^T \bar{R}_V^{-1} h_v$$

where the last term derives from the output energy constraint and $\bar{R}_V^{-1}$ is average autocorrelation function (taken over all images in the sequence). This term is more easily computed in the frequency domain (see [8]) and is equivalent to pre-whitening the images using the inverse of the average power spectrum. The scalar weighting terms $\alpha_v, \alpha_u, \beta$ were set using a data dependent heuristic for all experiments.

The interesting thing to note is that computing $h_v$ can be decomposed into three stages:
1. Pre-whiten the images **once** (using the average spectrum of the images) followed by iterations of
2. Updating the feature values, and
3. Solving for the projection coefficients using least squares and the $L_2$ penalty.

The pre-whitening interpretation makes intuitive sense in our case as it accentuates edges in the input image. It is the moving edges (lips, chin, etc.) which we expect to convey the most information about the audio. The projection coefficients related to the audio signal, $h_U$, are solved in a similar way (simultaneously) without the initial pre-whitening step.

### *The Implicit Statistical Model*

Estimating separate projections of the audio video measurements which have high mutual information with respect to each other makes intuitive sense from the perspective of information theory as such features will be predictive of each other. The advantage being that the form of those statistics are not subject to strong assumptions (e.g. joint gaussianity).

However, we now show that there is a statistical model for which such fusion is optimal. Consider the graphical models shown in figure 1.2. Figure 1.2a shows an independent cause model, where $\{A, B, C\}$ are unobserved random variables representing the causes of our (high-dimensional) observations $\{U, V\}$. In general there may be more causes and more measurements, but this simple case can be used to illustrate our algorithm. An important aspect is that the measurements have dependence on only one common cause. The joint statistical model consistent with the graph of figure 1.2a is

$$P(A,B,C,U,V) = P(A)P(B)P(C)P(U \mid A,B)P(V \mid B,C)$$

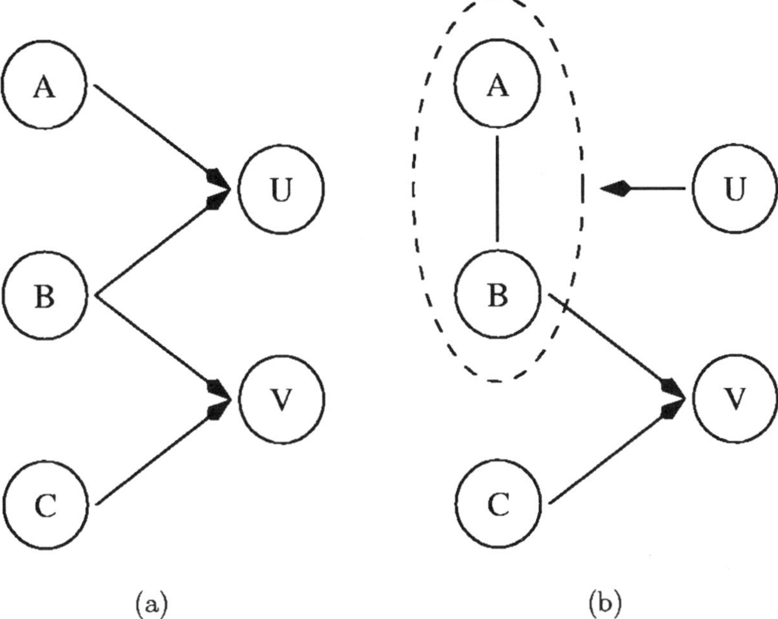


**Figure 1.2:** Graphs illustrating the various statistical models exploited by the algorithm: (a) the independent cause model - $U$ and $V$ are independent of each other conditioned on $\{A, B, C\}$, (b) information about $U$ contained in $V$ is conveyed through *joint* statistics of $A$ and $B$.

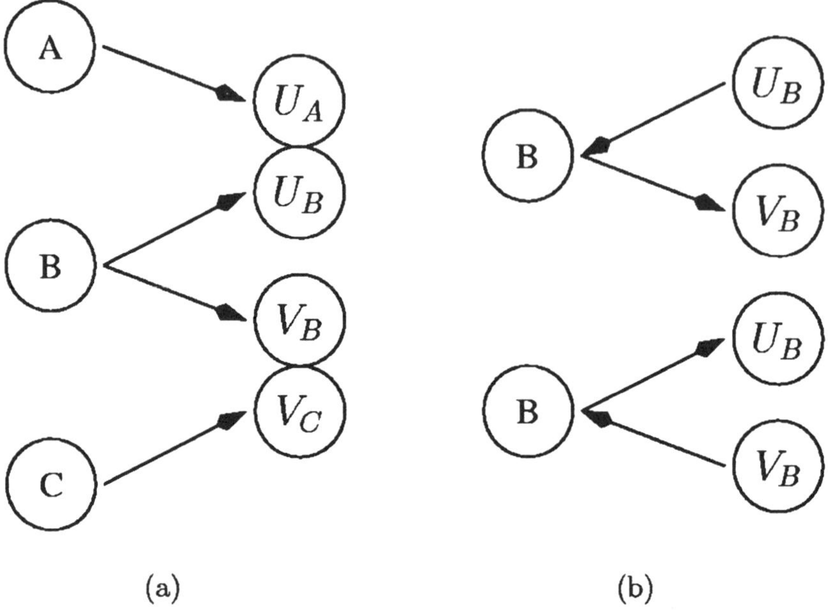

(a)                              (b)

**Figure 1.3:** Statistical models when (a) a separating function exists, and (b) two equivalent Markov chains which can be extracted from the graphs *if* the separating functions can be found.

Given the independent cause model a simple application of Bayes' rule (or the equivalent graphical manipulation) yields the graph of figure 1.2b which is consistent with

$$P(A, B, C, U, V) = P(U)P(C)P(A, B|\ U)P(V|\ B, C) \ ,$$

which shows that information about $U$ contained in $V$ is conveyed through the *joint* statistics of $A$ and $B$. The consequence being that, in general, we cannot disambiguate the influences that $A$ and $B$ have on the measurements. A similar graph is obtained by conditioning on $V$. Suppose decompositions of the measurement $U$ and $V$ *exist* such that the following joint densities can be written:

$$P(A,B,C,U,V) = P(A)P(B)P(C)P(U_A|A)$$
$$P(U_B|B)P(V_B|B)P(V_C|C)$$

where $U = [U_A, U_B]$ and $V = [V_B, V_C]$. An example for our specific application would be segmenting the video image (or filtering the audio signal). In this case we get the graph of figure 1.3a and from that graph we can extract the Markov chain which contains elements related only to $B$. Figure 1.3b shows equivalent graphs of the extracted Markov chain. As a consequence, there is no influence due to $A$ or $C$.

Of course, we are still left with the formidable task of finding a decomposition, but given the decomposition it can be shown, using the data processing inequality [1], that the following inequality holds:

$$I\left(f_U, f_V\right) \leq I\left(f_U, B\right)$$

$$I\left(f_U, f_V\right) \leq I\left(f_V, B\right)$$

So, by maximizing the mutual information between $I(f_U, f_V)$ we must necessarily increase the mutual information between $f_U$ and $B$ and $f_V$ and $B$. The implication is that fusion in such a manner discovers the underlying cause of the observations, that is, the joint density of $P(f_U, f_V)$ is strongly related to $B$. Furthermore, with an approximation, we can optimize this criterion without estimating the separating function directly. In the event that a perfect decomposition does not exist, it can be shown that the method will approach a ``good" solution in the Kullback-Leibler sense.


## Empirical Results

We now present experimental results in which the general method described previously is used to first to localize the speaker in the video and second to measure whether the audio signal is consistent with the video signal. We collected audio-video data from eight subjects. In all cases the video data was collected at 29.97 frames per second at a resolution of 360x240. The audio signal was collected at 48000 KHz, but only 10Khz of frequency content was used. All subjects were asked to utter the phrase ``How is the weather?". This typically yielded 2-2.5 seconds of data. Video frames were processed as is, while the audio signal was transformed to a series of periodograms. The window length of the periodogram was 2/29.97 seconds (i.e. spanning the width of two video frames). Upon estimating projections the mutual information between the projected audio and video data samples is used as the measure of consistency. All values for mutual information are in terms of the maximum possible value, which is the value obtained (in the limit) if the two variables are uniformly distributed and perfectly predict one another. In all cases we assume that there is not significant head movement on the part of the speaker. While this assumption might be violated in practice one might account for head movement using a tracking algorithm, in which case the algorithm as described would process the images after tracking.

## Video Localization of Speaker

Figure 1.4a shows a single video frame from one sequence of data. In the figure there is a single speaker and a video monitor. Thoughout the sequence the video monitor exhibits significant flicker. Figure 1.4c shows an image of the pixel-wise standard deviations of the image sequence. As can be seen, the energy associated with changes due to monitor flicker is greater than that due to the speaker. Figure 1.4b shows the absolute value of the output of the pre-whitening stage for the video frame in the same figure. Note that the output we use is signed. The absolute value is shown instead because it illustrates the enhancements of edges in the image.

Figure 1.6a shows the associated periodogram sequence where the horizontal axis is time and the vertical axis is frequency (0-10 Khz). Figure 1.4d shows the coefficients of the learned projection when fused with the audio signal. As can be seen the projection highlights the region about the speaker's lips.

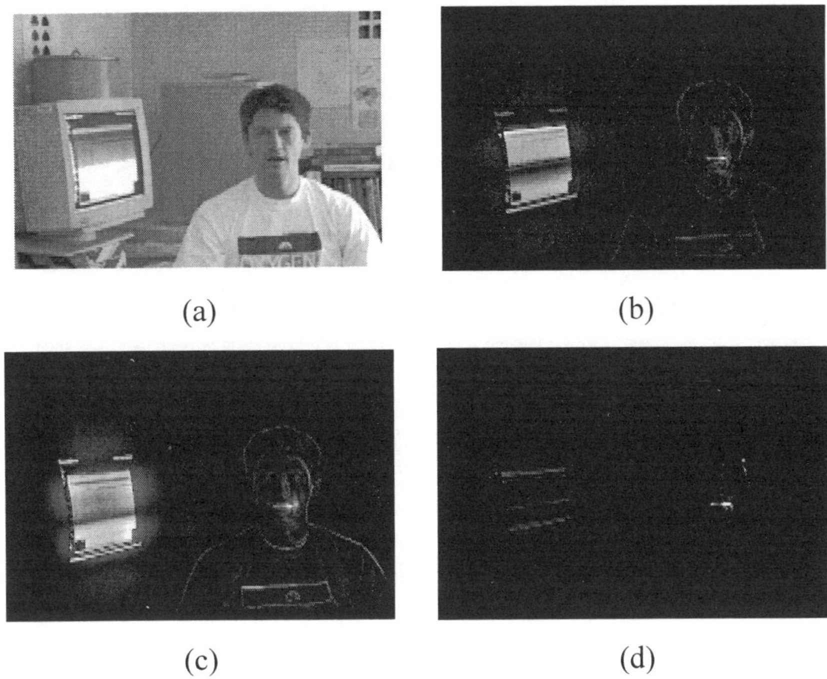

**Figure 1.4:** Video sequence contains one speaker and monitor which is flickering: (a) one image from the sequence, (b) magnitude of the image after pre-whitening, (c) pixel-wise image of standard deviations taken over the entire sequence, (d) image of the learned projection, $h_V$.

Figure 1.5a shows results from another sequence in which there are two people. The person on the left was asked to utter the test phrase, while the person on the right moved their lips, but did not speak. This sequence is interesting in that a simple face detector would not be sufficient to disambiguate the audio and video stream. Furthermore, viseme based approaches might be confused by the presence of two faces.

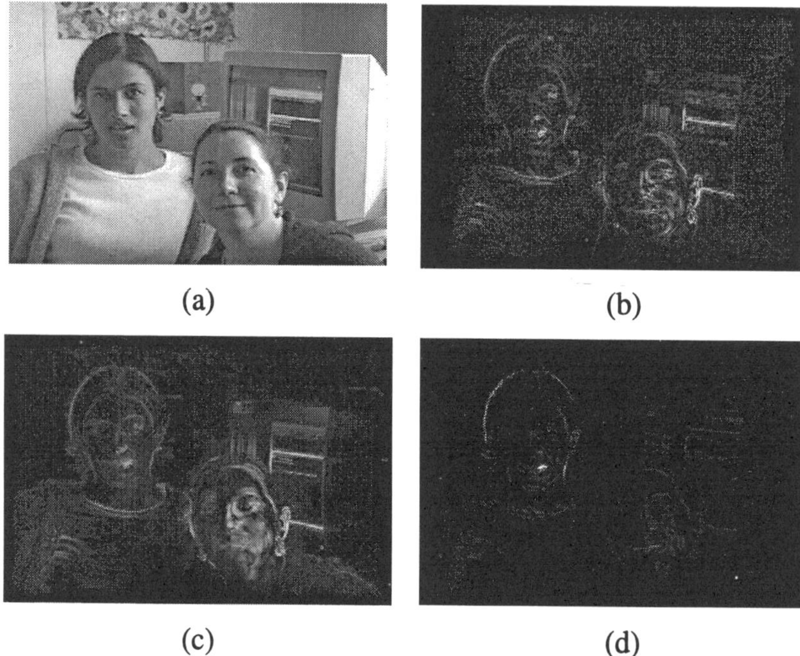

(a)

(b)

(c)

(d)

**Figure 1.5:** Video sequence containing one speaker (person on left) and one person who is randomly moving their mouth/head (but not speaking): (a) one image from the sequence, (b) magnitude of the image after pre-whitening, (c) pixel-wise image of standard deviations taken over the entire sequence, (d) image of the learned projection, $h_V$.

Figures 1.5b and 1.5c show the pre-whitened images as before. There are significant changes about both subjects lips. Figure 1.5d shows the coefficients of the learned projection when the video is fused with the audio and again the region about the correct speaker's lips is highlighted.

## *Quantifying Consistency Between the Audio and Video*

In addition to localizing the audio source in the image sequence we can also check for consistency between the audio and video. Such a test is useful in the case that the person to which a system is visually attending is not the person who actually spoke. Having learned a projection which optimizes MI in the output feature space, we can then estimate the resulting MI and use that estimate to quantify the audio/video consistency.

Using the sequence of figure $\underline{1.4}$ we compared the fusion result when using separately recorded audio sequence from another speaker. The periodogram of the alternate audio sequence is shown in figure $\underline{1.6}$b. Figure $\underline{1.7}$a (correct audio) and $\underline{1.7}$b (alternate audio) compares the resulting projections $h_v$. In the case that the alternate audio was used we see that coefficients related to the video monitor increase significantly. The estimate of mutual information was 0.68 relative to the maximum possible value for the correct audio sequence. In contrast when compared to the periodogram of $\underline{1.6}$b , the value drops to 0.08 of maximum. We repeat the same experiment with two speaker video sequence, shown in figure $\underline{1.7}$c (correct audio) and $\underline{1.7}$d (alternate audio) and again we see, not surprisingly, the speaker is not localized. The estimate of mutual information for this correct sequence was 0.61 relative to maximum, while it drops to 0.27 when the alternate audio is used.

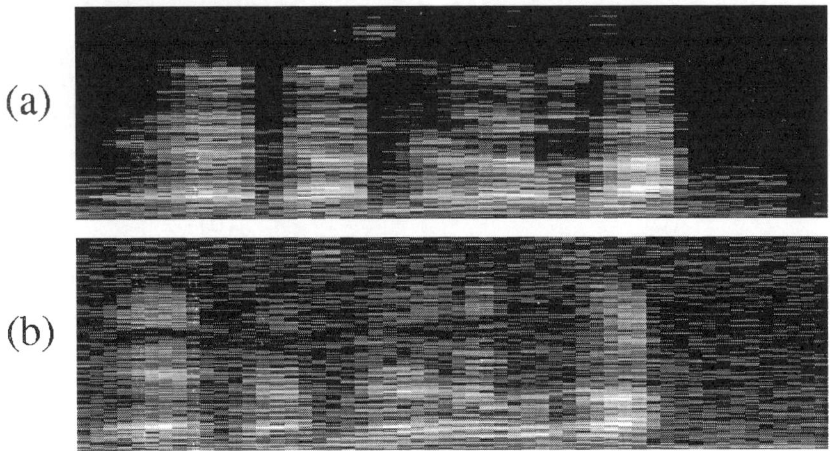

**Figure 1.6:** Images of periodogram sequences where the vertical axis is frequency and horizontal axis is time. The top image (a) corresponds to the ``correct'' audio for the sequence of $\underline{1.6}$ while the bottom (b) corresponds to a separately recorded audio signal from a different speaker.

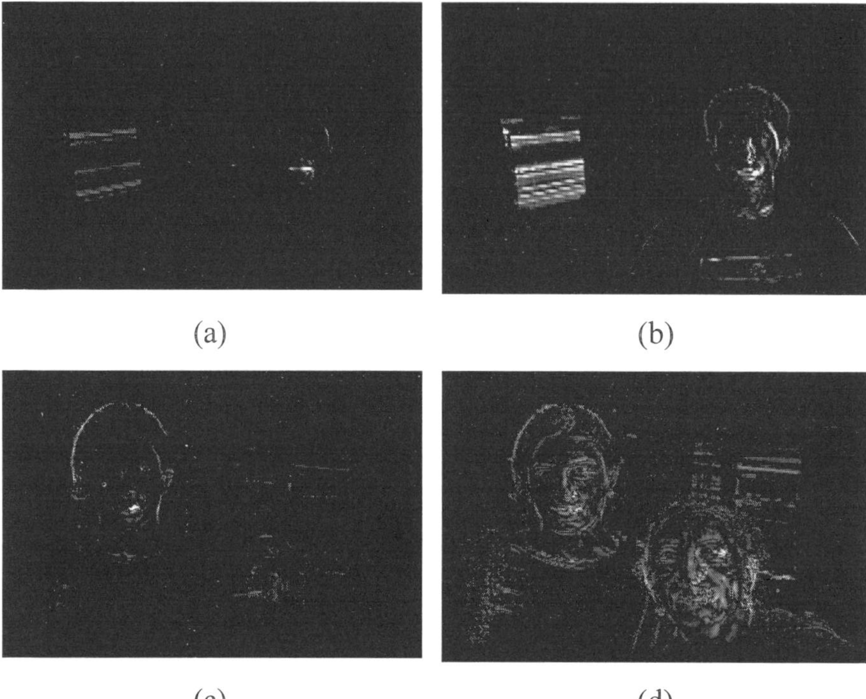

(a) (b)

(c) (d)

**Figure 1.7:** Comparison of projection images when $h_V$ when correct audio is used (a) and (c) to when separately recorded (or ``incorrect'') audio is used (b) and (d). As can be seen, when the audio is not associated with the image sequence (b) and (d) the projection energy is distributed throughout the image.

## *Eight-way Test*

Finally, data was collected from six additional subjects. These data were used to perform an eight-way test. Each video sequence was compared to each audio sequence. No attempt was made to optimally align the mismatched audio sequences. Table 1.1 summarizes the results. The previous sequences correspond to subjects 1 and 2 in the table. In every case the matching audio/video pairs exhibited the highest mutual information after estimating the projections.

|     | a1   | a2   | a3   | a4   | a5   | a6   | a7   | a8   |
| --- | ---- | ---- | ---- | ---- | ---- | ---- | ---- | ---- |
| v1  | 0.68 | 0.19 | 0.12 | 0.05 | 0.19 | 0.11 | 0.12 | 0.05 |
| v2  | 0.20 | 0.61 | 0.10 | 0.11 | 0.05 | 0.05 | 0.18 | 0.32 |
| v3  | 0.05 | 0.27 | 0.55 | 0.05 | 0.05 | 0.05 | 0.05 | 0.05 |
| v4  | 0.12 | 0.24 | 0.32 | 0.55 | 0.22 | 0.05 | 0.05 | 0.10 |
| v5  | 0.17 | 0.05 | 0.05 | 0.05 | 0.55 | 0.05 | 0.20 | 0.09 |
| v6  | 0.20 | 0.05 | 0.05 | 0.13 | 0.14 | 0.58 | 0.05 | 0.07 |
| v7  | 0.18 | 0.15 | 0.07 | 0.05 | 0.05 | 0.05 | 0.64 | 0.26 |
| v8  | 0.13 | 0.05 | 0.10 | 0.05 | 0.31 | 0.16 | 0.12 | 0.69 |

**Table 1.1**: Summary of results over eight video sequences. The columns indicate which audio sequence was used while the rows indicate which video sequence was used. In all cases the correct audio/video pair have the highest relative MI score.

## Discussion and Future Work

We have presented a method for information theoretic fusion of audio and video data. We have demonstrated over a small set of data, that the method shows promise for detecting audio-video consistency. We are not aware of equivalent results in the literature, although previous multi-modal methods might also work for this application. However, in contrast to previous approaches our method does not make strong assumptions about the underlying joint properties of the modalities being fused (e.g. Gaussian statistics). Consequently, it has the capacity to represent more complex structure which may be present in the data. Furthermore, our method makes no use of training data. While there is an adaptive element to the method, the adaptation occurs in an online fashion over a short sequence (approximately 2-2.5 seconds) of audio-video data. Consequently, the method is applicable when a prior model cannot be trained. As might happen when a multi-modal interface is moved to a new environment. Future work will address the robustness of the method over a larger corpus of data. Another area of interest is to determine the relationship between camera resolution, audio signal-to-noise ratio, and sampling rates for which the method maintains reliability.

# References


1. T. M. Cover and J. A. Thomas. *Elements of Information Theory.* John Wiley & Sons, Inc., New York, 1991.

2. J. Fisher and J. Principe. Unsupervised learning for nonlinear synthetic discriminant functions. In D. Casasent and T. Chao, editors, *Proc. SPIE, Optical Pattern Recognition VII*, volume 2752, pages 2-13, 1996.

3. J. W. Fisher III, T. Darrell, W. T. Freeman, and P. Viola. Learning joint statistical models for audio-visual fusion and segregation. In *Advances in Neural Information Processing Systems 13*, 2000.

4. J. W. Fisher III, A. T. Ihler, and P. A. Viola. Learning informative statistics: A nonparametric approach. In S. A. Solla, T. K. Leen, and K.-R. Müller, editors, *Advances in Neural Information Processing Systems 12*, 1999.

5. J. W. Fisher III and J. C. Principe. Entropy manipulation of arbitrary nonlinear mappings. In J. Principe, editor, *Proc. IEEE Workshop, Neural Networks for Signal Processing VII*, pages 14-23, 1997.

6. J. W. Fisher III and J. C. Principe. A methodology for information theoretic feature extraction. In A. Stuberud, editor, *Proceedings of the IEEE International Joint Conference on Neural Networks*, 1998.

7. J. Hershey and J. Movellan. Using audio-visual synchrony to locate sounds. In S. A. Solla, T. K. Leen, and K.-R. Müller, editors, *Advances in Neural Information Processing Systems 12*, pages 813-819, 1999.

8. Mahalanobis, B. Kumar, and D. Casasent. Minimum average correlation energy filters. *Applied Optics*, 26(17):3633-3640, 1987.

9. U. Meier, R. Stiefelhagen, J. Yang, and A. Waibel. Towards unrestricted lipreading. In *Second International Conference on Multimodal Interfaces (ICMI99)*, 1999.

10. E. Parzen. On estimation of a probability density function and mode. *Ann. of Math Stats.*, 33:1065-1076, 1962.

11. M. Slaney and M. Covell. Facesync: A linear operator for measuring synchronization of video facial images and audio tracks. In T. K. Leen, T. G. Dietterich, and V. Tresp, editors, *Advances in Neural Information Processing Systems 13*, 2000.

12. G. Wolff, K. V. Prasad, D. G. Stork, and M. Hennecke. Lipreading by neural networks: Visual preprocessing, learning and sensory integration. In *Proc. of Neural Information Proc. Sys. NIPS-6*, pages 1027-1034, 1994.

# Using Virtual Humans for Multimodal Communication in Virtual Reality and Augmented Reality

Daniel Thalmann

*Computer Graphics Lab, EPFL, Lausanne, Switzerland*

## Introduction

Virtual Reality techniques have introduced a wide range of new methods and metaphors of interaction with these Virtual Environments. Virtual Environments are generally composed of static and dynamic Virtual Entities and may include 3D graphics objects, 3D sounds, images, and videos. Inside these Virtual Environments, Virtual Humans are a key technology that can provide Virtual presenters, Virtual Guides, Virtual actors, and be used to show how humans should act in various situations (see Figure 1). Scenes involving Virtual Humans imply many complex problems we have been solving for several years [1]. With the new developments of digital and interactive television [2] and multimedia products, there is also a need for systems that provide designers with the capability for embedding real-time simulated humans in games, multimedia titles and film animations. In fact, there are many current and potential applications of human activities that may be part of a VR system involving virtual humans:

- simulation based learning and training (transportation, civil engineering etc.)
- simulation of ergonomic work environments
- virtual patient for surgery, plastic surgery

- orthopedy and prostheses and rehabilitation
- plastic surgery
- virtual psychotherapies
- architectural simulation with people, buildings, landscapes and lights etc.
- computer games involving people and "Virtual Worlds" for Lunaparks/casinos
- game and sport simulation
- interactive drama titles in which the user can interact with simulated characters and hence be involved in a scenario rather than simply watching it.

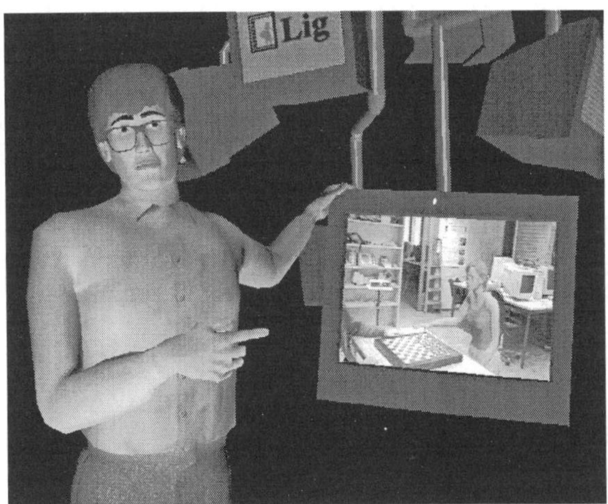


Figure 1. A Virtual Human interacting with a computer

We may identify several areas [3] where autonomous virtual humans are essential:

*Virtual people for Inhabited Virtual Environments.* Their role is very important in virtual environments with many people, like virtual airports or even virtual cities. In the next few years, we will see a lot of Humanoids or Virtual Humans in many applications. These virtual humans will be more and more autonomous. They will also tend to become intelligent.

*Virtual substitutes.* A virtual substitute is an intelligent computer-generated agent able to act instead of the real person and on behalf of this person on the network. The virtual substitute has the voice of the real person and his or her appearance. He/she will appear on the screen of the workstation/TV, communicate with people, and have predefined behaviours planned by the owner to answer to the requests of the people.

*Virtual medical assistance.* Nowadays, it seems very difficult to imagine an effective solution for chronic care without including the remote care of patients at home by a kind of Virtual Medical Doctor. The modelling of virtual patient with correspondence to medical images is also a key issue and a basis for telesurgery.

But mainly, telepresence is the future of multimedia systems and will allow participants to share professional and private experiences, meetings, games, and parties. Virtual Humans have a key role to play in these shared Virtual Environments and true interaction with them is a great challenge. Although a lot of research has been going on in the field of Networked Virtual Environments, most of the existing systems still use simple embodiments (avatars) for the representation of participants in the environments. More complex virtual human embodiment increases the natural interaction within the environment. The users' more natural perception of each other (and of autonomous actors) increases their sense of being together (Figure 2), and thus the overall sense of shared presence in the environment.

Figure 2. Avatars

## Face and body construction

Real-time representation and animation of virtual human figures has been a challenging and active area in Computer Graphics since early eighties. Typically, an articulated structure corresponding to the human skeleton is needed for the control of the body posture. Structures representing the body shape have to be attached to the skeleton, and clothes may be wrapped around the body shape. Typically, the skeleton is represented by a 3D articulated hierarchy of 50 or 70 joints, each with realistic maximum and minimum limits. The skeleton is encapsulated with geometrical, topological, and inertial characteristics of different body limbs. The body structure has a fixed topology template of joints, and different body instances may be created by specifying scaling parameters.

In order to represent the body shape, it is necessary to attach to the skeleton a structure which should be deformed during the motion. A solution is to represent only the skin as a surface; the problem is how to generate realistic shapes for any configuration of the skeleton. Another solution is to simulate the inner layers: muscles, bones, soft tissues. This approach is too expensive for real-time actors. A compromise solution is to approximate the muscles and the bones using primitives like ellipsoids or more generally kinds of implicit surfaces, called in the jargon of computer graphics, metaballs, blobs or soft objects. The skin or body shape is generated from the inner structure. One way of doing this is to cut the metaballs into cross sections and generate the skin from these sections. Figure 3 shows the principle.

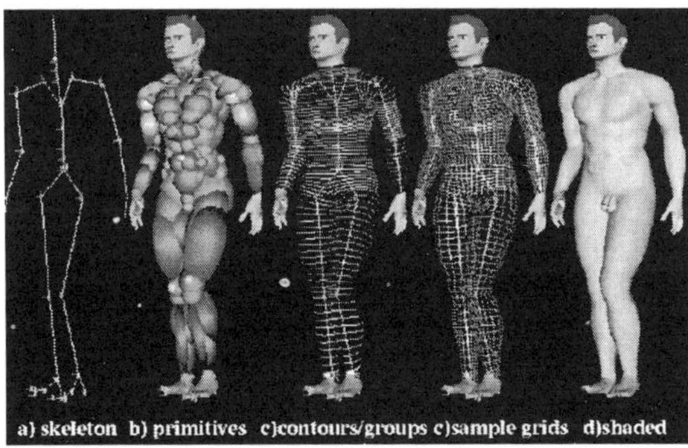


Figure 3. Modeling human body: skeleton, metaballs, metaballs with wireframe skin, rendered skin and clothes

For creating face shapes, tedious methods based on digitizing techniques have been first replaced by methods based on local deformations. For example, a realistic human character may be produced with a method similar to the modelling in clay, work which essentially consists of adding or eliminating bits of material, and turning the object around when the shape has been set up. An elegant solution is the use of a sculpting software based on an interactive 3D input device like the Spaceball.

More recently, new methods coming from Computer Vision have appeared. The goal of these methods is to automatically fit a complex facial animation model to image data obtained using orthogonal photographs [4] or regular video cameras [5] as opposed to sophisticated sensors such as laser range finders. For example, Fua et al. [6] starts with a set of stereo image pairs or a video sequence, and first extract stereo data and silhouette data. The system then fits to this image data a facial animation model. This model should allow us to produce sophisticated and realistic animations of a specific person in an automated fashion and using only cheap sensors.

In the example in Figure 4, the images have been registered using standard interactive photogrammetric techniques. First disparity maps are computed for each consecutive pair of images in the video sequence, then clouds of 3D points are derived and local surface patches fitted to these raw 3D points. Finally, a least-square adjustment technique is used to fit the animation mask to the 3--D data.

Figure 4. Reconstruction of a face

## *Avatar functions*

The avatar representation fulfils several important functions:

1. the visual embodiment of the user
2. means of interaction with the world
3. means of sensing various attributes of the world

It becomes even more important in multi-user Networked Virtual Environments [7], as participants' representation is used for communication. This avatar representation in NVEs has crucial functions in addition to those of single-user virtual environments [8 9]:

1. perception (to see if anyone is around)
2. localisation (to see where the other person is)
3. identification (to recognise the person)
4. visualisation of others' interest focus (to see where the person's attention is directed)

5. visualisation of other's actions (to see what the other person is doing and what is meant through gestures)
6. social representation of self through decoration of the avatar (to know what the other participants' task or status is)

Using articulated models for avatar representation fulfils these functionalities with realism, as it provides the direct relationship between how we control our avatar in the virtual world and how our avatar moves related to this control, allowing the user to use his/her real world experience. We chose to use complex virtual human models aiming for a high level of realism, but articulated "cartoon-like" characters could also be well suited to express ideas and feelings through the nonverbal channel in a more symbolic or metaphoric way.

*Motion control*

The main goal of computer animation is to synthesize the desired motion effect which is a mixing of natural phenomena, perception and imagination. The animator designs the object's dynamic behavior with his mental representation of causality. He/she imagines how it moves, gets out of shape or reacts when it is pushed, pressed, pulled, or twisted. So, the animation system has to provide the user with motion control tools able to translate his/her wishes from his/her own language.

In the context of Virtual Humans, a Motion Control Method (MCM) specifies how the Virtual Human is animated and may be characterized according to the type of information it privileged in animating this Virtual Human. For example, in a keyframe system for an articulated body, the privileged information to be manipulated is the angle. In a forward dynamics-based system, the privileged information is a set of forces and torques; of course, in solving the dynamic equations, joint angles are also obtained in this system, but we consider these as derived information. In fact, any MCM will eventually have to deal with geometric information (typically joint angles), but only geometric MCMs explicitly privilege this information at the level of animation control.

Many MCMs have been proposed: motion capture, keyframe, inverse kinematics, dynamics, walking models, grasping models, etc.. But, no method is perfect and only combination of blending of methods can provide good and flexible results.

The problem is basically to be able to generate variety among a finite set of motion requests and then to apply it to either an individual or a member of a crowd. A single autonomous agent and a member of the crowd present the same kind of 'individuality'. The only difference is at the level of the modules that control the main set of actions. With this formulation, one can also see that the personality of an agent (i.e. the set of noisy actions) can be preserved whenever it is in a crowd, alone.

## *High-level behavior*

Autonomous Virtual Humans should be able to have a behaviour, which means they must have a manner of conducting themselves. Typically, the Virtual Human should perceive the objects and the other Virtual Humans in the environment through virtual sensors [10]: visual, tactile and auditory sensors. Based on the perceived information, the actor's behavioural mechanism will determine the actions he will perform. An actor may simply evolve in his environment or he may interact with this environment or even communicate with other actors. In this latter case, we will consider the actor as a interactive perceptive actor.

The actor-environment interface, or the synthetic sensors, constitute an important part of a behavioral animation system. As sensorial information drastically influences behavior, the synthetic sensors should simulate the functionality of their organic counterparts. Due to real-time constraints, we did not make any attempt to model biological models of sensors. Therefore, synthetic vision only makes efficient visibility tests using SGI's graphics rendering hardware that produces a Z-buffered color image representing an agent's vision. A tactile point-like sensor will be represented by a simple function evaluating the global force field at its position. The synthetic "ear" of an agent will be represented by a function returning the on-going sound events. What is important for an actor's behavior is the functionality of a sensor and how it filters the information flow from the environment, and not the specific model of the sensor.

Another aspect of synthetic sensor design is its universality. The sensors should be as independent as possible from specific environment representations and they should be easily adjustable for interactive users. For example, the same Z-buffer based renderer displays the virtual world for an autonomous actor and an interactive user. The user and the autonomous actors perceive the virtual environment through rendered images, without knowing anything about the internal 3D environment representation or the rendering mechanism.

The sense of touch plays also an important role for humans. In order to model this sense, we use a physically based force field model. This model is close to reality, as the real sense of touch also perceives collision forces. By adding a physically-based animation of objects, we can extend the force field model to a physically based animation system where touch sensors correspond to special functions evaluating the global force field at their current position. This approach also solves the response problem of collisions, as they are handled automatically by the physics-based evolution system if both colliding objects - sensor and touched object - exert for example short range repulsion forces. We opted for a force field-based model to represent the sense of touch, as it integrates itself naturally into the physically-based particle system we already use for physical and behavioral animation. Of course, for real-time applications, the number of sensors and particles should be small, as the evolution of the particle system is computationally expensive. Another disadvantage of this approach is that the touch sensors only "sense" geometrical shapes that are explicitly bounded by appropriate force fields. Another difficulty arising due to the force field model is the fact that the parameterization of the force fields, the numerical integration of the system of differential equations, the time step and the speed of moving objects depend on each other, and that the adaptation of all parameters for a stable animation is not always trivial.

As pointed out above, we use a sound event framework for controlling the acoustic model of the animation system. The sound event handler maintains a table of the on-going sound events. Consequently, one can immediately model synthetic hearing by simple querying of this table of on-going sound events. An interactive user can also produce sound events in the virtual environment via a speech recognition module. Through a sound event, an autonomous actor can directly capture its semantic, position and emitting source. Figure 5 shows a complex behavior.

**Figure 5. A complex behavior**

## Speech Recognition

A considerable part of human communication is based on speech. Therefore, a believable virtual humanoid environment with user interaction should include speech recognition. In order to improve real time user interaction with autonomous actors we extended our system with a speech recognition feature that transmits spoken words, captured by a microphone, to the virtual acoustic environment by creating corresponding sound events perceptible by autonomous actors. This concept enables us to model behaviors of actors reacting directly to user-spoken commands. For speech recognition we use POST, the **P**arallel **O**bject oriented **S**peech **T**oolkit [11], developed for designing automatic speech recognition. POST is freely distributed to academic institutions. It can perform simple feature extraction, training and testing of word and sub-word Hidden Markov Models with discrete and multi Gaussian statistical modeling. We use a POST application for isolated word recognition.

The system can be trained by several users and its performance depends on the number of repetitions and the quality of word capture. This speech recognizing feature was recently added to the system and we don't have much experience with its performance. First tests, however, with a single user training, resulted in a satisfactory recognition rate for a vocabulary of about 50 isolated words.

A high level behavior uses in general sensorial input and special knowledge. A way of modeling behaviors is the use of an automata approach. Each actor has an internal state which can change each time step according to the currently active automata and its sensorial input. Abstraction mechanisms to simulate intelligent behaviours have been discussed in the AI (Artificial Intelligence) and AA (Autonomous Agents') literature. Several methods have been introduced to model learning processes, perceptions, actions, behaviours, etc, in order to build more intelligent and autonomous virtual agents.


*Interaction with objects*

The necessity to model interactions between an object and a virtual human agent (here after just referred to as an agent), appears in most applications of computer animation and simulation. Such applications encompass several domains, as for example: virtual autonomous agents living and working in virtual environments, human factors analysis, training, education, virtual prototyping, and simulation-based design. A good overview of such areas is presented by Badler [12]. An example of an application using agent-object interactions is presented by Johnson et al [13], whose purpose is to train equipment usage in a populated virtual environment.

Commonly, simulation systems perform agent-object interactions for specific tasks. Such approach is simple and direct, but most of the time, the core of the system needs to be updated whenever one needs to consider another class of objects.

To overcome such difficulties, a natural way is to include within the object description, more useful information than only intrinsic object properties. Some proposed systems already use this kind of approach. In particular, the object specific reasoning [14] creates a relational table to inform object purpose and, for each object graspable site, the appropriate hand shape and grasp approach direction. This set of information may be sufficient to perform a grasping task, but more information is needed to perform different types of interactions.

Another interesting way is to model general agent-object interactions based on objects containing interaction information of various kinds: intrinsic object properties, information on how-to-interact with it, object behaviors, and also expected agent behaviors. The smart object approach, introduced by Kallmann and Thalmann [15 16] extends the idea of having a database of interaction information. For each object modeled, we include the functionality of its moving parts and detailed commands describing each desired interaction, by means of a dedicated script language. A feature modeling approach [17] is used to include all desired information in objects. A graphical interface program permits the user to interactively specify different features in the object, and save them as a script file. Figure 6 shows an example.

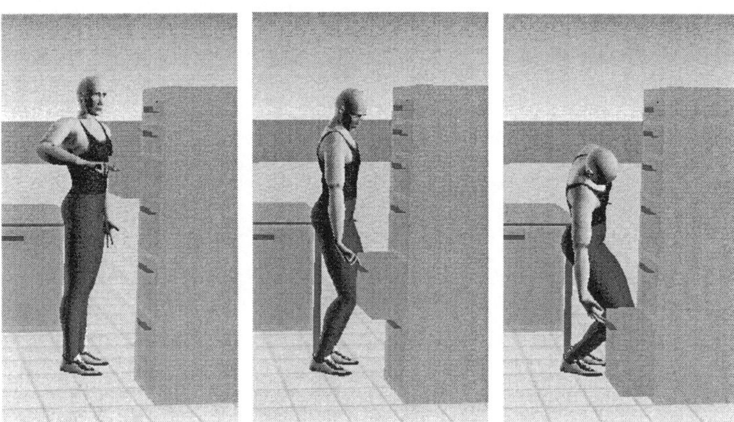

Figure 6. Interaction with objects

## Intercommunication

Behaviours may be also dependent on the emotional state of the actor. A non-verbal communication is concerned with postures and their indications on what people are feeling. Postures are the means to communicate and are defined by a specific position of the arms and legs and angles of the body. This non-verbal communication is essential to drive the interaction between people without contact or with contact.

What gives its real substance to face-to-face interaction in real life, beyond the speech, is the bodily activity of the interlocutors, the way they express their feelings or thoughts through the use of their body, facial expressions, tone of voice, etc. Some psychological researches have concluded that more than 65 percent of the information exchanged during a face-to-face interaction is expressed through nonverbal means [18]. A VR system that has the ambition to approach the fullness of real-world social interactions and to give to its participants the possibility to achieve a quality and realistic interpersonal communication has to address this point; and only realistic embodiment makes nonverbal communication possible. Figure 7 shows an example of intercommunication.

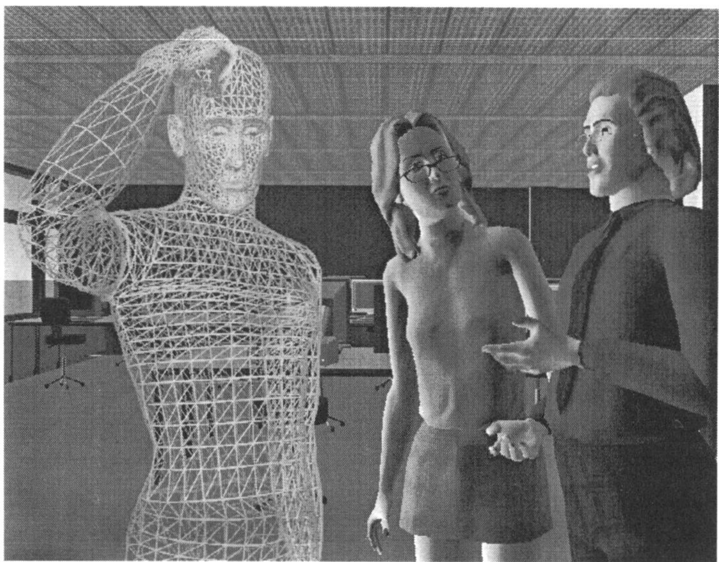

Figure 7. Intercommunication

## Interaction with user

The real people are of course easily aware of the actions of the Virtual Humans through VR tools like Head-mounted displays, but one major problem to solve is to make the virtual actors conscious of the behaviour of the real people. Virtual actors should sense the participants through their virtual sensors. Such a perceptive actor would be independent of each VR representation and he could in the same manner communicate with participants and other perceptive actors. Perceptive actors and participants may easily be. For virtual audition, we encounter the same problem as in virtual vision. The real time constraints in VR demand fast reaction to sound signals and fast recognition of the semantic it carries. For the interaction between virtual humans and real ones, gesture recognition is a key issue.

To date, basically two techniques exist to capture the human body posture in real-time. One uses video cameras which deliver either conventional or infrared pictures. This technique has been successfully used in the ALIVE system [19] to capture the user's image. The image is used for both the projection of the participant into the synthetic environment and the extraction of cartesian information of various body parts. If this system benefits from being wireless, it suffers from visibility constraints relative to the camera and a strong performance dependence on the vision module for information extraction.

The second technique is based on sensors which are attached to the user. Most common are sensors measuring the intensity of a magnetic field generated at a reference point. The measurements are transformed into position and orientation coordinates and sent to the computer. This raw data is matched to the rotation joints of a virtual skeleton by the means of an anatomical converter [20]. This is the approach we use currently for our interactive VR testbeds.

Figure 8 shows a snapshot of a life participant with ten sensors used to reconstruct the avatar in the virtual scene. The participant performs fight gestures which are recognized by the virtual opponent [21]. The latter responds by playing back a pre-recorded keyframe sequence. The most disturbing factors of this system are the setup time to fix all the sensors and the wires hanging around during the animation. However wireless systems are already available which solve these problems. For the interactive part of the VR testbed we developed a model of body actions as base of the recognition system.

Figure 8. Interactive environment with the video image of the participant using ten motion capture sensors (right of a & b), his avatar (middle of a & b) and the virtual opponent (left of a & b)

By analyzing human actions we have detected three important characteristics which inform us about the specification granularity needed for the action model. First, an action does not necessarily involve the whole body but may be performed with a set of body parts only. Second, multiple actions can be performed in parallel if they use non-intersecting sets of body parts. Finally a human action can already be identified by observing strategic body locations rather than skeleton joint movements. Based on these observations, a top-down refinement paradigm appears to be appropriate for the action model. The specification grain varies from coarse at the top level to very specialized at the lowest level. The number of levels in the hierarchy is related to the feature information used. At the lowest level, we use the skeleton degrees of freedom (DOF) which are the most precise feature information available (30-100 for a typical human model). At higher levels, we take advantage of strategic body locations like the center of mass and end effectors, i.e. hands, feet, the head and the spine root.

Human activity is composed of a continuous flow of actions. This continuity makes it difficult to define precise initial and in-between postures for an action. As a consequence we consider only actions defined by a gesture, a posture or a gesture followed by a posture.

The action model of relies on cartesian data and joint angle values. For a given action this data is not unique but depends on the anatomical differences of the live performers. A solution is, to normalize all cartesian action data by the body height of the performer. This is reasonable as statistical studies have measured a significant correlation between the body height and the major body segment lengths.

Each level of the action model defines action primitives. At the gesture level, an action primitive is the detection of the motion of the center of mass (CoM) or an End Effector (EE) along a specific direction. They are of the form (CoM, velocity direction) or (EEi, velocity direction), where i denotes one of the end effectors. If the average motion is above a normalized threshold, the velocity direction is assigned to one of the following values: upward, downward, forward, backward, leftward, rightward. For the head end effector it's preferable to use rotation directions of a 'look-at' vector rather than velocity directions, in order to specify messages like 'yes' or 'no'. Additionally a *not_moving* primitive detects a still CoM or EE. Thus the gesture of an action is described by an explicit boolean expression of gesture primitives, e.g.:

'Body downward motion' = (CoM, downward)
'Walking motion' = ((spine_root, forward) AND (left foot, forward))
                    OR ((spine_root, forward) AND (right foot, forward))

At the posture level an action primitive is the cartesian position of the CoM or the EE's or the joint values of the body posture. As it is not convenient to specify position or joint information explicitly, we use a 'specify-by-example' paradigm: we build a database of posture prototypes and extract the posture primitives automatically.

During the recognition phase we keep a trace of the actions which are potential candidates for the recognition result. Initially this Candidate Action Set (*CAS*) is a copy of the complete action database. Then the candidate selection is performed sequentially on the five levels of the action model, starting with level 1.

Figure 9 shows an interactive office environment with an avatar and an autonomous character: the employer. The employer's decision automata is completely coordinated by the recognition feedback of the performer's actions. For example the employer insists energetically on the fact of a non-smoking area if the performer wants to lit his cigarette. If the performer throws away his cigarette the employer invites him to take the contract files. The motions of the employer character consist of pre-recorded keyframe sequences, inverse kinematics and a procedural walking and grasping motors.

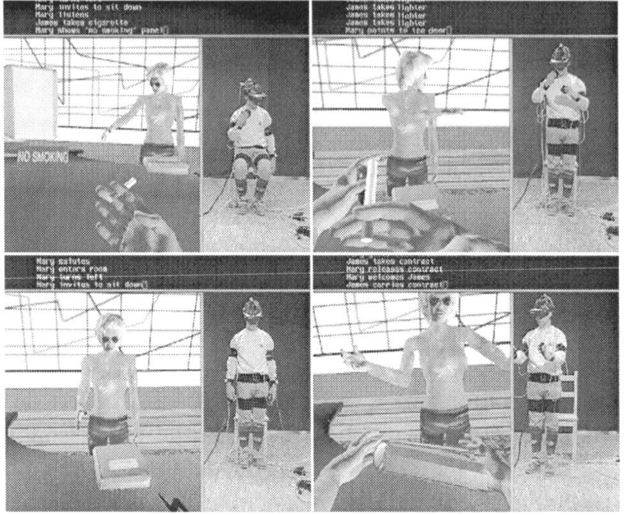

Figure 9. A scene with gesture recognition

## *Augmented reality*

To have a similar interactive application in a mixed environment than the fight in Figure 7 without any cumbersome tracking devices, would require a real-time non-invasive tracker for complete human body. Only a computer vision based tracking system would fit this specification, however current vision trackers are not up to full body tracking and giving similar results like a magnetic tracker. To overcome this limitation we decide to track simpler objects than a human, but still having a large range of interaction possibilities. We propose an approach, where tracked objects have semantic values known to real humans and to the mixed environment simulation.

In checkers game, like any other board game, all the interactions are happening on or very close to the game board. Additionally several objects on the board are moved by participants. A minimalist approach would be to let user play with his pieces and virtual pieces would change their places automatically similar to chess simulators from early 1980s. However we are accustomed to play against a real opponent in real life. A virtual human acting as an opponent will enrich the experience of playing the game, making it more realistic in several ways:

- **Perception of time**: Even if the checkers simulator would produce instant results, a virtual human will raise her hand, take a piece and make her move. The time needed for a move is analog for a real human, without considering time for thinking.
- **Perception of 3D space**: In a similar setup to our mixed reality setup, virtual pieces would change their places by themselves, in case of a virtual human, we can track her movements and have a longer time to follow which piece is played from where to where.
- **Perception of opponent**: A virtual human can be programmed or guided to speak and perform facial and body animation according to a situation. The game play is similar to a real game, with only major difference where virtual player can not move real pieces when they are eliminated from game, this has to be done by the real player.

To develop our checkers game simulator we need to track game play of the real participant and to place correctly a virtual human and virtual pieces in the mixed environment we need correct registration during the game play. We decide to use the checkers board as a feature object for this demonstration. The checkers board will be always in the center of the action due to the nature of the game play, and it is large enough to be tracked even from greater distance. Tracking the board is performed by our model-based tracker, the resulting position and orientation data is used to track the camera movements.

Tracking the movements of the real player is tracking the changes of positions of his pieces. As the game is played only on square of the same color, we need only to examine same colored squares, like white squares. As we have 3D coordinates of the checkers board from the camera tracker, and knowing relative coordinate of each and every white square, we can scan each white square and check if a different colored checkers piece is on it. A vision based scanner based for this purpose is build by Torre (Torre 00). The AR system uses a calibrated camera for correct registration of the board, the board coordinates are used to let the virtual camera follow the real one over the game play.

The Virtual Human is controlled by a text based checkers game simulator, which calculates the next move for the virtual human using the information on current game situation from the scanner. Figure 10 presents snap-shots from game play. This experiment shows that using available computer vision algorithms and virtual humans in a mixed environment, we can develop a natural interaction technique. In this case users manipulate real objects to trigger some meaningful actions in a mixed environment. Next example will present another interaction technique, where semi-autonomous virtual humans manipulate virtual objects and demonstrate some meaningful results in a mixed environment.

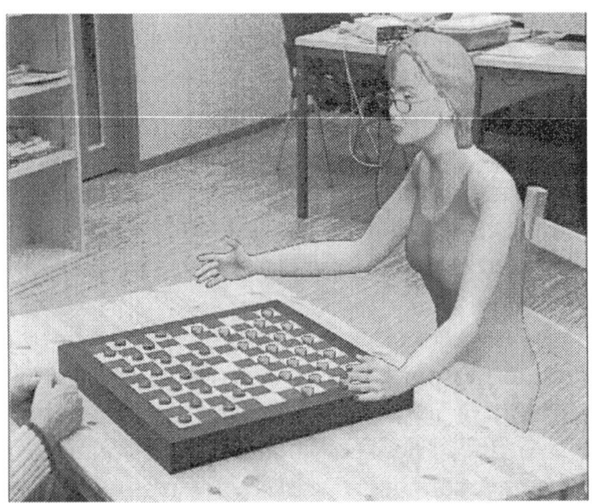

Figure 10. Snap-Shots from a Checkers Game between real and virtual humans.

## THE VIRTUAL HUMAN DIRECTOR SYSTEM

The Virtual Human Director (VHD) system [22] is a multimodal system jointly developed by EPFL (Computer Graphics Lab) and University of Geneva (MIRALab). It focuses on two important issues:

- Fully integrated virtual humans with facial and body animation, and speech.
- A straightforward user interface for designers and directors.

VHD provides a range of virtual human animation and interaction capabilities integrated into one single environment. The software architecture allows the addition of different interfaces from distinct environments into our software. VHD actors can be controlled via a standard TCP/IP connection over any network by using our virtual human message protocol. Possible high-level AI software can also be coded to control multiple actors.

The goal of the VHD interface was to provide an easy control of multiple actors and cameras in real-time. Thus, the user can create virtual stories by directing all the actions in real-time. It is similar to a producer directing actors during a shooting but with more controls given to the producer in the sense that everything is decided and controlled by the same person. To make this complicated task possible and useable, we provide high-level control of the virtual actors. Tools were developed to be able to predefine actions in advance so that during the real-time playing, the director can concentrate on the main guidelines of his scenario (sentences for example).

Only high-level actions can be used with the interface. It allows control of the speech by typing/selecting simple text-based sentences. The facial animation is controlled by pre-recorded sequences. These animations can be mixed in real-time and also mixed with the facial animation. Control of the body is done through keyframing and motion motors for the walking.

As soon as we have many virtual actors to control, the number of available actions will make the task of the director more and more complex. In order to ease this complicated task for the real-time interaction, we provide several tools for pre-programming actions in advance. The user can give a time after which the action will be played. Nevertheless, the idea is more useful for repeating actions. For example, we can program the eye blinking of an actor every five seconds plus a value between zero and two seconds. However all the actions cannot be programmed this way. As the goal is to be able to play scenario in real-time, we want to let the control of the main actions to be in the hands of the director. Nevertheless, a lot of actions result from a few main events. Let's consider the sentence "I am very pleased to be here with you today". The user may want to have the virtual actor smiling after something like one second (while saying: "pleased") and move the right hand after 1.5 seconds (saying: "here"). So the idea is to pre-program actions to be played after the beginning of a main event which is the sentence.

Then, just by selecting the main actions, complex behavior of the virtual actors will be completely determined. However the user will still be able to mix other actions to the pre-programmed ones.

Basic virtual camera tools are also given to the user. New camera positions can be fixed interactively from the interface. Cameras can be attached to virtual humans, so that we can have a total shot and a close-up of a virtual actor whatever his/her position is on the virtual scene. During real time, the list of camera positions is available on the interface, and the user can switch from one camera to the other just by clicking on it. An interpolation time can be easily set to provide zooming and traveling options between two camera positions. The cameras are also considered as an extension of the actions. They can be programmed in advance so when an actor says a sentence, the camera can be programmed to go directly to a given position

In order to improve the building of virtual stories, a scripting tool was developed for recording all the actions being played on an actor. Then, the user can adjust the sequence and play it again in real-time. As the saving is done independently for each actor and for the cameras, one can program the actors one by one, and play all the script together at the end. The other idea is to program background actors in order to be able to pay more attention to the main action being played in real-time.

We used one motion motor for the body locomotion. This walking motor was developed by Boulic et al. [23]. Current walking motor enables virtual humans to travel in the environment using instantaneous velocity of motion. One can compute the walking cycle length and time from which the necessary skeleton joint angles can be calculated for animation. This instantaneous speed oriented approach influenced VHD user interface design, where user is directly changing the speed. On the other hand VHD also supports another module for controlling walking, where users can control walking with simple commands like "WALK_FASTER". Figure 11 includes snapshots from a walking session.

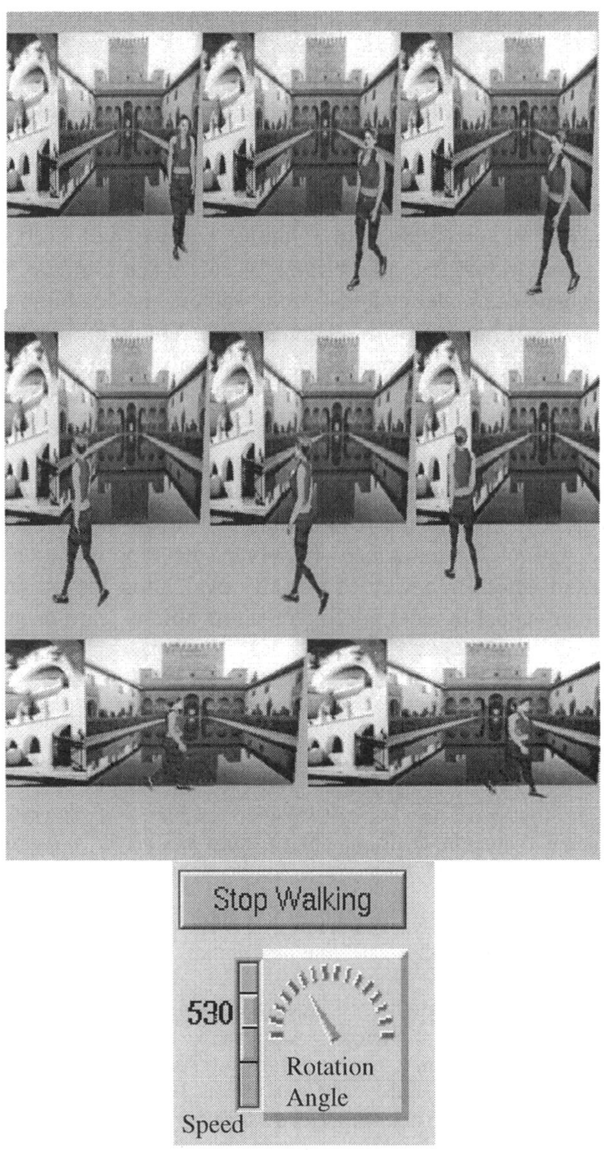


Figure 11. A walking example

## Conclusion

Telepresence is the future of multimedia systems and will allow participants to share professional and private experiences, meetings, games, parties. The concepts of Distributed Virtual Environments are a key technology to implement this telepresence. Using humanoids within the shared environment is a essential supporting tool for presence. Real-time realistic 3D avatars will be essential in the future, but we will need interactive perceptive actors to populate the Virtual Worlds. The ultimate objective in creating realistic and believable virtual actors is to build intelligent autonomous virtual humans with adaptation, perception and memory. These actors should be able to act freely and emotionally. Ideally, they should be conscious and unpredictable. But, how far are we from such a ideal situation? Our interactive perceptive actors are able to perceive the virtual world, the people living in this world and in the real world. They may act based on their perception in an autonomous manner. Their intelligence is constrained and limited to the results obtained in the development of new methods of Artificial Intelligence. However, the representation under the form of virtual actors is a way of visually evaluating the progress. In the future, we may expect to meet intelligent actors able to learn or understand a few situations.

## References


1.  N. Magnenat Thalmann, D. Thalmann, *Complex Models for Animating Synthetic Actors*, IEEE Computer Graphics and Applications, Vol.11, No5, 1991, pp.32-44.
2.  N. Magnenat Thalmann N., Thalmann D. (1995) *Digital Actors for Interactive Television*, Proc. IEEE, Special Issue on Digital Television, Part 2, July 1995, pp.1022-1031.
3.  D.Thalmann, L.Chiariglione, F.Fluckiger, E.H. Mamdani, M.Morganti, J.Ostermann, J.Sesena, L.Stenger, A.Stienstra, *Report on Panel 6: From Multimedia to Telepresence, Expert groups in Visionary Research in Advanced Communications*, ACTS, European Commission, 1997.
4.  W.S. Lee, N. Magnenat Thalmann, *Head Modeling from Pictures and Morphing in 3D with Image Metamorphosis based on triangulation*, Proc. Captech98 (Modelling and Motion Capture Techniques for Virtual Environments), (Springer LNAI LNCS Press), Geneva, 1998, pp.254-267.

5.  P. Fua, R. Plaenkers, and D. Thalmann, *From Synthesis to Analysis: Fitting Human Animation Models to Image Data*, Proc. Computer Graphics International, Canmore, Alberta, Canada, June 1999.

6.  P.Fua, *Face Models from Uncalibrated Video Sequences*, in: N.Magnenat-Thalmann, D.Thalmann (eds), "Modeling and Motion Capture Techniques for Virtual Environments" , Lecture Notes in Artificial Intelligence, No1537, Springer, 1998, pp.214-228.

7.  T. K. Capin, I.S. Panzic, N. Magnenat-Thalmann, D. Thalmann *Avatars in Networked Virtual Environments*, John Wiley and Sons, 1999.

8.  T. K. Capin, I.S. Panzic, N. Magnenat-Thalmann, D. Thalmann, *Virtual Human Representation and Communication in VLNET Networked Virtual Environment*, IEEE Computer Graphics and Applications, March 1997.

9.  S. D. Benford et al., *Embodiments, Avatars, Clones and Agents for Multi-user, Multi-sensory Virtual Worlds*, Multimedia Systems, Berlin, Germany: Springer-Verlag, 1997.

10. D. Thalmann, *Virtual Sensors: A Key Tool for the Artificial Life of Virtual Actors*, Proc. Pacific Graphics '95, Seoul, Korea, August 1995, pp.22-40.

11. Hennebert and Delacrétaz 1996 D.P., (1996) *POST: Parallel Object-Oriented Speech Toolkit*, Proc. ICSLP 96, Philadelphia

12. N. Badler, *Virtual Humans for Animation, Ergonomics, and Simulation*, IEEE Workshop on Non-Rigid and Articulated Motion, Puerto Rico, June 97.

13. W. L. Johnson, and J. Rickel, *Steve: An Animated Pedagogical Agent for Procedural Training in Virtual Environments*, Sigart Bulletin, ACM Press, vol. 8, number 1-4, 16-21, 1997.

14. L. Levison, *Connecting Planning and Acting via Object-Specific reasoning*, PhD thesis, Dept. of Computer & Information Science, University of Pennsylvania, 1996.

15. M. Kallmann, D. Thalmann, *Modeling Objects for Interaction Tasks*, Proc. Eurographics Workshop on Animation and Simulation, Springer, 1998

16. M. Kallmann, D.Thalmann, *A Behavioral Interface to Simulate Agent-Object Interactions in Real-Time*, Proc. Computer Animation 99, IEEE Computer Society Press

17. J.J. Shah, and M. Mäntylä, *Parametric and Feature-Based CAD/CAM*, John Wiley & Sons, inc. 1995, ISBN 0-471-00214-3.

18. M. Argyle, Bodily *Communication*, New York: Methuen & Co., 1988.

19. P. Maes, T.r Darrell, B. Blumberg, A. Pentland, *The ALIVE system: Full-body interaction with Autonomous Agents*, Proc. Computer Animation '95, Geneva, Switzerland, IEEE CS Press, April 1995

20. T.Molet, R.Boulic, D.Thalmann, *Human Motion Capture Driven by Orientation Measurements*, Presence, MIT, Vol.8, No2, 1999, pp.187-203.

21. L. Emering, R. Boulic, D. Thalmann, *Interacting with Virtual Humans through Body Actions*, IEEE Computer Graphics and Applications, 1998 , Vol.18, No1, pp.8-11.

22. G. Sannier, S. Balcisoy, N. Magnenat-Thalmann, D. Thalmann, VHD: *A System for Directing Real-Time Virtual Actors*, The Visual Computer, Springer, Vol.15, No 7/8, 1999, pp.320-329.
23. R. Boulic, P. Becheiraz, L. Emering, D. Thalmann (1997) *Integration of Motion Control Techniques for Virtual Human and Avatar Real-Time Animation*, Proc. VRST'97, pp. 111-118.